THE SEXTANTS OF BEIJING

Also by

JOANNA WALEY-COHEN

EXILE IN MID-QING CHINA:
BANISHMENT TO XINJIANG, 1758–1820

JOANNA WALEY-COHEN

THE SEXTANTS OF BEIJING

GLOBAL CURRENTS IN CHINESE HISTORY

W· W· NORTON & COMPANY
New York London

for BRAD, KIT, *and* ISABEL

First published as a Norton paperback 2000

For information about permission to reproduce selections from this book, write to Permissions, W. W. Norton & Company, Inc., 500 Fifth Avenue, New York, NY 10110.

The text of this book is composed in Galliard
with the display set in Galliard
Desktop composition by Gina Webster
Manufacturing by Courier Companies, Inc.
Book design by Jacques Chazaud

Library of Congress Cataloging-in-Publication Data

Waley-Cohen, Joanna.
The sextants of Beijing : global currents in Chinese history / Joanna Waley-Cohen.
p. cm.
Includes bibliographical references and index.
ISBN 0-393-04693-1
1. China—Civilization—Western influences. 2. China—Relations—Europe. 3. Europe—Relations—China. I. Title.
DS721.W268 1999
951—dc21 98-36897
CIP

ISBN 0-393-32051-0 pbk.

W. W. Norton & Company, Inc., 500 Fifth Avenue, New York, N.Y. 10110
www.wwnorton.com

W. W. Norton & Company Ltd., 10 Coptic Street, London WC1A 1PU

1 2 3 4 5 6 7 8 9 0

Acknowledgments

Over the long-drawn-out process of writing this book, I have accumulated intellectual and personal debts to many more than the usual band of suspects. Without them the task would certainly have been both impossible and intolerable.

For their detailed reading and comments on parts or all of the manuscript, I thank Kristin Bayer, Pamela Kyle Crossley, Brad Gallant, Rebecca Karl, Iona Man-cheong, Peter Perdue, Lucia Pierce, Kenneth Pomeranz, Jonathan Spence, and Griselda Warr. For making their work available to me, I thank Timothy Barrett, Jane Elliott, Robert Entenmann, Allen Fung, John Herman, Thomas Kennedy, and John Zou. For references, helpful suggestions, and endless encouragement, I am grateful to Jane Baun, Nicola di Cosmo, Antonio Feros, Valerie Hansen, Harry Harootunian, Jonathan Hay, Ronnie Po-chia Hsia, Walter Johnson, Ben Kiernan, Liu Yuan, Molly Nolan, Moss Roberts, Nathan Sivin, King-fai Tam, Joyce Waley-Cohen, Xu Haoyuan, Louise Young, and Marilyn Young. For practical help at critical moments, I owe thanks to Kathryn Aldridge, Evelyne Dumanchin, Anne Gallant, Claire Gallant, Edward Gallant, Samantha Lewin, Gabriele Serruya, Susan Waller, and Rubina Zesner; and for making the details of daily life easier in countless ways, and infinitely more pleasant, thanks to Karin Burrell, Rachel Goldman, Delverlon Hall, Ben Maddox, and Daniel Olson. For unflagging support, and for several very careful and constructive readings of the manuscript as it developed, I thank my editor at Norton, Steven Forman.

For financial and institutional support while I was conducting the original research out of which the book grew, I wish to acknowledge the History of Christianity in China Project and the Henry Luce Foundation; the Columbia Society of Fellows in the Humanities, the John M. Olin Postdoctoral Fellowship in Military and Strategic History at Yale University; and New York University.

The last should be first—as they have often felt over the past few years. In addition to placing on record here my profound and loving gratitude to them, I dedicate the book to Brad, Kit, and Isabel Gallant.

Contents

MAPS

THE SEXTANTS OF BEIJING

R U S S I A
KAZAKHSTAN
L. Balkhash
Khobdo
MON
KYRGYZSTAN
Ürümqi
Barkul
Turfan
Hami
TAJIKISTAN
Kashgar
AFG.
Yarkand
XINJIANG
Dunhuang
Yumen
PAKISTAN
QINGHAI
Xining
XIZANG
(TIBET)
New Delhi
SIC
Lhasa
NEPAL
Kathmandu
Ganges
Brahmaputra
Kunmin
INDIA
Dhaka
Calcutta
YUNNA
Mandalay
BANGLADESH
BURMA
(MYANMAR)
Bay of
Bengal
THAILAND

L. Baikal
RUSSIA
HEILONGJIANG
Harbin
Ulan Bator
JILIN
Changchun
Vladivostok
INNER MONGOLIA
Shenyang
Zhangjiakou
LIAONING
Sea of Japan
NORTH KOREA
Hohhot
Pyongyang
Yellow R.
BEIJING
Datong
Tangshan
GREAT WALL
Tianjin
HEBEI
Seoul
Shijiazhuang
Yinchuan
Yellow Sea
SOUTH KOREA
Taiyuan
Jinan
NINGXIA
Yan'an
SHANXI
Qingdao
SHANDONG
JAPAN
Zhengzhou
Kaifeng
Baoji
SHAANXI
Xi'an
JIANGSU
HENAN
East China Sea
Hefei
Nanjing
ANHUI
Shanghai
HUBEI
Yangtze R.
Hangzhou
Wuhan
ZHEJIANG
Jingdezhen
Nanchang
Changsha
Zunyi
HUNAN
JIANGXI
GUIZHOU
Fuzhou
FUJIAN
Guiyang
Taipei
Guilin
TAIWAN
GUANGDONG
GUANGXI
Guangzhou
(Canton)
Tainan
Nanning
Hong Kong
Macao
(Port.)
Contemporary China
Hanoi
South China Sea
Haikou
HAINAN
0
1000 km
0
600 miles
Chazaud

Introduction

In the first decade of the nineteenth century a confederation of pirates plagued the waters off China's southeastern coast. At their height they numbered at least fifty thousand men and women, with some two thousand junks, organized into two fleets, based in the port of Jiangping (Giang Binh) on the Vietnamese border. Their daring was legendary. In 1805, for instance, they blockaded the Portuguese island enclave of Macao for several weeks, reducing the panicked occupants to a few days' food supply. Three years later they held hostage three large Siamese junks on a tribute mission and drove five American ships to take refuge within range of Macao's artillery defenses. They capped it all by capturing the brig of the visiting Portuguese colonial governor of Timor, and to add insult to injury, the pirates towed the vessel ignominiously past Macao city, trailing its flag in the water.

Solving the piracy problem was in the interest of both the Manchu Qing rulers of China (1644–1911) and the various foreign traders whose merchantmen were vulnerable to pirate attack. The Qing insisted that it was their prerogative alone to patrol the Chinese coast, but they were unable to clear the seaways. So, in line with numerous predecessors, who over the centuries had called on foreign fighting forces and military technology, the Qing enlisted the aid of armed Portuguese and British ships in the area. But their occasional joint expeditions were not terribly successful and led to mutual recriminations. The Europeans accused the Chinese of being in league with the pirates, while the Chinese blamed the Europeans because their deep-draft boats could not sail in shallow coastal waters, thus usually allowing the pirates to slip away.

The pirates themselves—fishermen, peddlers, grass cutters, shopkeepers, rice dealers, sailors, and others from the lowest echelons of Chinese society—were just as willing to make use of the foreigners and their skills as were the Qing authorities. After pirate leader

Zhang Bao's vessel fled from a broadside of twenty-four-pound shot administered by a British ship, for instance, he is said to have examined the size of the cannonball with astonished respect. Only a few months later, his ship boasted its own twenty-four-pounder. And pirates often spared the lives of foreigners they captured so as to co-opt their expertise in gunnery, medicine, or just literacy.

Two significant points emerge from these facts. First, it is obvious that at the dawn of the nineteenth century China's involvement with the wider world was already routine. Second, and as a corollary, clearly few Chinese, whether government officials or common folk, cared whether the skills and technology they needed had a foreign origin. In other words, the traditional isolationism, hostility to innovation, and xenophobic sentiment often sweepingly attributed to all Chinese, seem to have played little part in their calculations.

Unfortunately, however, even by the early 1800s this kind of misdiagnosis was fast becoming a habit among a majority of the Europeans arriving on China's shores. Whatever these observers may have seen with their own eyes, their opinions of China and Chinese civilization were affected rather more by their own prejudices. These prejudices themselves were primarily influenced by the context in which they formed: by the Enlightenment, by industrialization, and by the new passion for political liberty evidenced by the American and French revolutions, among other things. Their judgments still profoundly influence our understanding of China today.

China shares responsibility for the formation of these notions. For one thing, there has been a wide chasm between propaganda and reality. Lofty public utterances emanating from the Chinese side led many observers to draw the conclusion that China regarded its own civilization as vastly superior to all other contenders. But the reality is that this rhetoric disguised considerable flexibility and open-mindedness. When we examine Chinese acts rather than Chinese words, it becomes evident that since earliest times China has displayed no greater cultural chauvinism than most other societies.

Old habits die hard. Much of what we once thought we knew about China now seems little more than a set of stereotypes, yet the promotion of this "knowledge" to the level of certainty has been extremely influential. Thus apparently well-informed people commonly, but inaccurately, still refer to the diverse and dynamic vastness of China as monolithic and perennially isolated from the rest of the world. These misconceptions, largely reflections of the views of the colonial Western powers, have even become a part of Chinese self-perception, for the extraordinary success of the West in undermining the Chinese sense of national identity and self-confidence led many Chinese to accept as accurate Western descriptions of China, particularly its relations with the rest of the world.

This book springs from the conviction that we must lay to rest some long-cherished myths, including the assumption that the Western nations "opened up" a hitherto "closed" China. Above all, it argues that time out of mind, China—Chinese emperors, Chinese governments, and Chinese people across the social spectrum—has been energetically and enthusiastically engaged with the outside world, permitting, encouraging, and seeking the circulation of foreign goods and ideas. At the same time, however, those in authority have been consistently reluctant to allow free rein to any kind of foreign ideology, for fear of losing political and moral control over that portion of the population for whom the foreign ideology might come to prevail over Chinese values and traditions.

The book is thus primarily about how China has taken the measure of the world and about the goods and ideas that have flowed into and out of China during the past several centuries. Readers should not, however, be misled into thinking that the book's focus on foreign influences is intended to suggest that all of China's development, especially in the modern era, has been externally driven. To the contrary, the contention of this book is that much of China's historical experience has involved the complicated interplay of, on the one hand, indigenous developments and, on the other, foreign imports and influences of all kinds.

The book opens with a broad overview of China's early contacts with other civilizations, from around 200 B.C., when surviving records enable us to begin to reconstruct the countless connections that existed, down to the advent of Europeans to East Asia in the sixteenth century. The principal theme of Chapter One is China's active participation in a complex network of international exchange that stretched from Syria in the west to Japan in the east and from Korea in the north to Indonesia in the south and, by the sixteenth century, included Europe and the New World. Among the most influential features of this traffic was the spread of Buddhism from India to China; from China it spread across East Asia, particularly to Korea, Japan, and Vietnam, taking with it elements of Confucianism and other cultural, intellectual, political, commercial, and artistic aspects of Chinese civilization.

Chapters Two and Three are primarily devoted to China's first sustained interaction with Europe and European culture, in the sixteenth through the eighteenth centuries. These initial encounters between Europe and China in the early modern age took place largely through the medium of Jesuit missionaries. Chapter Two focuses on China and Catholicism from the late sixteenth to the early eighteenth century and demonstrates that China's reluctance to embrace Christianity stemmed from a variety of causes. First, traditional Chinese religious eclecticism was ultimately irreconcilable with Christian requirements of exclusivity. Second, in a context in which religion either directly served the state or was specifically subversive, many Chinese suspected that the foreign religion might turn out to represent the advance guard of a foreign invasion. Third, set against the highly charged political atmosphere of the mid-seventeenth-century dynastic transition from Ming to Qing, Jesuit service at the new Qing court appeared to some Chinese like collaboration with the enemy and cost them vital support, especially among the elite. Finally, bitter disputes within the European Church establishment bore some responsibility for Jesuit missionaries' inability fully to achieve their goals in China.

Chapter Three, focused mainly on the late seventeenth and eighteenth centuries, refutes the still-tenacious belief that China at that time was implacably hostile to foreign trade and to imported ideas in any form, a notion symbolized by the memorable assertion that "we have no need for [English] manufactures," made in 1793 by the Qianlong Emperor (r. 1736–1795). The chapter describes Jesuits' wide-ranging secular activities at the courts of Qianlong and his grandfather Kangxi (r. 1662–1722), among which was the construction by the Flemish Jesuit Ferdinand Verbiest (1623–1688) of the sextant and other astronomical instruments that can still be seen today at the Observatory near the center of Beijing. Imperial enthusiasm for European and other imports—a preoccupation that mirrored the eighteenth-century European craze for chinoiserie—was intense and spearheaded a widespread passion for things European among the elite in China. Chapter Three also discusses the connections of the substantial inter-Asian trade to the growing Chinese settlements abroad, primarily in Southeast Asia, and this trade's proliferating links to European nations through their colonial activities in Asia.

Chapters Four and Five cover the "long nineteenth century," from the death of Qianlong in 1799 to the outbreak of World War

One in Europe in 1914. During this period China suffered the imposition of a series of "unequal treaties" that gave the Western powers wide-ranging special rights in China. In retrospect historians have castigated the powers for imposing these treaties, but at the time these did not at first seem particularly onerous, even to China, because their provisions closely resembled arrangements made a few years earlier between China and its neighbors in Central Asia. Before long, however, China found that the cumulative effect of the treaties was to ride roughshod over Chinese sovereignty in all spheres, in an attempt to force China to become more "modern" or, put otherwise, to become more like the West. These treaties fundamentally affected the view of Europe, America, and later Japan held by Chinese men and women. Other international agreements China concluded during the nineteenth century, however, sought with some success to protect the by now huge number of Chinese migrants around the world, thus giving the lie to an oft-repeated view of a China that was debilitated at home and apathetic toward its diaspora.

By the late nineteenth century many educated Chinese had become deeply disillusioned with their culture, because neither Confucianism nor anything else within the Chinese tradition seemed adequate to meet the challenge of Western and Japanese imperialism. They came to feel both awed by these countries' wealth and power, which they strongly desired to emulate and eventually match, and profoundly resentful. The potent fear, that the foreigners would carve China up "like a melon," until it ceased to exist as an independent entity, together with increasing despair over the ineptitude of China's Manchu rulers, encouraged the growth of nationalist sentiment whose ultimate goal was a return to autonomy. In short, China hoped selectively to adopt Western ways so as to overcome the West and preserve its own civilization.

Chapters Six and Seven cover the period from 1914 to 1997. The year 1914 marked the culmination of a shift in emphasis among the serried ranks of those threatening China. The slow buildup of hostilities among the European powers in the first years of the twentieth century diverted their attention just at the same time that newly modernized Meiji Japan had shown, by its defeat of first China (in 1895) and then Russia (in 1905), that it had become a significant force meriting both respect and fear. With the outbreak of World War One, the European powers altogether yielded pride of place in China to Japan, which from then on became China's principal imperialist foe, arranging pretexts to encroach on Chinese territory and periodically launching limited military attacks. In 1937 Japan invaded China, compelling the Nationalist (Guomindang) government to retreat far inland and establish a temporary wartime capital in Chongqing, Sichuan province. At the same time, the Nationalists, led by Chiang Kaishek, passionately desired to eliminate the threat posed to their authority by the Chinese Communist Party, founded in 1921.

War with Japan merged into World War Two, in which China's resistance against Japan played a vital part in the Allied victory. The end of that war in 1945 was followed almost at once by a bitter civil war between the Nationalists and the Communists that in turn culminated in the departure of the Nationalists for Taiwan and the establishment by the Chinese Communist Party of the People's Republic in 1949, marked by Mao Zedong's ringing assertion that China would "never again be an insulted nation." Over the next few decades, against the shifting politics of the Cold War era, much of China's domestic and international agenda concerned its determination to slough off forever the economic and cultural residue of the century of domination by the Western powers and Japan.

The book ends in 1997, the year in which China resumed control over Hong Kong, an island off the south China coast under British colonial rule since 1842. The reversion of Hong Kong raised anew the question of once-independent Tibet, under Chinese control for most of the past 250 years, and of the island of Taiwan, lost in 1895 to the Qing empire that had annexed it in 1683, then a Japanese colony until 1945, and since then neither part of China nor independent.

Twentieth-century China has displayed a complicated mixture of fascination and ambivalence about foreign cultures. Politically China has often adopted a contradictory stance involving, on the one hand, the outward expression of enormous hostility to foreigners, especially the United States, and, on the other, a willingness to engage. But Americans, in particular, long rejected any engagement with China because of extraordinarily strong anti-Communist sentiment stoked by the "loss" of China, Guomindang lobbying, and the politics of the Vietnam War era.

A few definitions are necessary. In referring to "China," one appears to be papering over immense regional differences, as well as considerable change over time in what constituted "China." At its simplest, for instance, the impact of foreign imperialism in China was much different in coastal areas, where by the late nineteenth century foreigners had become commonplace, from its impact far inland, where foreigners often were still a rarity, although the advent of newspapers and telegraphs went some considerable way toward changing that situation. Similarly, in the late eighteenth century the boundaries of the empire, also constituting what is today regarded as properly part of the nation, ranged as far west as the Pamir Mountains bordering Kashmir and Afghanistan and as far north as the Amur River on the Russian frontier, whereas in the later nineteenth century the boundaries of the empire contracted from their eighteenth-century extent. At other times, for instance, under the Song (960–1276), "China" included neither the area now known as Manchuria nor the regions beyond the western terminus of the Great Wall in Gansu province. But to hedge every reference to "China" with qualification and clarification would be altogether too cumbersome, so readers must simply bear these spatial and temporal variations in mind.

The same is true of the term "the West." From the fifteenth to the late eighteenth century, this expression denotes Europe and Europeans, in a shifting configuration that began with the arrival of Portuguese and Spaniards, who established their Asian colonial bases, and ended with the domination of England and the Netherlands, although other Europeans were also present in Asia during this period. After the 1780s "the West" includes Americans, although on the whole they played a secondary role in Chinese history and consciousness down to the end of the nineteenth century. From then on, for a number of reasons, the United States took over the leading position among the nations of "the West," and Europeans generally took second place.

This book is not intended for specialists in Chinese history, European imperialism, or world history, although it may have something to offer some or all of them. Rather, it is addressed to the general reader wishing to learn more about China's engagement with the world in historical perspective and to those for whom the old saw, about China's perennial preference for isolation and its antagonism to outsiders, just does not ring true. Although it is impossible to overcome deeply held stereotypes with a single work, it is the author's hope that this book will go far toward undermining inaccurate conceptions about the history of China's relations with the outside world, particularly but not exclusively Europe and the United States.

China has a long history and, until the last two hundred years, has been accustomed to exert authority over foreigners wishing to interact with it, at either the official or the individual level, as well as over those who live within its boundaries. This does not mean that China has been inimical to knowledge and ideas that come from abroad, merely that it has preferred to exercise caution in allowing the free circulation of notions potentially subversive to the ability to operate on its own terms. The ongoing quest to strike a balance between the absorption of foreign influences and the retention of autonomy and a distinctive national identity in many ways represents a more sophisticated continuation of past struggles, even though the playing fields of global power have leveled out considerably in the last part of the twentieth century.

CHAPTER ONE

Early Chinese Cosmopolitanism

Between the years 629 and 645, during the Tang dynasty (618–907), a Chinese monk named Xuanzang traveled to India in search of Buddhist scriptures. On his return he translated more than a thousand rolls of text from the Sanskrit and wrote an account of his journey that remains an invaluable description of Central Asia at that time. Xuanzang's epic journey, soon dramatized for stage performance and recounted by storytellers all over China, became a standard theme of popular literature. In the sixteenth century it formed the centerpiece of the great Chinese novel *Journey to the West*, in English sometimes known as *Monkey* after the adventures of the magical monkey-king who in the novel accompanies Xuanzang on his travels and protects him from peril. As the saga of Xuanzang's journey was told and retold, it embedded the idea of international exchange into the Chinese tradition from a very early period.

In the early twentieth century Xuanzang unwittingly played a part in illuminating once more some early links between China and the civilizations to its west. In 1907 a Hungarian-British explorer,

Aurel Stein, traveled across Central Asia as far as the west China oasis of Dunhuang. Dunhuang was an important staging post on the old Silk Road, along which, since time immemorial, traders and religious believers had traveled between China and points west. Nearby was a huge temple complex whose walls had been lavishly decorated over the centuries with frescoes depicting Buddhist paradises. Within the complex also were thousands of ancient manuscripts and decorated textiles, concealed in a side room walled up almost nine hundred years earlier. Wishing to persuade the priest in charge to allow him access to these ancient texts, Stein described how he had retraced Xuanzang's footsteps across Asia. His evident familiarity with and admiration for this popular figure of the Chinese past successfully established a bond with the priest, who that same night showed the explorer a small sampling of the treasures under his care. The first texts to emerge from the walled-up library in this way turned out to be none other than some of the scriptures Xuanzang had brought back from India and translated into Chinese so long before. These documents were followed by many more. Most, like the frescoes, were Buddhist, but there were also Confucian, Daoist, Zoroastrian, and Nestorian Christian materials showing links to Persia, Tocharia (in modern Afghanistan) and Sogdiana (in modern Uzbekistan), as well as to China, and still other texts that had little connection to religion. Some were in languages never before encountered. Paintings on silk from Dunhuang also testified to an abundant blending of cultures. They depicted figures whose faces showed traces of the so-called Greco-Buddhist tradition—that is, in an Indian style known to have been influenced by Hellenistic art—while the drapes of their clothes and the landscapes they dwelt in were done in distinctly Chinese style. Probably these paintings were done by several different artists. Thus the heritage of the Tang priest Xuanzang, himself a representative of the rich interchange between China and the rest of Asia, helped in this century to expose to the light the cultural diversity these exchanges brought about more than a thousand years ago.

Early Chinese contact with other civilizations occurred in three broad overlapping categories of equal importance: politics, including both diplomacy and warfare; religion and intellectual exchange; and trade, in which Chinese silk and later porcelain figured prominently. Chinese diplomacy and warfare usually involved programs of national security and expansion, which often created trade opportunities. At the same time, peaceful commercial exchange often resulted in expansion without any fighting or negotiation—for instance, when Chinese merchants involved in long-distance trade settled permanently in outlying areas and founded new communities. Trade was further linked to politics because of the preferred Chinese method of conducting foreign relations; since this involved the formal exchange of goods with foreigners, it was in effect a politicized form of international trade.

Similarly, international trade was tightly interwoven with the flow of ideas into and out of China. Buddhism, for instance, an originally Indian religion, entered China both with priests and missionaries and with merchants who came across Central Asia. Other religions, including Islam and Christianity, followed in Buddhism's wake, but none proved able to match its tenacity. In this realm of intellectual transmission too, much more than religion crossed the world with the caravans and carracks of international trade. Many travelers carried with them news of the latest breakthroughs in astronomy, mathematics, philosophy, and technology. Nor was China simply the passive recipient of imported goods and ideas. Over time countless elements of Chinese culture, both material and spiritual, and including such originally foreign aspects as Buddhism, found their way to other parts of Asia, notably Korea, Japan, and Vietnam.

The final overlap between categories of early contact with other civilizations was between the realms of religion and politics. In China, as in Europe, these were sometimes associated in the realm of early foreign policy—for instance, when missionaries doubled as ambassadors to other countries—but unlike in Europe, wars of religion were virtually unknown. This was because there was no single established state religion and because those religions that at different times were prevalent in China lacked Christianity's strong evangelical element. Nor was the emperor considered divine in China, as was his counterpart in Japan, but his position as the Son of Heaven gave him special qualities that contributed in important ways to the environment of international trade, as we shall see in the next section.

The Idealized Chinese Worldview

Ancient Chinese, as represented by their monarch, claimed to hold a Mandate of Heaven according to which they had a valid claim to preside over everyone else by virtue of their unequivocal political, cultural, and moral authority. That principle remained intact even under an alien ruler; it was moral integrity and benevolent leadership rather than ethnic origins that were important. Originally this cultural self-confidence had perhaps been in some degree justified by the relatively high level of ancient Chinese civilization and its sophisticated political organization, in comparison with the peoples surrounding it. For at least in antiquity China's neighbors were in most cases unsettled tribes; many were nomads rather than sedentary farmers like the Chinese. Their culture was not well developed—for example, few had written scripts of their own—and their political organization was unstable enough that none could describe itself as a state.

By the time of the early empire (second century B.C. to second century A.D.), the premises underlying this worldview had been many centuries in the making. They envisaged a universe divided into an inner and an outer zone, sometimes conceived of more specifically as a series of graduated concentric circles. Within this universe one's degree of civilization depended on one's relationship to the center of the inner zone. In common with many other societies, China placed itself at the center; in other words, it regarded itself as the most civilized and regarded those farthest away as the most barbarous. At least in theory, the assumption was that most outsiders aspired to be "more like Chinese" and would eventually become assimilated to a greater or lesser extent. There was a fatal weakness in this argument, however, for taken to its logical conclusion, it implied that most, if not all, Chinese were descended from outsiders who had previously undergone the process of acculturation.

Han China (206 B.C.– A.D. 220) established an ideal formula for dealing with outsiders that, it hoped, would overcome the disagreeable reality that some of them showed no particular inclination to assimilate or to abandon their own cultures. The formula became known to historians as the tributary system. This was in effect a bundle of practices intended to symbolize outsiders' submission to Chinese overlordship. Its most important features were as follows. First, the tributary ruler or his representative had to go to China to pay homage. In particular the envoy had to prostrate himself before the Chinese emperor, in ritual acknowledgment of his vassal status. Second, the tributary state had to send a significant hostage, such as its crown prince, to the Chinese court. Third, the tributary state had to send gifts of native goods, always described as the payment of tribute, to the Chinese emperor.

The system functioned reciprocally. In return for the tributary's symbolic submission, China guaranteed its security, although actual military intervention tended to depend on China's stake in the tributary's stability. China also bestowed extravagant gifts, together with elaborate honors and titles. These were intended to buy off the tributary, and although often cripplingly expensive, they still cost less than raising and maintaining a standing army that could compel submission. Finally, the foreigners were permitted to engage in carefully controlled trade for a few days before being conducted back to the frontier and sent on their way.

This formula was, however, optimistic, for although China claimed that the ritual homage and the offering of local goods demonstrated submission to Chinese political overlordship, the tributary did not necessarily see it that way. Rather, for tributary states the entire process primarily represented a peaceful way to acquire essential Chinese goods without having to steal them in border raids. The question of relative status did not much concern them, although in some cases recognition by the Chinese emperor may have enhanced a leader's prestige in local disputes.

Moreover, a fundamental paradox flawed the tributary framework. For it functioned properly only when others acquiesced in it or at least agreed not openly to dispute the Chinese version. Such acquiescence was possible only when China was strong enough to compel compliance. When, as frequently happened, this was not the case, China simply adapted to reality. Indeed, Chinese leaders were well aware from early times that their empire and its environs formed only a small part of the civilized world and that other comparable cultures existed. For instance, the Han accorded the easternmost territories of the Roman Empire, in contemporary Syria, the respectful title of Great Qin, dispensing altogether with the patronizing vocabulary that they preferred to use in all their dealings with other states.

Many of the preconditions of China's assumed superiority over its neighbors simply withered away over time. Particularly after the fall of the Han in 220, China itself often was politically divided into a number of small states, none of which had sufficient power to demand deference from any other. Moreover, although it claimed that foreigners longed to revolve in China's political and cultural orbit, the reality suggested otherwise. This was not least because the surrounding states were becoming much stronger and more stable, with highly literate elites whom it was no longer feasible for China to patronize.

In short, while the ideals embodied in the tributary system have endured down to the present century, China has necessarily, and often, departed from that ideal since very early times. That is, China's approach to relations with other states and civilizations has been highly pragmatic, whatever its theoretical underpinnings and however firmly it may have asserted its superiority in public.

THE EARLY IMPERIAL AGE 206 B.C.–A.D. 581

Traffic between China, Southeast Asia, the kingdoms of Central Asia, and India, if not farther afield, certainly began informally in the preimperial age. But our story begins with the Han empire, which about the year 200 B.C. established its capital at the eastern terminus of the Silk Road, located at Chang'an (on the site of which contemporary Xi'an stands) in northwest China. This was around the same time that both Rome and Alexandria were rising to political and cultural prominence, respectively, in the Mediterranean world.

Han China was distinctly interested in establishing political and commercial relationships with other states, through diplomatic missions and both official and unofficial trade. In the latter part of the second century B.C. the expansion-minded emperor Wudi (r. 141–87) twice sent his emissary Zhang Qian (fl. ca. 125 B.C.) to explore the diplomatic and commercial prospects to the west. Zhang Qian spent some years in captivity among China's longtime enemies, the Xiongnu confederation of nomads, who rightly regarded him as a spy. Eventually he returned home, bringing a great deal of information about living conditions in Central Asia and in places farther to the west that he either visited himself or sent his agents to investigate. Partly as a result of his journeys and those of later Han emissaries to the "Western Regions," China began trading with Central Asia on a regular basis.

Han China's primary exports were silk and gold. In return China imported spices, woolen fabrics, and the horses essential to its military projects. On occasion, inevitably, foreign germs sneaked in with foreign commodities; smallpox, for example, is thought to have reached China from India sometime in the first century.

Warfare and trade fed on each other in a variety of ways. For one thing, Han armies sometimes recruited Central Asian merchants to join their forces as they advanced westward. For another, ordinary soldiers stationed on the frontier certainly exchanged some of their government issue clothing for cash; probably they also smuggled arms and other goods across the frontiers between China and its hostile neighbors, but we do not know about these activities in any detail. Knowledge of the distant regions in which these far-flung campaigns took place also inspired, in at least one instance, the urge to acquire exotic foreign luxuries, as we know from an exchange between the Ban twins, one an eminent historian and the other a senior general campaigning in Central Asia. The historian urged his brother to get him some of those fine local rugs and send them on home.

It was sometimes hard to distinguish diplomatic from commercial missions, for the exchange of goods formed an important part of Han relationships with other states, and the roles of merchant and official envoy could be interchangeable. Several delegations came to China from Parthia in northern Persia, which the Chinese called Anxi. One such embassy, which appeared in A.D. 10, was renowned for having presented an ostrich to the Chinese emperor; it followed a seaborne mission from an unidentified state eight years earlier that had brought the no less remarkable gift of a rhinoceros. Later that century a Chinese envoy was said to have been prevented from reaching Rome by the Parthians, who, according to Chinese tradition, tried hard to maintain their role as middlemen between the two great empires by luridly painting the difficulties of the journey to any who sought to make it himself. The Roman upper classes greatly desired Chinese silk and referred to China as Seres, the "land of silk," while the Chinese valued Mediterranean glass and coral.

Although the Parthians seem to have been largely successful in their efforts to discourage direct contact between the Chinese and Roman empires, in 166 a famous embassy did reach Han China from "Antun," who has been identified as the Roman emperor Marcus Aurelius (121–180). The envoys brought gifts of ivory, rhinoceros horn, and tortoiseshell, perhaps acquired in North African ports they passed through on their long voyage.

By the end of the Han, China had begun to consolidate its earlier sporadic connections to those states accessible by sea. This development derived both from the growing uncertainty of the overland route (the Silk Road) as the Han empire retracted and from the fact that after the Han collapse the reconstituted states in southern China were, in any case, cut off altogether from direct access to the Silk Road, so they had to find some other way to reach the source of the imported luxuries they wanted. For these reasons, by no later than the third century Canton (Guangzhou) had become a flourishing port for overseas trade. At the same time, Chinese started to migrate overseas, especially to Japan and Southeast Asia, as well as along the overland trade routes. From this period, as the result of migrations, commercial exchange, military expeditions, and the growing numbers of Buddhist priests and pilgrims journeying between China and India, a considerable literature about foreign countries and their cultures began to appear, making it possible for those at home to learn more about the world.

EARLY BUDDHISM

Buddhism was first recorded in China in the first century, although Chinese may have been aware of it earlier. It came by way of Dunhuang on the Silk Road, home of the frescoed temples with which this chapter opens. At first it had few Chinese converts and primarily served the foreign community of merchants and others, but as the Han empire began to disintegrate toward the end of the second century, a Buddhist establishment had been set up in the capital at Luoyang, systematic translation of texts into Chinese had begun, and the foreign religion was steadily becoming more widely accepted.

The central tenet of Buddhism was that the world was neither fixed nor real and that the self did not exist. Buddhism held that such illusions lay at the root of human suffering, causing people to be mired in such worldly emotions as envy, lust, hate, and pride. This led them to carry out those evil actions that caused suffering to others, which in turn condemned them to an endless cycle of rebirths into horrendous misery. Claiming to offer a path to salvation from this inexorable process, Buddhism called for people to renounce this world of illusion and adopt a monastic existence given over to devotion, spiritual purification, and good works.

Many of Buddhism's tenets, originating in the profoundly different culture of India, were incompatible with traditional beliefs associated with Confucianism concerning the harmonious functioning of the family and society. These beliefs, already prevalent in China, later became permanently incorporated into the predominant state ideology. For instance, Buddhism's call for a monastic existence and for celibacy ran directly counter to Confucian requirements of filial piety within a family-oriented social structure, including the important obligation to perpetuate one's family line. Just as important was the fact that Confucianism focused on this world, not the next; compellingly the sage had asked: "You are not even able to serve man; how can you serve the spirits . . . you do not understand even life; how can you understand death?"[1] By contrast, one of Buddhism's central concerns was the endless cycle of life, death, and reincarnation to which humans were committed; it taught that what one did in this life directly affected what happened to one in the next. For some Chinese, the subordination of the here and now to a theoretical future existence was unacceptable, while the notion of perpetual reincarnation was profoundly subversive because it implied that a person's position in life, as a monarch or a beggar, a human or an ant, was not fixed.

Early Buddhist missionaries tried, with some success, to persuade Chinese that Buddhism was akin to the indigenous Chinese religion of Daoism, which similarly called for spiritual purification as a means to transcend the evils of the world and attain a golden age. Thus they used certain Daoist ideas and vocabulary to introduce Buddhist notions. This strategy of "grafting the alien onto native roots" was fairly successful in that it helped Buddhism spread among existing Daoist communities, which in turn probably helped spread Buddhist symbols and ideas farther afield. In time Buddhism established an independent existence and became one of China's major religions. Its particular attraction was precisely that it filled a gaping vacuum of spiritual support left both by this-worldly Confucianism and by Daoism, which for a time became increasingly abstract.

Buddhism was especially successful in making inroads into China after the fall of the Han in 220. The profound social dislocations of the ensuing civil wars indirectly promoted Buddhism's growth by securing the monasteries' position in local communities as agencies of social welfare, making it possible to refute the criticisms of those who questioned Buddhism's social utility. For instance, many women widowed in the fighting resorted for protection to religious life in Buddhist nunneries. Numerous other needy people availed themselves of the programs Buddhist establishments began increasingly to operate, providing food and shelter for the destitute. In short, women and the lowly, to whom traditional Chinese society offered little in the way of material or spiritual benefit, often found that Buddhism and the monastic life could offer greater opportunities for self-fulfillment than life within a Confucian framework.

Buddhist monasteries also began to play an important economic role. For example, they held religious festivals for which Buddhist paraphernalia were in demand. Many such commodities could be obtained only abroad, so that fragrant plants for incense, jewels, and precious metals came to form an important sector of the long-distance trade. In other words, Buddhism helped bolster trade and raise prices. The monasteries also operated pawnshops and mutual financing associations and actively boosted handicrafts industries by, for example, sponsoring the production of thousands of statues. These multiple roles served both to integrate the Buddhist establishments in Chinese society and, almost imperceptibly at first, to strengthen their political significance.

Buddhism's growing influence in China spread to the world of art and architecture. Gradually the distinctively Indian artistic forms and styles of the earliest Chinese Buddhist temples, with the place of worship focused in a central tower, began to undergo a long process of adaptation to China. For example, what in India was a Buddhist stupa eventually transmuted into the multistory Chinese pagoda that came to epitomize a classic Chinese landscape.[2] Along with the new architecture came monumental stone sculptures and highly elaborate paintings and murals, often incorporating Buddhist motifs. In the earliest of these representations the features of Buddha and his disciples and the statuary style show traces of Indian, Persian, and even Greco-Roman influence, but in the course of time this evidence of foreign origin dwindled away. The Dunhuang murals, painted over a period of centuries, offer one illustration of this tendency.

The Buddhist religion benefited in other ways from the post-Han political division of China. The southern kingdoms, which regarded themselves as more "purely" Chinese, used it as a tool in the assimilation of "wild natives" previously little exposed to Chinese culture.

The northern kingdoms, often dominated by alien groups, found Buddhism a convenient alternative to existing Chinese ideologies to which they were often hostile. In general, rulers openly employed Buddhism to bolster their claims to legitimacy because Buddhist legend offered highly appealing models of kingly behavior, in which devotion to the religion ensured earthly success as a ruler while generous donations to its institutions purchased semidivine status. Such models neatly complemented ancient Chinese theories of universal rulership.

In practical terms, monarchs struck deals whereby in return for their investment in religious institutions and for letting the Buddhist establishments operate more or less without restriction, they arranged for prominent clergymen to declare them incarnations of the Buddha. They hoped of course that this assumption of divine status would make them politically unassailable as rulers, while the Buddhists hoped that the imperial imprimatur would make them unassailable by Daoist and Confucian competitors. To a considerable extent, these strategies worked for both sides. This political cooptation of the Buddhist religion made it extremely difficult for rulers to restrain the growth of Buddhism on any level. In sum, the foreign religion became both widespread as a belief system and extremely powerful as an institution, and it spread into China simultaneously among members of the ruling classes and a wide range of ordinary people.

The Multicultural Ambience of Tang China, 618–907

Historians describe the Tang empire as a "native" empire, to align it with the Han and distinguish it from some of the "non-native" kingdoms of the preceding centuries of division and from the later Mongol and Manchu dynasties. Yet such a description is deceptive partly because it implies the existence of a fixed "Chineseness" unsullied by foreign influence and partly because of the complex origins and habits of the Tang imperial family itself. Descended from the Tuoba Xianbei, a Turco-Mongol group that had ruled much of north China a century earlier as the Northern Wei dynasty, Tang emperors preferred to speak the language of their forefathers among themselves, rather than Chinese, and their matrimonial and

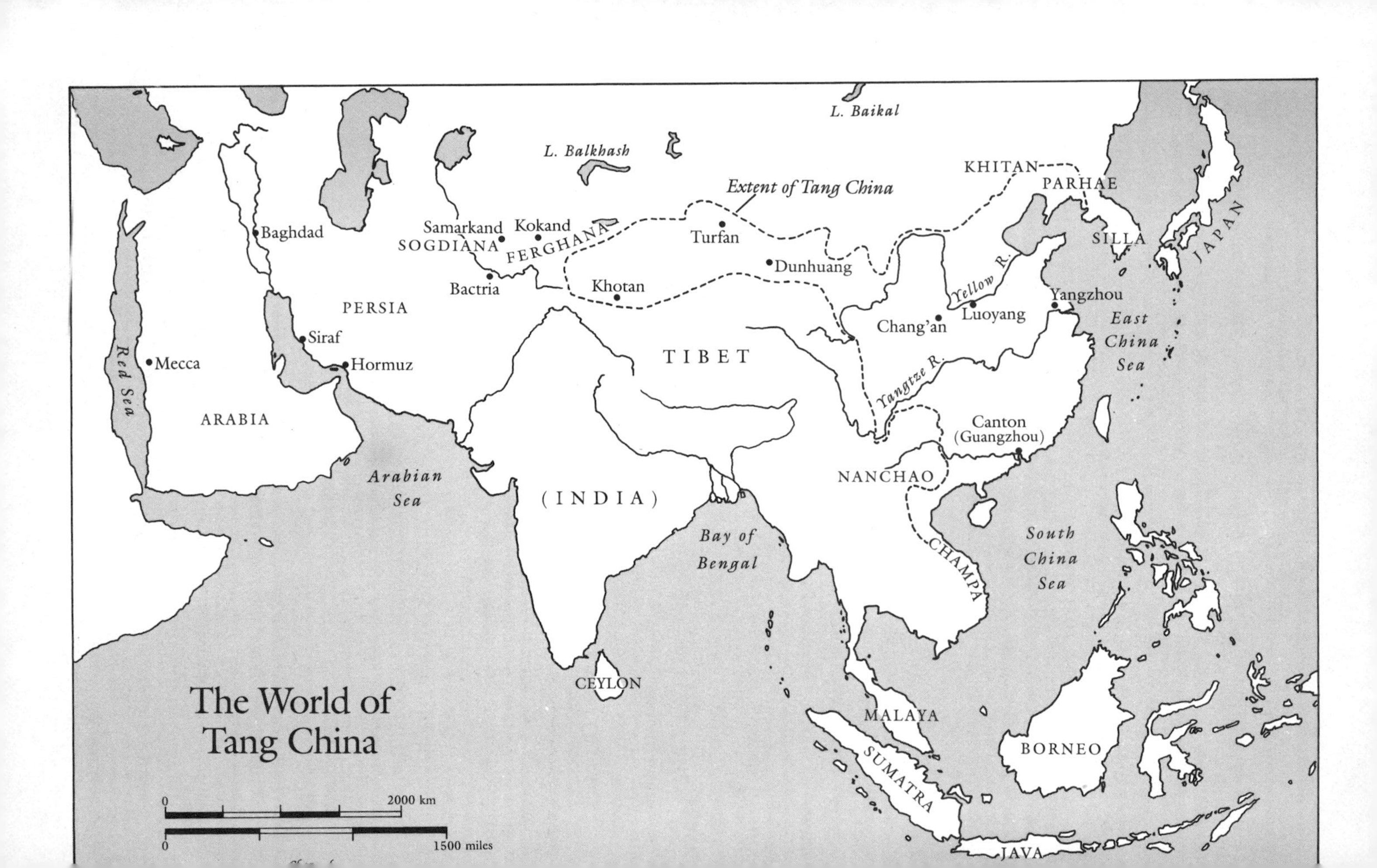
The World of Tang China
L. Baikal
L. Balkhash
KHITAN
PARHAE
SILLA
JAPAN
Extent of Tang China
Samarkand
Kokand
SOGDIANA
FERGHANA
Baghdad
Turfan
Dunhuang
Bactria
Khotan
Yellow R.
Yangzhou
Luoyang
Chang'an
East China Sea
PERSIA
Siraf
Hormuz
Mecca
Red Sea
TIBET
Yangtze R.
ARABIA
Canton (Guangzhou)
NANCHAO
Arabian Sea
(INDIA)
Bay of Bengal
CHAMPA
South China Sea
CEYLON
MALAYA
BORNEO
SUMATRA
JAVA
0
2000 km
0
1500 miles

clan practices and social customs differed from the indigenous Chinese tradition. They shunned close association with the native aristocracy, which in turn for some time resisted forming any imperial connections. Anxious to demonstrate their legitimacy, Tang rulers successfully established their credentials as a thoroughly Chinese house and suppressed evidence to the contrary. They were also highly receptive to foreign influence, appreciating imported goods and freely making use of foreigners' services.

For example, foreigners abounded in the Tang military. Imperial expansion in the seventh century, an important component of Tang China's power and prestige, owed much to the destruction of China's external enemies by the great emperor Taizong (r. 627–649), under whom China imposed political control over the numerous kingdoms along the Silk Road almost as far west as the Persian frontier. Among other foreigners in Taizong's armies, for instance, were several thousand Nepalese and Tibetan troops serving under a Chinese commander in northern India. A century later a Tang general of Korean origin defeated a Tibetan army on the frontier at about the same time as, in the heartland, another multinational Tang army under a Khitan general from the northeast defeated a major rebellion led by a Tang military governor named An Lushan (703–757). An himself was part Sogdian and part Turkish; his armies included numbers of non-Chinese frontier forces. One of the major problems with which the shattered Tang had to contend after suppressing the rebellion was the restlessness of many of these foreign troops.

At its height in the decades before An Lushan's rebellion, the Tang capital at Chang'an was the largest, most sophisticated, and most cosmopolitan city in the world, with a taxable population of nearly two million people. Only Baghdad and Constantinople even remotely approached it. Chang'an's population came from all over the world. There were western and eastern Turks from Central Asia (sometimes called Turkestan); Persians from the collapsing Sassanian empire; Uighurs from China's northwest frontiers; and Sogdians from the Samarkand area, whose language was the lingua franca of the Silk Road. There were also Arabs and Jews; Indians, both Hindu and Buddhist; Koreans; Tibetans; Malays; Japanese; and a host of other foreigners of sometimes uncertain origin. With them they brought their merchandise, religions, languages, customs, and cultures. When they returned to their own countries, they took back with them Chinese artifacts, institutions, and systems of belief.

Many journeyed overland, from Syria and Persia along the various routes of the Silk Road through Central Asia. These well-beaten tracks went either north, by way of Samarkand in Sogdiana and Kokand in Ferghana, or farther to the south, by way of Bactria, to the edges of contemporary Xinjiang. From there it was again possible to take a northern or southern route. The northern route skirted the great Taklamakan desert and ran along the edges of the Tianshan mountain range, onward to the oases of Turfan and Hami. The southern route went from the Pamirs via Khotan along the foothills of the Kunlun Mountains and intersected with the northern route at the Dunhuang oasis. There were other, less traveled routes. One went much farther south, from India through Burma to Yunnan in southwest China, at least until the rise of the hostile kingdom of Nanzhao in the eighth century made this route too dangerous. Another, especially favored by Buddhist pilgrims, went by way of Nepal and Tibet.

Others came by sea, from Siraf and Ubullah in the Persian Gulf and from southern India and Ceylon, going by way of Malaya, Java, and other Southeast Asian entrepôts. Still others sailed south from Korea and Japan. Canton continued to be the major port for overseas trade, but foreign merchant communities sprang into existence all up and down China's eastern seaboard.

As in Chang'an, Tang Canton's foreign population ran into the tens of thousands. There were Khmers from present-day Cambodia, Javanese from modern Indonesia, Singhalese and Tamils from what is today Sri Lanka, Chams from what is now Vietnam, Indians, Arabs, and Persians. Canton could claim with some justification to be a truly multicultural city, with a veritable babel of languages, among which Persian, the sailors' common language, probably came second only to Chinese.

From Canton it was possible to travel all over China by an extensive network of roads and waterways, many newly built to accommodate the burgeoning traffic. Most proceeded to Yangzhou, a thriving commercial center at the intersection of the Yangzi River and the Grand Canal connecting north and south China, through which almost all seaborne imports passed. From Yangzhou they went on to the great political centers of north China. As in towns such as Turfan and Dunhuang along the Silk Road and in the seaports, settlements of foreigners plied their wares in many of the towns along the way. These communities played a considerable role in the spread of towns and cities beyond the old administrative centers, and helped disseminate foreign objects and ideas throughout the land.

Tang Chinese, for all their cosmopolitanism, seem to have felt some ambivalence about foreigners. They were fascinated and enthused by what the strangers brought, whether intellectual excitement or material culture, but they did not always like or trust the messenger. Sometimes, like so many others, they took refuge in stereotypes. Thus they tended to characterize Persians as "wealthy (and therefore enviable)," Malays as "black (and therefore ugly)," and Chams as "naked (and therefore immoral)."

For the literate it was possible to gain some considerable sense of the world beyond China from the accounts of soldiers, merchants, and religious travelers. Such works—still only in manuscript in this preprinting age—must have been available in the bookstores of large Tang cities, along with multilingual dictionaries and imported books in translation. Some accounts were of course more well informed and less fanciful than others. For example, the imperial archivist and collector Duan Chengshi (d. 863), who delighted in learning about strange and wonderful matters, reported about the people of East Africa that they "do not eat the Five Grains, but only meat. They are given to sticking a needle into the veins of their cattle and drawing out the blood, which they mix with milk and consume raw. They wear no clothes, but merely use goatskins to cover the parts below their waists. Their women are clean and of proper behavior."[3]

Although Duan's work was grounded in reality, others produced imaginative works that included the names of actual places or events to lend an air of veracity. Duan himself wrote fiction as well as descriptive geographies. His fairy story "The King of Persia's Daughter" was set in a foreign place and reflected his sense of the magical potential of the outside world.

Tang poetry abounded in references to foreigners, foreign styles, and foreign ways. Some poets were neutral but others condemned the apparently wholesale embracing of foreign cultures:

> Ever since the alien horsemen began raising smut and dust,
> Fur and fleece, rank and rancid, have filled Xian and Luo.
> Women make themselves alien matrons by the study of alien makeup,
> Entertainers present alien tunes, in their devotion to alien music.[4]

In this poem by Yuan Zhen (799–831) the term "alien" (*hu*) was used in the pejorative sense of "uncivilized." Xian and Luo referred to the two Tang capitals, Chang'an (anciently Xianyang) and Luoyang. "Alien music" refers to a type of music called *faqu* introduced during the Sui (581–607) and extremely popular during the Tang. Another poem, by Yuan Zhen's contemporary Bai Juyi (Po Chü-i), explicitly blames Xuanzong's passion for this type of music for the decline of the Tang.

Foreign residents in Tang China lived and conducted business in specially designated areas. They were somewhat independent of local authority. They had their own community heads, and they enjoyed some degree of extraterritoriality, applying their own rather than Chinese laws in cases that affected only members of their own community. They were allowed to worship their own gods, as we shall see. But so far as commerce was concerned, they were given far less latitude.

TRADE AND INTERNATIONAL EXCHANGE UNDER THE TANG

By Tang times China was beginning to build ships capable of undertaking long journeys. Their vessels excited admiring comment in southern India and the Persian Gulf and may even have traveled as far as the Americas. Tang coins and fragments of porcelain have been found on the north and east coasts of Africa, although we cannot tell if they got there on Chinese ships. Other Chinese goods, especially written texts and artifacts connected to Buddhism, found their way to Japan, Korea, and Southeast Asia in great quantity with the steady trickle of migrants and with the envoys and merchants who traveled to and fro.

Trade expanded enormously, for a number of reasons. The first was simply the magnetism of the prosperous and cosmopolitan Tang court and society. The second was an increase in seafaring skill and adventurousness on the part of the Arabs, who still dominated the maritime trade. The third was a change in the goods China was exporting. Silks had once been China's most wanted product, but ceramics now began to compete as a leading category of exports, to compensate for China's loss of the world monopoly on silk production. This loss had occurred when silkworm cocoons were smuggled out to Syria, where Damascus provided the English name for the fine-quality fabric known as damask; sericulture had soon spread across Asia Minor and parts of southern Europe, and from the seventh century the silk industry, centered in Constantinople, had become a mainstay of the Byzantine economy. Although fine Chinese silks remained in great demand and were still traded around the world, both the need for diversification and technical advances leading to the development of a true porcelain that was much finer than earlier products greatly boosted the trade in ceramics. Because of their bulk and weight, it was much more practical to transport them by sea than by the well-worn camel route overland. As a result, by the latter part of the Tang, China's entire orientation had begun to shift from the plains of the northwest and the continental routes across the Silk Road toward the southeastern seaboard. Increasingly, maritime trade became as important as that carried overland.

Tang China regulated foreign commerce strictly. In Canton all foreign imports and all Chinese goods destined for sale abroad were supposed to pass through a Bureau of Merchant Shipping (*shibosi*), headed by a customs inspector. This system enabled the government to maintain its lucrative monopolies on such expensive imports as pearls, gold, fine silks, and tapestries; to collect customs duties, which sometimes ran as high as 30 percent, and hence were a major source of revenue; and to limit smuggling of such valuable commodities as gold and fancy silks or iron, which alien states could use to forge weapons they might one day use against China.

The numerous restrictions and controls on foreigners sometimes provoked protest and even on occasion led to violence. In the late seventh century, for instance, a foreign shipowner murdered a Canton official whose depredations, thinly disguised as government regulation, had become intolerable. But for most foreign merchants the vast profits of the China trade apparently outweighed the expenses and inconveniences of doing business in China on Chinese terms.

Under the Tang, imported objects became so fully absorbed into Chinese material culture that their foreign origins were sometimes forgotten. One example of such incorporation was the chair, adopted from Central Asia and by Tang times regarded as quintessentially Chinese as well as something of a status symbol. Its use was thought to distinguish Chinese from those who continued to sit on mats on the floor—for instance, Koreans, Thai, Vietnamese, and Japanese.

The most elaborate of all imported objects were those presented by visiting dignitaries to the emperor. These included peacocks from India; ostriches from Tocharia; goshawks, sables, and leopard skins from the northeast, brought by Koreans and Mongolians; elephants from Indochina; hunting mastiffs from Tibet; and the reputedly blood-sweating horses of Ferghana. These last China coveted mainly for military use, for it had no breed to match them.

Within the cities, especially Chang'an, specialized bazaars sold exotica of all kinds. There were aromatics, such as Arabian or African myrrh and frankincense; pigments and dyes, such as indigo and henna; weapons, in which there was a considerable clandestine commerce; and jewels, such as pearls and corals, lapis lazuli and malachite, jade and cornelian, sold by Persian merchants. There were new foods: such plants as spinach, and sesame buns similar to those that Muslim restaurants now serve in Beijing. There were peach trees from Samarkand; date palms from Persia, whose fruits were not only savored but also used to enhance the complexion; grapes for wine, a pleasure newly learned or relearned from abroad; Indian cotton, still something of a luxury in China; cloves for toothache; aloe for salves; and saffron, a highly valued import used as a perfume, as a dye, and for medicinal purposes.

Foreigners themselves came into the category of exotic imports, though this was controversial. A few foreign slaves, Africans, Turks, and Malays traded by Arabs or Southeast Asians, appeared in the major cities and at court. Dwarfs of uncertain origin titillated the court's passion for curiosities. Foreign prostitutes were quite widespread, including young Korean women in the imperial harem and boys from the "Western Regions," perhaps Sogdiana or Tocharia:

> The Western boy with curly hair and green-irised eyes
> In the high tower, when the night is quiet, blows the transverse bamboo.[5]

Surviving pottery figurines of the period include many foreigners—soldiers, grooms, magicians, exorcists, musicians, dancers, and so on—with the bushy hair or large, hooked noses of western Asians. Their draperies reveal Persian or Turkish influences, including lapels; leopard-skin hats; tight-sleeved tunics; close-fitting dresses; long scarves; long, pleated skirts; boots, for women as well as for soldiers in the field; headdresses shaped like the characteristic Turkish onion domes; small Turkish-type caps; and piled-up hairstyles and "Uighur chignons." Soon imported styles became quite fashionable in Chinese high society.

This trend aroused some objections. Conservatives accused modish Chinese of both sexes of an unseemly lack of decorum, especially deploring the tendency of some women to show themselves bare-headed in public, and in general they criticized the trend away from traditional Chinese modes of dress and decoration. The renowned ninth-century poet Bai Juyi condemned the fashion, popular among contemporary women, of applying orange beauty spots in the style of the Turfan oasis. Yet Bai himself was not immune from the allure of foreign exotica and had a Turkish-style blue felt tent erected for a garden party.

Chinese enjoyed foreign dance styles, often highly erotic, accompanied by unfamiliar melodies with strange musical notations. They watched performances by all-female orchestras and troupes from the "Western Regions." They acquired a taste for the Persian game of polo, played on horseback by men and women alike, and sent it on to Japan and Korea. Even those who could not afford to purchase luxury goods for themselves were able to see and hear people from other cultures and to gain a sense of the world beyond their own civilization.

THE EXCHANGE OF IDEAS UNDER THE TANG

Buddhist monks were one major conduit of ideas; often they were men of immense learning. In addition to transmitting their religion, they acted as an important vehicle for the transfer of ideas and of scientific knowledge between China and elsewhere. Those from India were especially renowned for their medical skills. More than once Tang emperors commissioned Indian monks to lead expeditions to such distant places as Java and Sumatra, to collect rare medicinal herbs and resins known to be efficacious remedies. Many upper-class Chinese were attracted not only to those who professed knowledge of mainstream medicine—ophthalmology for instance—but also to gurus, hypnotists, yoga masters, ascetics, and other would-be miracle workers, including the spellbinders associated with the magical branch of Buddhism known as Tantrism, introduced from India in the eighth century.

Some Indian wise men found that the quest for longevity, something long associated in China with Daoist alchemists, especially appealed to their Chinese patrons. Thus in 648 a Chinese diplomat-general brought back from engagements in India not only a defeated king come to pay homage but a magician who claimed that he was two hundred years old and knew how to make an elixir of long life. Emperor Taizong provided him with space in the palace in which to brew his alchemical concoctions and assigned a senior official to attend to his every need. Although the emperor's health did in fact improve after he took the elixir, he eventually decided that the improvement was due to his pious works, not to the medicine. He dismissed the monk, whose death soon afterward brought him total discredit.

Foreign influence in the realm of ideas extended to philosophy, mathematics, and astronomy. Around this time China adopted foreign notions of logic and trigonometry, although for the time being they rejected the use of zero, another foreign import. In particular Indian knowledge of astronomy—itself influenced by Persian and Hellenistic ideas—became dominant in China. One of the greatest of early Chinese astronomers was the Tantric Buddhist monk Yixing (fl. 720s), who organized teams to map the constellations and measure the altitude of the stars. Astronomy was politically important beyond its considerable significance as a science because the ability to predict such phenomena as eclipses and control over the calendar were imperial prerogatives, so that accurate knowledge of the heavens amounted to a tool of government. During most of the eighth century Chinese official astronomy was dominated by three Indian families, but in the long term Indian influence in the field of Chinese astronomy was relatively inconsequential.

Foreign monks also helped China develop gunpowder, one of its most famous "inventions." China had used smoke both in warfare and for purposes of fumigation or disinfection at least as early as the fourth century B.C., but the refinement of the mixture of ingredients needed to make explosives seems to have developed toward the end of the Tang. It was, ironically, a side effect of the chemical experiments of Daoists seeking an elixir of immortality. Tang period Daoist texts indicate that Chinese knowledge of the chemical properties of saltpeter, one of gunpowder's key components, was indebted to information garnered from monks who hailed from Sogdiana. Like much else, then, gunpowder did not simply appear in isolation but was instead a product of China's contact with the Middle East.

DIPLOMACY

Foreign dignitaries visiting Tang China were treated differently from foreign residents. They came under the aegis of the Court of State Ceremonial (*honglusi*), located in Chang'an and operated under the general supervision of the Board of Rites, one of the six main ministries of state. This agency took overall charge of official foreign visitors and their needs. In cooperation with military personnel, *honglusi* officials interviewed all official foreign delegates immediately upon their arrival, interrogating them about the geography, living conditions, and customs of their countries. They then had maps drawn on the basis of what they had learned and presented them to the emperor, with copies to the Bureau of Operations (*zhifang*) of the Board of War. These maps often included very extensive annotation in addition to simply expressing measurements. Along with local products, some embassies offered maps of their own territories as gifts to the Tang court, as a mark of their submission.

In exchange they took home Chinese goods to present to their rulers or to sell on the home market; with those goods, inevitably, went some of the culture that had produced them. This was particularly marked in the case of Japan. In the fifth century Japan had adopted China's writing system, and during the Tang it took on many more of the distinctive features of Chinese civilization, including its centralized political structure, its city planning—the Japanese capitals at Nara and later Heian were modeled on Tang Chang'an—and its system of land tenure. Several of the frequent Japanese embassies to Tang China took with them large numbers of Buddhist monks as well as political envoys, for by this time Buddhism, accompanied by elements of Confucianism and Chinese culture, had spread to Japan, by way of Korea, and to Vietnam. Just as Chinese Buddhists traveled to India in search of texts and learned masters, so Japanese Buddhists journeyed to China. Thus the network of international contacts forged in the Tang did not merely draw foreign imports into China but also spawned the outward extension of Chinese influence into much of East Asia.

Embassies thus were an instrument of both trade and intellectual exchange. They were also major sources of information about the outside world. Jia Dan (730–805), reputedly Tang China's greatest cartographer, including of marine routes, was famous for his extensive geographical knowledge. Jia headed the *honglusi* for several years in the late eighth century and produced a number of maps that incorporated information he gained while interviewing visiting dignitaries in his professional capacity. Unfortunately none of his work, nor other contemporary work known to have been written about foreign lands and civilizations, has survived. We do, however, still have a few paintings done by such court artists as Yan Liben—probably commissioned to display Tang power—depicting such subjects as the presentation of "tribute" by foreign emissaries and the newly conquered "Western Regions."

Just as incoming embassies were carefully interrogated, so Chinese missions sent abroad were specifically expected to gather geographic and other information about the places they visited, on both land and sea. For example, the seventh-century emperor Gaozong (r. 650–683) sent emissaries to Sogdiana and Tocharia to collect information on local customs and products and to draw detailed maps. The resulting work in sixty scrolls, entitled "Illustrated Treatise on the Western Regions," written up by the Court Historiographical Office, was presented to the throne in 658.

Diplomacy thus included a strong element of espionage. Chinese leaders had no illusions that such practices could work both ways. Well aware of their own envoys' reconnaissance activities, they often worried that tributary missions and other visitors from abroad might use for hostile purposes what they learned while in China. They regarded with the utmost suspicion any foreigner found asking too many questions or, worse, drawing maps.

There were other ways to learn about the world beyond China. For example, some of those who fought in the far-flung Tang military campaigns traveled even farther from home. One Tang officer captured near Samarkand in 751 eventually found his way back to China by way of what are now Eritrea and Iraq, bringing with him firsthand tales of these distant lands and their ways of life.

The fairly regular traffic of religious pilgrims between China and India at this time provided another major source of information. When Xuanzang, with whose epic journey in search of Buddhist scriptures this chapter opens, returned after a journey of several years, Emperor Taizong personally debriefed him in two audiences.

Appreciating the advantages of obtaining a firsthand account, the emperor questioned Xuanzang closely about Indian history, customs, geography, climate, and products and later built an Indian-style brick tower in Chang'an—the Wild Goose Pagoda, successors of which can still be visited today in Xi'an—to house the texts brought back. Complete freedom of movement was, however, far from universal. For most ordinary Chinese at this time, travel beyond China required express government permission. Even Xuanzang, whose departure had not been officially sanctioned, made sure to apply for permission to reenter China as he approached the imperial border posts.

We can draw two major conclusions about the circulation of information about other lands and civilizations in Tang China. First, there was an enormous flow of people, goods, and ideas into and out of China that together provided rich possibilities for the mutual harvesting of knowledge. Second, the emperor and his government played so active a role in collecting information of this kind that we can be certain that from very early times Chinese leaders clearly grasped the value of knowing as much as possible about other countries.

Foreign Religions

A number of foreign religions thrived in the first couple of centuries of Tang rule. Among these was Buddhism, but by now it was so pervasive and so politically powerful that Chinese usually disregarded its alien origins.

The early Tang were tolerant toward foreign religions on the whole, although they discouraged Chinese from joining them and appointed a special official to keep an eye on them. Their approach to these foreign religions varied, depending on shifts in their perception of the nature and extent of the religions' influence. During the Tang period Jewish, Muslim, Zoroastrian, Manichaean, and Nestorian Christian foreign traders routinely built their own houses of worship in China; other religions, such as Hinduism, may also have been represented. In early-eighth-century Chang'an alone, for instance, there were four Persian temples, Zoroastrian or Manichaean.

Zoroastrianism, a Persian religion based on belief in a fierce tension between cosmic forces for good and evil, had been patronized by the Tuoba Wei, ancestors of the Tang royal house, in the early sixth century. After Emperor Taizong of the Tang granted asylum to Crown Prince Firuz of the collapsing Sassanian empire, he permitted him to establish a Zoroastrian temple in Chang'an to service his court in exile. With this apparent imperial toleration, if not endorsement, Zoroastrianism gained a certain following in China, but its chief constituency remained the Persian merchant population. Manichaeism, another Persian religion that combined elements of Eastern Christianity, Buddhism, and Zoroastrian dualism, reached China in 694, but within forty years it had been banned among native Chinese for "falsely appropriating the name of Buddha and misleading the people." Foreigners were still permitted to practice Manichaeism, however, and some credence was given to adherents' claims to be able to influence celestial patterns. In the late eighth century, for example, Manichaeans, whose knowledge of astronomy Chinese scholars appreciated, were invited to use their magical formulas to bring rain to the parched countryside. In this respect, and in the Tang's ambivalent attitude toward them, the Manichaeans prefigured seventeenth- and eighteenth-century Jesuit missionaries, whose apparent rainmaking skills commoners admired as much as Qing emperors admired their knowledge of astronomy.

The earliest mention of Christianity in China dates from the early fourth century, but at the time its impact was limited. Most early Christianity in China was Nestorianism. This branch of Christianity had seceded from Rome and established its own patriarch in Baghdad after having been condemned in the fifth century as heretical because it taught that Christ's human and divine natures were distinct, relegating Christ the man and the Virgin Mary to positions inferior to those assigned by orthodox Catholicism. Nestorian missionaries reached China in the seventh century, as recorded in a 781 inscription written in Syriac and Persian and erected in Chang'an. Much later the discovery that these early Christians had once flourished in China aroused enormous excitement—their status as heretics notwithstanding—among European missionaries hoping to convert the whole of China.

Finally, foreign traders brought both Islam and Judaism into China, as we can see from the presence of mosques and synagogues in such commercial cities as Canton. The first Muslim mosque in China, for example, was established in Canton in 627, five years before the death of the prophet Muhammad. But for the time being the spread of these faiths among native Chinese remained relatively limited.

From the mid-eighth century a surge of xenophobia marked the beginning of the end of Tang religious tolerance and a shift in favor of indigenous religions and beliefs. This shift derived in part from the foreign origins of the rebel An Lushan, whose uprising caused widespread suffering as well as a major downturn in Tang imperial fortunes. Not coincidentally, during the rebellion Chinese in Canton and Yangzhou massacred tens of thousands of foreign businessmen, Muslim Arabs, Jews, and Persians, resented for their great prosperity and occasionally avaricious practices. The government started to issue increasingly stringent restrictions on foreign communities. In such a climate some intellectuals began to recall the alien origins of the Buddhist religion and to feel apprehensive about the political strength of the Buddhist establishment.

This hostility to Buddhism was not entirely new. Buddhism's association with the early-eighth-century empresses Wu and Wei, whose names became bywords for extreme corruption, had first begun to tip the balance against the foreign religion. Then, in Xuanzong's reign (712–756), various monastic abuses came to public notice. For instance, wealthy families were able to evade paying taxes either by becoming ordained as Buddhist priests or novices or by founding private temples. Nor was the problem confined to the wealthy. In 714, for example, the government ordered tens of thousands of people, who called themselves monks or nuns so as to gain exemptions from tax and service requirements, to return to lay life and hence to the tax and service registers. These abuses, and the growing influence of Buddhist institutions, prompted the Tang authorities to seek ways to restrict the power of Buddhism. They transferred overall control to the *honglusi* (Court of State Ceremonial), a move intended to undermine Buddhist influence by clearly characterizing it as foreign. At the same time, the emperor became increasingly interested in Daoism, Buddhism's chief competitor.

The fall from favor of outsiders and their religious ideas culminated in a wide-ranging proscription of all foreign religions, promulgated in 845. Several thousand foreign monks, an undifferentiated group from all the foreign religions then present in China, were returned to lay life. None of the foreign religions, not even Buddhism, ever fully recovered its former position in China.

Confucians were at the forefront of this backlash. In a famous diatribe the great Confucian statesman and essayist Han Yu (786–824) criticized the display of a Buddhist relic in the imperial palace. Han Yu objected to Buddhism both because he found it superstitious and opposed to Confucian morality and because it was foreign. His attack reads in part:

> Now Buddha was a man of the barbarians who did not speak the language of China and wore clothes of a different fashion. His sayings did not concern the ways of our ancient kings, nor did his manner of dress conform to their laws. He understood neither the duties that bind sovereign and subject, nor the affections of father and son. If he were still alive today and came to our court by order of his ruler, Your Majesty might condescend to receive him, but it would amount to no more than one audience in the Xuanzheng Hall, a banquet by the Office of Diplomatic Relations [part of the *honglusi*], the presentation of a suit of clothes, and he would then be escorted to the borders of the empire, dismissed, and not allowed to delude the masses. How then, when he has long been dead, could his rotten bones, the foul and unlucky remains of his body, be rightly admitted to the palace? Confucius said: "Respect ghosts and spirits, but keep them at a distance. . . ."[6]

Much of the remainder of this famous memorial is even more emphatic in tone. For so boldly speaking out, Han Yu was banished to the far south. But his sentiments were in line with the rising tide of public opinion.

The Tang empire collapsed in 907. After a hiatus of sixty years—a single calendrical cycle by Chinese reckoning—during which several small states vied with one another for supremacy, it was succeeded by the Song empire (960–1276).

Beginning in that interregnum, regional and international commerce expanded greatly, for two main reasons. First, technical advances had prompted a great increase of agricultural and handicraft production, especially in the ceramics industry. As a result, a surplus was available for trade either with other Chinese regions or overseas. At the same time, demand for foreign luxuries also increased. The second reason for the expansion of trade was that the various states into which the Tang empire disintegrated, taking advantage of a period of relative peace resulting from their own military weakness, tried to use trade to form political connections and shore up their support wherever they could. This trend to the expansion of trade continued unabated after the Song empire assumed power.

Commercial and Maritime Expansion under the Song, 960–1276

The Song was a period of extraordinary economic, cultural, and social change during which, in the estimation of many scholars, Chinese civilization was preeminent in the entire world. The Song capital was at Kaifeng, in north China, until 1127, when the Song were driven south by invaders from the northeast. From 1127 until its overthrow in 1276 the Southern Song ruled a reduced empire from its reconstituted capital in Hangzhou, while in north China, the alien invaders proclaimed a Jin empire, which lasted until the Jin themselves were driven out by the Mongols, in the early thirteenth century. The Southern Song lasted until their overthrow by the Mongols in 1276.

As we have seen, China during the Tang had become integrated into the flow of seaborne trade that went to and from its own east coast, traveling by way of the kingdoms of Southeast Asia to India and onward to the Middle East. At the same time, the installation of various foreign communities in China, the adoption of Chinese institutions by other states, and the establishment of Chinese communities overseas had reinforced China's presence in the Asian trading world, long before the advent of Europeans in any number.

In the centuries following the fall of the Tang, China rose to the leading position on the seas. Chinese shipbuilders began to build massive oceangoing junks, up to 300 feet long, with a capacity of approximately 1,250 tons, and able to carry from five hundred to a thousand people. These ships, the technology for which partly drew on Arab models, were capable of undertaking very long-distance voyages and transporting vast cargoes. At about the same time, the Indians, Persians, and Arabs who had dominated the seaborne trade at the height of the Tang became distracted by other concerns nearer to home, and the volume of foreign shipping reaching China diminished. This left a vacuum that the newly competent Chinese merchant marine was ready and able to fill.

Song Chinese made a series of major technical advances related to their improved knowledge of geography, astronomy, mapmaking, and shipbuilding. They invented the compass, which radically improved their ability to navigate; soon every Chinese ship carried one. They instituted lighthouses and beacons. Far more accurately than before they observed tides, winds, weather patterns, and stars; calculated distances; and plumbed depths. Experienced sailors made records of all this new knowledge, and a new genre of technical literature came into existence, consisting, among other things, of marine charts and itineraries and records of islands, currents, and reefs with precise bearings.

Writers of the Song period also produced informative and up-to-date accounts of foreign countries. Some of this new information, which circulated widely, was largely technical, but Song scholars were ready to expand their own more limited literary horizons by studying the contributions of Arab and Hindu navigators and geographers, thus making it possible for Chinese bound overseas to benefit from foreigners' experiences. Among the most famous of this type of work was Zhao Rugua's *Zhufan Zhi* ("Records of Foreign Peoples"), written after 1225. Zhao had been superintendent of the Office of Merchant Marine in Quanzhou on the Fujian coast, which by then had surpassed Canton as China's leading port for foreign trade. Among other things Quanzhou housed both Muslim and Hindu temples for the use of merchants from Southeast Asia, the Indian subcontinent, and beyond, and it honored the Muslim custom of allowing foreigners to be governed by their own laws, indicating a considerable Muslim presence. In his account Zhao discussed in detail such topics as commerce, foreign countries, and the exotic products he had come across in the course of his work. His description of Egypt, for example, was the first known in any Chinese work. It reads in part:

> The country of Wusili [Egypt] is under the dominion of Baida [Baghdad]. The king is fair; he wears a turban, a jacket, and black boots. When he shows himself in public he is on horseback, and before him go three hundred led horses with saddles and bridles ornamented with gold and jewels. There go also ten tigers held with iron chains; an hundred men watch them, and fifty men hold the chains. There are also an hundred club-bearers and thirty hawk-bearers. Furthermore a thousand horsemen surround and guard him, and three hundred body-slaves bear bucklers [*sic*] and swords. Two men carry the king's arms before him, and a hundred

> kettle-drummers follow him on horseback. The whole pageant is very grand!
>
> The people live on cakes, and flesh; they eat no rice. Dry weather usually prevails. The government extends over sixteen provinces with a circumference of over sixty stages. When rain falls the people's farming (is not helped thereby but on the contrary) is washed out and destroyed. There is a river (in this country) of very clear and sweet water, and the source whence springs this river is not known. If there is a year of drought, the rivers of all other countries get low, this river alone remains as usual, with abundance of water for farming purposes, and the people avail themselves of it in their agriculture . . .[7]

The Song authorities decisively promoted international trade because it was such a valuable source of revenue. Their policy, initiated soon after the founding of the dynasty, was to "invite and stimulate" foreign merchants. Song commercial activism took various forms. In 988 the emperor dispatched a mission to various foreign countries, bearing elaborate gifts with which to lure merchants to China. At the same time the Song envoys purchased valuable goods, such as ivory and pearls, plants and animal horns for medicinal use, and perfumes, to sell upon their return. In China itself government officials in the main trading ports held annual farewell banquets and other celebrations for the encouragement of foreign sailors and traders. Merchant shipping that was blown onto the coast or damaged was taken under Chinese government protection, which included protection from ill-treatment by local officials. If, however, those officials succeeded in encouraging foreign trade, they might be rewarded by banquets or promotions.

In this way foreign trade expanded rapidly, but so did Chinese government control over it, both to maintain its function as an important source of revenue and to restrict the outward flow of hard currency. Customs duties on imports ran at about 10 percent. The central government maintained monopolies on the most profitable goods, such as ivory, coral, rhinoceros horn, and crocodile skins. They banned any private traffic in a number of luxury commodities and retained an option for preferential purchase of anything imported. The government also kept a close watch on exports. A Chinese merchant going overseas had to declare his intended destination. If subsequently he claimed to have been blown off course to some other place, he had to report it promptly and, if possible, produce evidence. He needed an inventory for export items and a receipt for taxes already paid. As in the Tang, products that could be used to make weapons could not be exported legally, although illicit commerce in iron with Southeast Asia flourished steadily; nor could rice, presumably in case the surplus should be needed in times of famine or war. To guard against the threat of piracy, merchants engaged in the overseas trade were allowed to carry arms, but they had to deposit their weapons when they returned to China; if they went overseas again, they could reclaim them.

These restrictions prompted some merchants to emigrate, mainly to the commercial entrepôts of Southeast Asia. Others became pirates. Throughout the Asian seas piracy was endemic, as was smuggling. Both could be enormously lucrative. Such outlawry presented bona fide merchants with a strong temptation as well as a threat. But legal investment in the overseas trade was also attractive; contemporary sources record the willingness of not particularly rich people to put what little spare funds they had into the overseas trade.

The range of goods flowing in and out of Song China was immense. Different markets sought and offered different goods, of course, but overall the most sought-after Chinese exports continued to be silk and other textiles; silk thread; metals, including gold, silver, pewter, copper, tin, and lead; ceramic wares, from fine porcelains to coarse earthenware; and tea. Other exports included lacquerware, semiprecious stones, paper, bamboo, lichees, and books.

China took in as wide a variety of goods as it sent out. From the Khitan Liao empire in southern Manchuria, China imported horses, furs, wool, and slaves; from Japan it brought in sulfur for gunpowder, pearls and antlers for medicinal purposes, coffin woods, weapons, and decorative handicrafts; from Southeast Asia China imported such spices as cloves and cardamom, sandalwood and aloe, fruits, and tortoiseshell; from Tibet, horses in exchange for Sichuanese tea; from India and East Africa, ivory and rhinoceros horn; from Syria, glassware; from the Persian Gulf, pearls; and from the Mediterranean, coral. Some of these imports, such as ivory and rhinoceros horn, were subject to government monopolies, but as in the case of the iron trade, private merchants often were prepared to risk arrest for illicit trading because of the scale of potential profits.

One vital consequence of China's involvement with other parts of Asia during the Song period was the tenth-century introduction of early-ripening rice from Champa, a state in central Indochina. Over the long term government efforts to disseminate this relatively drought-resistant strain of rice, which could be cropped twice a year, revolutionized land utilization and created the preconditions for population growth. Early-ripening rice, in other words, was one of China's most influential foreign imports.

Intellectual interaction with other civilizations continued during the Song, although relatively little is known about it. Knowledge about medicine was still an important area of exchange. An early-fourteenth-century Persian manuscript, for instance, reproduced illustrations from an earlier Chinese text on anatomy, demonstrating that others valued Chinese expertise in this field just as China valued that of others. Also, sometime in the eleventh century techniques for inoculation against smallpox reached China, probably from India or Persia.

One side effect of the flourishing foreign trade was the reintroduction of foreign religious communities, which in some cases perhaps had never died out altogether. In Kaifeng a community of Jews established itself before the Song shifted their capital south in 1127. They came from Persia, Palestine, and Yemen; they mainly used Persian, the common language in much of Central Asia; and they sold "western cloth," perhaps cotton. By 1163 they had built their first synagogue in Kaifeng, which survived until it was destroyed in the mid-nineteenth century. The Kaifeng Jewish community never surpassed perhaps fifteen hundred members, divided into seven clans. But it maintained a distinct identity despite intermarriage, partly because the Chinese authorities tolerated the Jews as a sect of Islam, which continued to flourish quietly in China. Some Chinese Jews did convert to Islam—they had in common at least their abstention from pork, a Chinese staple—and even today Kaifeng Muslims can be divided into two groups: some claim descent from Muhammad while others, presumably the descendants of the old Jewish community, identify their ancestor as Abraham.

The Mongol Yuan, 1276–1368

After the Mongol leader Khubilai Khan conquered China in 1276 and established the Yuan dynasty, China in effect formed part of a huge empire that stretched right across Asia: from Korea and Manchuria in the northeast across Turkestan and parts of Siberia to Mesopotamia and the Caucasus in the west. In those circumstances it was not surprising that Chinese contact with lands to the west was frequent and extensive. The Venetian Marco Polo, whose claims to have lived in Yuan China remain to this day subject to debate, certainly was accurate enough when he reported China's astonishing cosmopolitanism and prosperity in the thirteenth century:

> To this port [Quanzhou, Fujian] come all the ships of India with quantities of costly merchandise, priceless precious stones and large, fine pearls. Here too all the merchants from south China, or at least those from the surrounding regions, stand out to sea. . . . I tell you, that for every ship loaded with pepper that goes to Alexandria or some other place, to be transported to Christendom, more than a hundred come to Zayton [Quanzhou]. The massive amount of merchandise assembled in this town is almost unbelievable. . . .[8]

The surging trade patterns and the taste for luxury that had become commonplace during the Song dynasty in many ways continued their momentum after the Mongol invasion. Merchants from all over the world came to China. Up and down the east coast, to the ports of Shandong, Zhejiang, Fujian, and Guangdong provinces, navigators and traders came from Vietnam, Borneo, Java, Sumatra, Pagan, India, and the Middle East, as well as from Korea and Japan and from farther afield.

The Mongols inhibited commercial exchange more than the Song had done because, wishing to reap vast profits, they tried to monopolize international trade. In 1284 they banned Chinese merchants from going overseas to trade unless specifically selected by the government and furnished with ships and capital by it. The Mongols took 70 percent of the profits of foreign trade and imposed more and heavier taxes. The net result was that international trade, though still significant, fell into a relative recession.

The vastness of the Mongol empire facilitated the flow of information as well as commodities. Yuan China absorbed ideas about astronomy from Persia, where, toward 1260, scholars from all countries manned an international astronomical observatory. In 1267 the Persian astronomer and geographer Jamal al-Din established a new calendar for Khubilai, although it eventually was replaced by a Chinese one that may have been put together under Arab influence. He also brought him a Persian terrestrial globe, together with various astronomical instruments and designs for them, including an armillary sphere, a celestial globe, a gnomon, and an astrolabe. A few years later the Chinese astronomer Guo Shoujing (1231–1316) adapted some of these designs to specific Chinese needs, for the Chinese system was different from the Muslim one. Guo made the astronomical instruments for the Beijing observatory that remained in use until a new one was built by Jesuit missionaries four hundred years later.

Meanwhile Chinese cartographers continued to make more wide-ranging and increasingly accurate maps. Helped both by the vast extent of territory that the Mongols controlled and by advances in astronomy, they correctly measured the latitudes of more and more places: Pyongyang in Korea; Lake Baikal in Siberia; Karakorum in Mongolia; Hainan Island off the south China coast. About 1320 the cartographer Zhu Siben (1273–1337) made a map that formed the foundation for Chinese knowledge of the world for the next several hundred years. Zhu's map included phonetic designations for about one hundred place-names in Europe ("A-lu-mang-ni-a" [approximating modern Germany, "Allemagne"] and "Fa-li-hsi-na" [modern France]). It shows a town situated approximately where Budapest now is and depicts the Mediterranean Sea. Unlike contemporary European maps, Zhu's map also gives the correct shape and orientation of Africa, with some detail for the north of that continent. It depicts both the Sahara and the Gobi Deserts in black, it indicates Alexandria by a pagoda showing the pharaohs, and it gives about thirty-five African place-names. Chinese maps of the world continued to be closely based on Zhu's work for at least another century.

Under the Mongols, "Arabs," a term primarily denoting Persians and Central Asians, dominated Chinese science and technology as for a time Indians had done under the Tang. Yuan histories record that Muslim gunners helped the Yuan finally overwhelm the Song in the 1270s; they may well have transmitted military and other information to China. Such knowledge traveled in two directions: tradition holds that it was the Mongols who conveyed the formula for gunpowder from China across their vast Asian empire to Europe, where it utterly transformed the face of warfare.

Another important development in Yuan China was the rapid expansion of the cotton industry, whose advantages the Mongols had perhaps learned to appreciate in other parts of their vast empire. Previously cotton cultivation in China had been more or less limited to border areas in the south, but with Mongol encouragement in the form of tax incentives and the dissemination of technical information, it now became an important factor in China's economy. State efforts to promote cotton were aided by the work of Huang Daopo (b. about 1245), a woman later canonized as cotton's patron saint, who spread the techniques of cleaning and spinning the raw cotton to the lower Yangzi region, which became a major center of cotton cultivation and manufacture.

Nestorian Christianity enjoyed considerable success among the Mongols, who also regarded the rulers of Western Christendom as promising allies against the Muslims, whose political power obstructed Mongol plans for world empire. Most Christians in China under the Mongols were Nestorians, including Khubilai Khan's mother, who encouraged her sons to exercise religious toleration. The Nestorians built several churches in south China and maintained a number of flourishing communities, to the chagrin of the pope's appointee as archbishop of Beijing, the Franciscan John of Monte Corvino, who reached China in 1294 and built two churches in Beijing in the hope of converting many Chinese to orthodox Catholicism.

Perhaps under his mother's influence, Khubilai did not persecute his subjects on religious grounds. Instead he encouraged religious diversity in his realm, in part as a counterweight to the influence of Confucianism. He himself privately acknowledged the Tibetan lama 'Phags-pa as his teacher and established joint spiritual and secular rule with him over Tibet.

In the 1280s a Nestorian monk became the first person from China ever known to have reached Europe. Rabban Sauma set off with a student on a pilgrimage to the tombs of the Nestorian martyrs and the Fathers of the Nestorian Church in the Holy Land. With support from their church and the Mongol court, the two pilgrims crossed Central Asia, journeying from oasis to oasis until eventually they reached Baghdad, where they became embroiled in local religious and political affairs. Rabban Sauma eventually traveled on alone to Rome and Paris, charged with a diplomatic mission by Persia's Mongol ruler, who wanted him to persuade the pope and the French and English kings to launch a crusade with him against Islam. The two kings received Rabban Sauma in audience and apparently pledged to join the desired alliance, but the monk reached Rome just as a new pope was being chosen and so was unable to fulfill his mission. He died in Persia without returning to China.

The adventures of Rabban Sauma—the very idea that a Christian monk from the eastern end of the vast Mongol empire should be conducting diplomacy in the courts of Western Europe—are less astonishing when viewed in the context of Mongol internationalism. In China the Mongols reorganized society along broadly ethnic lines. There were four tiers. The first rank was composed of Mongols; the second was composed of *semu*, or Western and Central Asians. The third rank was composed of those Chinese from the north who had lived under Jurchen Jin rule after the Song moved south in 1127. The lowest level consisted of the former Chinese subjects of the Southern Song. The Mongols preferred to employ *semu*, whom they found more reliable than Chinese, in high government office. Apart from Rabban Sauma, at different times their government included Muslims from Central Asia, Tibetans, Western Asians, and, according to Marco Polo, the Venetian merchant himself. Although it was not customary under the Chinese bureaucratic system to give this type of responsibility to foreigners, the practice was widespread by this time throughout Asia, where states often were only loosely defined.

Mongol open-mindedness extended to the arts. One of Khubilai's protégés, for instance, was the Nepalese painter and architect A'nige (1224–1306), who, in addition to painting the emperor's portrait, designed a number of temples and pavilions that introduced elements of Tibetan and Nepalese architecture into China.

Whether the Chinese scholars were as cosmopolitan as were their Mongol overlords remains open to debate. The trauma of alien conquest tended to encourage Chinese claims that foreigners, including the Mongols, whom Chinese disparaged as barbaric, longed to acquire Chinese culture. But the evidence indicates that under alien rule cultural influences flowed in both directions.

The Ming Empire, 1368–1644

In the mid-fourteenth century Chinese rebels overthrew the Mongol Yuan and established the Ming in its place. The Ming was the last native empire of imperial China, sandwiched between the Mongol Yuan and the Manchu Qing that succeeded it. Initial encouragement of overseas trade as a source of revenue was followed by a half century of tight restrictions intended mainly to stem the outflow of precious metals. Then, between 1405 and the early 1430s, the Yongle Emperor (r. 1402–1424) dispatched a series of seven major fleets, over a period of twenty years. Led by Zheng He (1371–1433), a Muslim eunuch, the Ming fleets sailed through the seas of Southeast Asia to India, Hormuz in the Persian Gulf, and on as far as Malindi on the east coast of Africa, which they reached only a few decades before Portuguese vessels arrived from the opposite direction in search of a passage eastward to the Indies.

At their largest the fleets comprised more than three hundred ships, sixty-two of which were more than 400 feet long and 180 feet wide, with three decks and nine masts with twelve sails. The Chinese "treasure ships" would have vastly overshadowed the single-decked, much more compact ships with which Christopher Columbus sailed to the Americas less than a century later. The fleet also included water tankers, for there was great concern about maintaining a supply of fresh water to keep the travelers healthy. It carried almost twenty-eight thousand people. There were armed troops, including cavalry; eunuchs and civil officials to conduct diplomatic exchanges; translators and imams to deal with the ubiquitous Muslim traders; doctors and herbalists to identify herbs whose therapeutic properties were already known in China and to locate possible new cures in the wake of a string of epidemics; engineers; sailors; and merchants.

Officially Yongle launched these voyages to find out if there was any truth to the rumors that his predecessor, whose position he had usurped, was still alive and planning his revenge. But the expeditions served many other purposes. First, they were intended to impress Ming power upon foreign rulers and to establish diplomatic relations with them along tributary lines, with a view to creating a universal empire that was maritime as well as land-based like that of the Mongols. In this way China could also show the world that the Mongol threat had now been permanently resolved. For the same reason overland missions also went forth—to Korea, Tibet, and across Central Asia—and tributary exchanges were conducted with Japan, from which China garnered, among other things, large quantities of weapons, particularly swords, in exchange for fine art objects, literary texts, and other cultural and practical items.

Trade was another important part of the voyages. Zheng He's fleet brought back to China tribute-bearing envoys from a number of places it visited, including Bengal, Java, Calicut, and Cochin. The gifts they brought included a giraffe, given to the king of Bengal by the ruler of Malindi. Yongle was so enchanted by this offering that later missions brought more exotic creatures: zebras, ostriches, another giraffe, leopards, and so on. The expeditions both established overseas markets for Chinese goods—notably silks, embroideries, and fine porcelains—and brought back a host of other foreign goods, particularly spices. Yet the circulation of foreign goods in early-fourteenth-century China was much less widespread than it had been under the Tang and Song empires, partly because of conservative criticism of the expeditions' extravagance.

To underscore the theory that a tributary relationship involved developing cultural affinity as well as economic attachment to China, the expeditions also took with them thousands of copies of educational texts. One such work, *Lienü Zhuan*, was a series of biographies of model women of the past, originally produced for the edification of women in China. By disseminating works such as this, the emperor noted, the "barbarians" could begin the process of becoming civilized. This approach offers a particularly clear illustration of Chinese notions about the centrality of women as the repository of civilized behavior; it also illuminates how imperial China's tendency publicly to patronize other cultures, while privately acknowledging their worth, resembled the attitude of traditional Chinese men toward their womenfolk.

Every expedition carried Arabic speakers recruited from mosques in China, whose job was to translate and to convey the clear message that China was friendly toward Islam. This was necessary both because the early Ming had been extremely hostile toward Muslims, owing to their former role as tax collectors for the Mongols in China, and because Muslim merchants now vied with Chinese for control over many of the trade routes. The goal of protecting merchant shipping and securing the maritime passage to India and the Middle East was greatly furthered when Zheng He's navy destroyed a powerful pirate fleet near Sumatra, in modern Indonesia.

Through the expeditions Ming China gathered immense amounts of information about the world as far as Africa. Officials questioned incoming envoys about the geography of their countries and drew maps on the basis of the responses they received. They asked about their customs, and if they found their appearance especially exotic, they made drawings of their faces and their costumes, in a kind of primitive ethnography. Several of Zheng He's companions also wrote accounts of what at the time were by far the most extensive maritime explorations in world history. Such works as Gong Zhen's 1434 "Record of Foreign Countries in the Western Ocean," Fei Xin's 1436 "Captivating Views from a Star-Guided Vessel," and Ma Huan's 1451 "Description of the Coasts of the Ocean" described Chinese relations with and attitudes toward the cultures of many of the places the fleets visited, particularly in the South China Sea, along the Strait of Malacca, and along the edge of the Indian Ocean. Chinese maps now also began to depict the shape of the Indian subcontinent with some accuracy, marking an advance from Zhu Siben's work a century before.

Taken together, these provide the most detailed accounts of travel in Asia between Marco Polo's *Travels* of 1298 and the notoriously unreliable records of Ibn Battuta, who may have visited China in the early sixteenth century. They also provided a wealth of information on Chinese shipping, navigation, and trade, as we can see from the account of the holy Islamic city of Mecca written by Zheng He's Muslim adviser and Arabic translator, Ma Huan:

> [The Country of the Heavenly Square] is the country of Moqie [Mecca]. Setting sail from the country of Guli (Calicut), you proceed towards the south-west—the point *shen* on the compass—the ship travels for three moons, and then reaches the jetty of this country. The foreign name for it is Zhida [Jedda], and there is a great chief who controls it. From Zhida you go west, and after traveling for one day you reach the city where the king resides; it is named the capital city of Moqie.
>
> They profess the Muslim religion. A holy man first expounded and spread the doctrine of his teaching in this country, and right down to the present day the people of the country all observe the regulations of the doctrine in their actions, not daring to commit the slightest transgression.
>
> The people of this country are stalwart and fine-looking, and their limbs and faces are of a very dark purple color.
>
> The menfolk bind up their heads; they wear long garments; and on their feet they put leather shoes. The women all wear a covering over their heads, and you cannot see their faces.

> They speak the A-la-pi [Arabic] language. The law of the country prohibits wine-drinking. . . .[9]

The voyages of the Chinese treasure fleets ended with Zheng He's death in 1433, when, in any event, China's navy was entering a period of decline. The conclusion of the expeditions came about as the result of a combination of circumstances. The Ming lost enormous prestige when the Mongols captured the emperor at the infamous Battle of Tumu in 1449. The Mongols released the emperor only a year later and in the meantime were greatly emboldened, necessitating a refocusing of Ming attention on the inland frontiers to the north. At the same time, the steady expansion of private trade at the expense of government monopolies meant that goods were harder to obtain and prices were higher. As the result of these developments, the value of paper money collapsed so that the Ming could no longer use it for foreign trade; instead they had to pay market value or offer goods in kind in order to acquire the horses they needed to fight the Mongols and other necessary imports. For these reasons, and also because of a diminishing tax base resulting from natural disasters and spreading bureaucratic corruption, the imperial treasury was depleted, priorities changed, and the dispatch of elaborate fleets came to an end. Nonetheless, within Asia maritime trade continued, drawing China into contact with a range of merchant groups from all over Asia and North Africa. Until the coming of the Portuguese in the early sixteenth century, China remained the most significant external power in the region.

The Advent of Europeans and the Impact of the Silver Trade

Portuguese ships reached the China coast in the early sixteenth century, but for some time relations between Chinese authorities and European merchants remained, if not downright hostile, distinctly cool as the result of the inevitable mutual misunderstandings. The Portuguese hoped to export both their material goods and their religion, but for a number of reasons they were less successful in China than in Japan, where the more centralized government exercised tighter control. The European China trade remained for the time being clandestine.

By mid-century the steady deterioration of relations between China and Japan had provided an opening for Portuguese merchants. Coastal raids by "Japanese" pirates, who in reality were both Chinese and Japanese smugglers trading illicitly with Japan, and demands for trade and recognition made by various contenders for power in Japan prompted China first to restrict trade with Japan and then, in 1560, to ban it altogether. But Chinese demand for cheap silver from Japan, where extremely rich deposits had recently been found, and Japanese demand for silks and other luxury Chinese goods both remained extremely strong. The formal ban did not therefore put an end to the China-Japan trade; it continued virtually uninterrupted, indirectly through Southeast Asian ports, by Chinese acting clandestinely, or on Portuguese vessels. The Portuguese middlemen's role in the silver trade was highly lucrative; the profits they made financed Macao, the toehold Portugal established off the southeast coast of China, with tacit Chinese consent, in 1557, and helped fund the Jesuit missions in East Asia. For

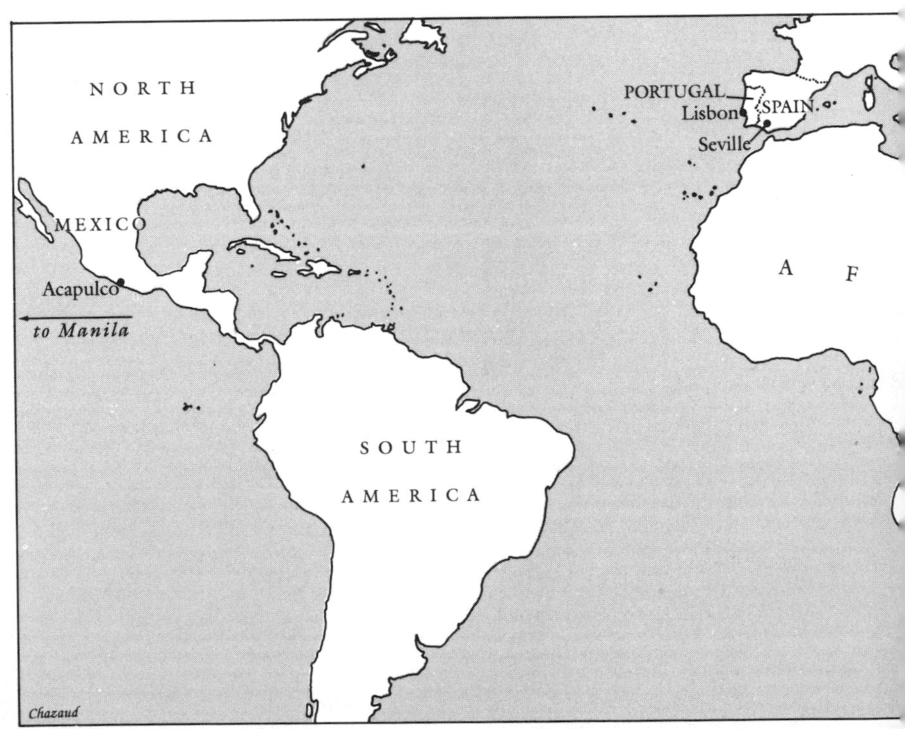

Japan, the enormous profits from the silver trade enabled those who controlled it to gain political power and ultimately to retreat from China's tributary orbit and in effect establish a commercial capitalism in Asia.

Silver from the New World began to compete with Japanese silver for the market in China. China, as we have seen, had long been integrated into the complex networks of trade within Asia. Now, however, proliferating links between Asia, Europe, and the Americas, including the establishment of European colonies in Southeast Asia, added a new dimension to international trade. Moreover, China hankered for silver just as Europe craved Chinese silks and porcelains. It was greatly in demand both as currency and as a commodity in its own right. The net result was that its value in China was as much as double its worth anywhere else. Thus adventurous traders willing to risk repeated long-distance journeys could make their fortune by selling silver bought, say, in Europe for twice the price in China and then exchanging the money made in China for twice the amount of silver in Europe, and so on.

The scale of international silver flows was massive. Silver entering

The World of Late Ming China

China from the Spanish Americas soon vastly outstripped that imported from Japan. In the early 1600s perhaps as much as one-half the silver mined in the Spanish Americas, where new technology had further reduced production costs, found its way to China. Some went directly across the Pacific in the so-called Manila Galleons, which sailed from Acapulco to the Philippines, under Spanish control from 1571; from Manila it was transshipped to China on Chinese junks. More New World silver reached China by way of Europe, either by sea or across the Central Asian trading routes. Toward the middle of the seventeenth century the laws of supply and demand brought the value of silver in China more in line with its value elsewhere, so that profits and shipments began to decline.

The point here is that because of silver, local economies around the world became more and more tightly connected through a highly elaborate network of international trade, in which Europeans acted primarily as middlemen. Chinese demand for silver in effect financed the Spanish empire, Tokugawa Japan, and, more indirectly, the Atlantic slave trade, in that in parts of the Americas, African slaves were exchanged for silver that eventually found its way to China. In short, as the sixteenth century turned into the seventeenth, China was already irredeemably integrated into the rapidly expanding global economy.

The changing configuration of world trade flows and the depredations of pirates along the Chinese coast spurred further Chinese emigration to Southeast Asia. Overseas Chinese settlement had grown substantially since the Song period and had continued thereafter. Some had migrated to escape the devastating Mongol invasions of the thirteenth century, while more recently others, including Chinese Muslims, had deserted from the massive Ming fleets and dispersed throughout the region. As Chinese communities expanded, they began to acquire political influence. By the sixteenth century Chinese could be found in powerful positions in Vietnam, where in Ming times Confucianism had become the state ideology; in the kingdoms of Indonesia and their successor Dutch colonies; and in the Philippines.

European colonists often felt threatened by the Chinese presence. Yet at the same time they could not do without their services, both as intermediaries in their dealings with native populations—for instance, in such unpopular occupations as pawnbrokers and rent collectors—and as an entrée to the lucrative China trade. Chinese merchants in Manila, for example, became crucial to the trade between China and the Spanish American colonies because the Chinese government refused to allow Spain to establish an outpost in China.

By 1603 Chinese in Manila were numerous enough to convince the Spanish that an uprising was imminent. To preempt it, the Spanish carried out a massacre in which perhaps twenty thousand Chinese died. The atrocity remained unrequited by the already declining Ming government. Yet the contacts that survivors and new settlers retained with their families at home helped forge new kinds of links between China and the outside world that became more and more important as time went on.

In sum, since very early times China has formed part of an international network that ranged from Syria to Japan and from Korea to Indonesia. The links that bound this network together were commercial, religious, intellectual, and simply human. Both formally and informally, China initiated contacts with foreign countries at least as often as it was on the receiving end. Well aware of the existence of other powerful and civilized nations, China pragmatically sought to establish relations with many of them through diplomacy, sometimes backed by warfare, and through trade. In international commercial circles China's monopoly on the production first of silk and then of porcelain gave its merchants a preeminent position. Long-distance travel took place both by land and by sea. The accounts of returning travelers made it possible for those who remained in China to learn a great deal about the larger world, often stimulating considerable interest in other civilizations.

Not only did China reach out to the world, but also representatives of many foreign countries journeyed to China in pursuit of Chinese specialties that were the envy of other civilizations. In exchange they brought to China a huge variety of their own native products, which Chinese people relished and adopted with great interest and pleasure. Foreigners introduced new religions, shared scientific knowledge, and established diplomatic ties. In the process China enormously refined its awareness and knowledge of the world. No less important, a whole range of Chinese goods, ideas, and people went abroad, diffusing Chinese intellectual and material influence as well as some of China's most characteristic institutions, such as its system of government. In short, the flow went in both directions, into and out of China, creating a mesh of relationships that spread right across Asia. China was ineluctably caught up in this network in innumerable ways well before Europeans appeared on the scene; their arrival extended its reach over even greater distances.

CHAPTER TWO

❦ ❦ ❦

China and Catholicism in the Sixteenth through Eighteenth Centuries

> . . .What would you say if I sent a troop of Buddhist monks into your country to preach their doctrines? You want all Chinese to become Christians. Your Law demands it, I know. But in that case what will become of us? Shall we become subjects of your king? The converts you make recognize only you in time of trouble. They will listen to no other voice but yours. I know that at the present time there is nothing to fear, but when your ships come by the thousands then there will probably be great disorder. . . . The emperor, my father, lost a great deal of his reputation among scholars by the condescension with which he let you establish yourselves here. . . .[1]
>
> The Yongzheng Emperor (1723–1735)

Portugal, seizing on the rich possibilities for European expansion suggested by the exploratory voyages of such men as Ferdinand Magellan and Vasco da Gama, had by the late fifteenth century identified two main goals in Asia. The first was economic: it wanted to wrest control of the lucrative spice trade between Asia and Europe from the Muslim traders who had dominated the sea routes since the decline of Ming naval power. The second was religious: it hoped to regain in Asia, as well as in Africa and in Brazil, some of the ground the Catholic Church had lost in Europe as a consequence of the Protestant Reformation.

In the late fifteenth century Portugal and Spain reached a general agreement to divide the world outside Europe between them. In the 1494 Treaty of Tordesillas, Pope Alexander VI purported to give formal recognition to Spanish and Portuguese domination of world trade routes by allocating to Portugal Asia, except the Philippines, as its sphere of influence, and to Spain the New World, except Brazil. This was a remarkable formula to draw up before all the newly discovered territories had been thoroughly mapped. In effect, it aimed to deliver control over European expansion into Catholic hands just as Catholic authority was undergoing the first assaults of the Protestant Reformation.

Portugal and Spain were, however, unable to exclude other Europeans from East Asian markets. They remained the principal European traders in East Asia—the Portuguese in Macao, with a more substantial colonial center in the Indian port of Goa, and the Spanish in the Philippines—only until the British and Dutch East India companies, founded in 1600 and 1602 respectively, successfully took over part of the market in spices. The Dutch soon established rival colonial trading bases in Batavia, Indonesia, and on the island of Taiwan, where Spain also maintained an outpost. Iberian and hence Catholic domination of the "market" in Asian souls proved more tenacious. Although the expansion of Islam offered Catholicism some competition in parts of Southeast Asia, in China Islam was less pervasive, and moreover, no European Protestants challenged Catholicism's monopoly for another two centuries. Thus the period from roughly 1600 to 1800 has been described as China's "Catholic centuries."

This chapter examines the introduction of European Catholicism into China, focusing in particular on its most conspicuous proponents, missionaries of the Society of Jesus. Although it is hard to separate the reception of Western religion, on the one hand, from the exchange of goods and secular knowledge, on the other—as the Chinese themselves often found—for clarity's sake we shall examine them more or less separately in this and the next chapter. Although this approach requires some unavoidable chronological overlap, this chapter deals primarily with Christianity during the period from the late sixteenth century, when the Ming was entering its declining phases, to the early eighteenth century, when for a number of reasons the tide turned decisively against the foreign religion. The next chapter focuses on the international exchange of goods and ideas and principally covers the reign (1736–1795) of Qianlong, under whose watch both foreign trade and the interest in European secular knowledge reached new heights.

Contrary to conventional wisdom, China rarely rejected foreign knowledge on the ground of pure outlandishness. Foreign origins were neither a recommendation nor an absolute bar to acceptance. China's reception of Christianity was influenced mainly by three factors. The first was the degree of compatibility between certain traditional Chinese beliefs and the Christian requirement that devotees should venerate the Christian God alone. The second factor related to the way Jesuit missionaries—Christianity's leading exponents in China—used their knowledge of such secular topics as mathematics and astronomy to attract Chinese interest before they ever raised the issue of religion. Attract interest they did, but this approach backfired because it raised doubts about their true intentions. The third factor influencing China's reception of Christianity was the momentous political changes taking place in China. In 1644 the Ming empire (1368–1644) which had expelled the Mongols from China, itself was replaced by Manchu invaders from the northeast, who established the Qing empire (1644–1911). To the majority of ordinary Chinese, the dynastic transition may have meant little more than the cessation of military activity and the resumption of the normal cycles of their lives. But for the educated classes, who were the prime targets of Jesuit mission efforts, the devastating experience of Manchu occupation completely colored their outlook, among other things disinclining them toward foreigners and foreign cultures. We turn now to a sketch of the situation in China at the time European missionaries first arrived in 1583.

LATE MING CHINA

On the surface late Ming China appeared truly thriving. Its population surpassed 150 million, far more than that of Europe at the time, which China roughly resembled in geographic size. Unprecedented agricultural prosperity gave commercial transactions a new importance, fueling the expansion of both regional and national markets. At the same time, the government consolidated the old forms of taxation in kind and in labor services into a single payment in silver, into which people converted the copper currency they used in everyday life. In other words, at about the same moment, the use of money, and silver in particular, became much more prevalent, both in the newly vital market economy and in the system of state revenues.

These currents contributed to a trend toward urbanization, particularly in the prosperous lower Yangzi area of Jiangnan. Urbanization in turn added momentum to a series of related developments, including the spread of literacy among both men and women; the much wider availability of books of all kinds; and a new attention to education for women, highly innovative in a world where up until then the main purpose of education had been preparation for the civil service examinations, which were reserved for men.

The same period saw the rapid expansion of a consumer culture, which endowed the possession of material goods with a new social significance. Members of the upper classes began to collect art objects and antiquities on a much larger scale than previously, as a yardstick of good taste and as a status symbol. Luxury goods, not least including exotic imports, were all the rage. Fine Japanese crafts, especially lacquer and metal wares, became a mainstay of luxury consumption (in Japan, Chinese luxury imports were equally prized). Other fashionable collectors' items at the time included turkeys from the New World, to be kept as pets; Tibetan religious texts (for purposes more of prestige than devotion); and paper and brushes from Korea to add cachet to the display of artistic prowess. Late Ming culture, in short, was hostile neither to foreign trade nor to outside influence.

The late Ming also saw a relaxation in the sphere of intellectual life. Over the centuries Confucianism had been forced to make some adaptations to counter competition from Buddhism. Under the Song in the eleventh and twelfth centuries, the scholar Zhu Xi (1130–1200) and others had developed a revised philosophy that was much more metaphysical than original Confucianism. Neo-Confucianism, as Westerners later called this new version, laid particular emphasis on moral rigor, the pursuit of self-cultivation through education and study, and public-spirited activism. It successfully fended off the Buddhist challenge and became the orthodox ideology upon which the civil service examinations were based. Hence it formed the foundation of every ambitious young man's education until the examination system was abolished in 1905.

In the fifteenth century the influential philosopher Wang Yangming (1472–1529) had sought to modify Zhu Xi's arguments by proposing that true moral knowledge exists within every person and hence that everyone is innately capable of understanding the meaning of life. This suggested that the pursuit of Confucian virtue might, after all, not require intensive education or even any formal education at all. For some late Ming scholars, Wang's ideas also raised the possibility that greater individualism and egalitarianism might be feasible within a Confucian framework, albeit a relatively unconventional one. At the same time, others who sought fresh approaches experimented with various creative and innovative syntheses of Confucian, Daoist, and Buddhist ideas.

This spirit of eclecticism met with strong disapproval on the part of some scholars, who feared that abandoning the orthodox tradition would lead straight to corruption and self-interest. But the point is that culturally and intellectually as well as economically and socially, the late Ming was in many ways a dynamic time and one of real open-mindedness about the possibilities of departure from traditional modes of life and thought. It created a fertile soil into which to plant the seeds of Christianity.

Beneath its veneer of prosperity the Ming was starting to show signs of trouble. The emperor lost interest in government and retreated into the pleasures of palace life, leaving court eunuchs and civil servants to run the country. Factional squabbles and extreme corruption became the political order of the day, seeming to confirm the worst fears of Confucian scholars. The central government's once iron grip over the empire grew steadily weaker, and the infrastructure began to fall apart.

Natural disasters compounded the difficulties caused by human neglect. Exceptionally severe weather in the early part of the seventeenth century, now thought to be part of a worldwide Little Ice Age, destroyed crops, and with them many people's food supply and livelihood. The government could no longer provide relief because it had failed to maintain the state granaries. Then a series of horrendous epidemics of some form of plague ravaged large parts of China. Some areas lost half their inhabitants; corpses lay everywhere. The overall population, a measure of prosperity, began to show marked decline. Survivors often were profoundly impoverished and close to despair. Some came together in armed associations that local officials were powerless to prevent or suppress. Uprisings sprang up in many different parts of the country.

Such groups were often extremely disparate and had no particular ideology or revolutionary goal. But as more and more disaffected people swelled their numbers, they began to occupy large portions of territory, preying on the inhabitants and destroying even the appearance of government authority or control. At the same time, along the southeast coast the expansion of maritime commerce was leading to long-term problems in the realms of both defense and the economy, while along the northern borders external enemies found little resistance to their increasingly frequent infringements into Ming territory.

QING CONQUEST, MING LOYALISM

In 1644 the Ming finally collapsed in the face of widespread peasant rebellions. They were replaced by Manchu invaders from the northeast, who proclaimed a new Qing empire. It took another forty years before the Qing could convincingly assert legitimacy as the bearers of the Mandate of Heaven to rule all China, for the country remained deeply disunited. Remnants of the Ming court fled south and tried repeatedly to reconstitute the old regime, with loyalist forces offering stiff resistance, but gradually the Manchus overwhelmed all opposition. In 1673 Wu Sangui (1612–1678), a former Ming general whose defection to the Qing had made possible the Manchu invasion, rebelled with two other southern satraps, whose combined military power and territorial control extended right across south and southwest China. It took the Manchus until 1681 to suppress this rebellion and establish their authority over south China.

In the meantime the island of Taiwan had become a base for anti-Qing activity. Taiwan had not been a part of the Ming empire, in whose imagination it remained a largely savage and isolated spot, but Spanish and Dutch traders and "Japanese" pirates all used it as a base. In the 1640s Dutch forces expelled the last of the Spanish settlers and the local pirates, only to be driven out with relative ease in 1662, when Zheng Cheng'gong, known in the West as Coxinga, established his own stronghold on the island.

The son of a Japanese mother and a Ming loyalist who had defected to the Qing in 1646, Zheng was a pirate entrepreneur who alternately supported the defeated Ming and negotiated with the conquering Qing. He operated in an unusually international ambience. Raised in Hirado, the Japanese port where the Dutch maintained a trading post, Zheng grasped the potential of the European weaponry he saw there and later used it effectively against both the Qing and the Dutch. In his campaigns against the Qing, he purchased arms, gunners, and vital supplies from both the Dutch and the British, in return for trading rights. He manned his bodyguard with African slaves escaped from Portuguese Macao.

During the 1650s Zheng conquered major portions of southeast and southwest China on behalf of the Ming remnants from his base at Xiamen (Amoy) on the Fujian coast. Alarmed at the prospects, the fledgling Qing were relatively receptive to Dutch embassies seeking trading concessions, hoping to enlist their military support. But having failed to recapture the former Ming capital of Nanjing from the Manchus, Zheng retreated to Taiwan, where the Dutch were no match for his forces. The Qing perceived little advantage in further alliance with the Dutch and accordingly gave short shrift to later embassies' requests for more frequent commercial exchanges in more locations.

Zheng died in Taiwan in 1662. His descendants remained there in defiance of Qing authority until 1683, when Taiwan was finally brought under Qing control. Chinese assertions of sovereignty over the island date from this last act in the consolidation of Manchu power in China, which marked the beginning of large-scale Chinese migration to the island. In later years Zheng Cheng'gong attained mythic status in both China and Japan. He has been honored variously as a Confucian loyalist, an anti-imperialist, a Japanese nationalist, a Chinese nationalist, and a hero of the Taiwan independence movement. Thus both actually and symbolically he represents a key figure in the shifting relationships between East Asia and the West.

Devotion to the fallen Ming aroused profound ambivalence among educated Chinese. Those steeped in the morally compelling Chinese traditions of loyalty had to resolve the emotional issue of whether or not they could possibly transfer their allegiance to the conquering regime. The chaos of national disintegration and the devastating experience of conquest completely demoralized Ming intelligentsia. Many now took refuge in loyalism, a key component of traditional morality that called for men and women identified with an overthrown ruler or dynasty to sacrifice their lives, if necessary, as an expression of their continuing devotion.

In practice Ming loyalism took two main forms. The first involved active armed resistance and often resulted in death. The second, longer-term and more subtle, led to a significant shift in the intellectual environment. Many scholars debated, in an agony of self-reproach and wide-ranging recriminations, the reasons for the cataclysmic Ming collapse. As they searched for explanations, many condemned what they saw as the loose intellectual and moral atmosphere of the late Ming, when, they believed, there had perhaps been too much of a sense that "anything goes" and too little emphasis on pursuing practical goals for the benefit of the country. As a consequence, a revival of the rigorous moral ethic of orthodoxy, accompanied by renewed interest in classical studies and practical statecraft, returned to the ascendant among Han Chinese intellectuals, who hoped to find a way to compensate for having tolerated the fatal laxity of the Ming's declining years. From this point of view, support for the new regime was particularly objectionable.

Such issues also resonated with the new Qing rulers. Without intellectuals' support, the new regime's legitimacy remained open to question. Besides, the Manchus were so much in the minority that they desperately needed a degree of cooperation from Chinese scholar-officials just to enable them to rule. Hence intellectual orthodoxy also received official encouragement from the Qing because it helped to identify them as upholders of Chinese traditions and thus to confound those who might question their legitimacy.

Overall neither the champions of the fallen Ming nor the new incumbents regarded a neutral stance as sufficient. Choices made in this volatile atmosphere determined the all-important judgment both of contemporaries and of history. These issues had much to do with the fate of the Catholic religion in China.

THE EARLY CATHOLIC MISSIONS TO CHINA

Catholic missionaries were at the forefront of China's introduction to Europe and its culture. Among the members of the several different religious orders that sent missionaries to China at this time, the most numerous and conspicuous were priests of the Society of Jesus (the Jesuit order), founded in 1540 with the express purpose of converting the heathen overseas. The first Jesuits took up residence in China in 1583 in the hope of gaining vast numbers of converts to their version of Christianity. Many spent the rest of their lives in China, living among Chinese people, speaking their language, and learning about their culture.

Constituted in 1540 by the soldier-mystic Ignatius of Loyola (1491–1556) as a highly militant order with the specific goal of converting "infidels" overseas, the Society of Jesus led the mission field in China. Sometimes referred to as the Shock Troops of the Counter-Reformation, the Jesuits called their leader a general and conceived of their overarching purpose as the conquest of the world for Christ. Christ himself was "transformed from an object of quiet reverence into a militant figure leading his disciplined order into battle against the devil."[2]

The Jesuits placed great stress on education. They used their colleges both to promote the Catholic education of the European upper classes and to provide future missionaries with a thorough grounding in the Western classics, history, theology, mathematics, physics, metaphysics, astronomy, logic, and moral philosophy, among other topics. Young Jesuits also were rigorously trained to draw connections between the different branches of their knowledge in order to be able to analyze and defend their faith. In short, the missionaries, who were often among the first to represent European culture abroad, came from the intellectual vanguard of their times. In China this was particularly appropriate because of the longevity and sophistication of its civilization, and because of the resulting cultural self-assurance of the Chinese intellectuals, who the missionaries hoped would lead the way in converting to Christianity.

Some nine hundred Jesuits worked in China in the seventeenth and eighteenth centuries. Other orders—Franciscans, Dominicans, Augustinians, and the secular French Society of Foreign Missions—also were well represented in China, but their numbers were consistently fewer, and they kept comparatively low profiles. Members of different religious orders often vehemently disagreed with one another on doctrinal or tactical matters, and on some points contention existed even within a single order. The bickering and mutual antagonism such disagreements generated had significant repercussions for the long-term goals of the missions in China because they undermined respect for the people involved and for the cause of Christianity.

The total number of Chinese converts is hard to fix with any certainty since missionaries sometimes retrieved and converted the dying while some converts later renounced the faith; besides, we cannot always assess the accuracy of missionary claims. The numbers of converted Chinese probably amounted to at least tens of thousands in the first half of the seventeenth century. At the end of that century, according to the estimate of a contemporary Jesuit observer, the 60 or so missionaries from all orders working in China were converting perhaps as many as 500 or 600 people each every year, making an annual total of more than 30,000, not including the additional several thousand abandoned children whom missionaries took under their wing each year. During the course of the eighteenth century periodic repressions caused considerable attrition; nonetheless, it is estimated that by 1800 200,000 to 250,000 thousand converts to Christianity may have been spread across China. This result was in no small measure due to the efforts of Jesuit missionaries.

JESUIT MISSION POLICIES

I: THE TOP-DOWN STRATEGY

The policies of the Jesuit missionaries brought them both their greatest successes and their greatest failures. Credit for many of the most significant is usually attributed to Matteo Ricci (1552–1610), among the first Jesuits to reach China in 1583, who set the standard for Jesuit mission work in China for the next two hundred years. The first policy we consider is that of focusing attention on educated, upper-class Chinese rather than on the ordinary people targeted by other religious orders. It was as the result of this top-down strategy that Jesuit missionaries were ensconced at the court of the emperor of China.

A two-fold rationale underlay the top-down strategy. First, the Jesuits wished to gain Chinese political support for the introduction of Christianity. Second, they hoped for a snowball effect. Jesuits assumed that once the elite converted, the common people would follow their social superiors into the foreign religion's fold. Of course, Jesuits did not abide rigidly by Ricci's guidelines. Even during his lifetime some of his colleagues were actively proselytizing among ordinary people, and by the end of the seventeenth century the vast majority of their converts were commoners.

Ricci's conversion of three leading scholars, all of whom gained high political office, was the most conspicuous vindication of the top-down strategy. Known to posterity as the Three Pillars of the Early Christian Church in China (*kaijiao san dazhushi*), together they provided the missionaries with powerful patronage. Each was impressed by the personal qualities of the European missionaries they came to know, and all were deeply interested in Western scientific knowledge. But that was also true of many Chinese who did not in the end adopt Christianity. What seems to have tipped the balance for these men, and other highly educated converts of this first generation of Chinese Catholics, was Christianity's promise to provide moral certainty at a highly unsettling time.

The first of the three to be baptized was Xu Guangqi (1562–1633), whose native place of Xujiahui, now part of the city of Shanghai, later housed a Jesuit library and the Cathedral of St. Ignatius. Xu was deeply impressed by Ricci when they first met in 1600 and was baptized in Nanjing a few years later. Shortly thereafter he passed the highest level of the civil service examinations and was assigned to work at the prestigious Hanlin Academy in Beijing. Xu then embarked on a collaboration with Ricci that produced some of the first translations of European books into Chinese. Together they translated works on Western geography, astronomy, hydraulics, and mathematics, notably the reworking of the first six books of Euclid's *Elements of Geometry* done earlier in the century by Ricci's own teacher in Rome, Christopher Clavius. Xu also adapted Western ideas in some of his original work on agriculture and trigonometry. He later became a grand secretary, one of the highest political offices in the empire. He was thus well placed to promote the Jesuits' cause.

The second of the Three Pillars was Li Zhizao (d. 1630), a native of Hangzhou whom Ricci himself baptized in 1610. By then the two men had been acquainted for nine years. Li, whose initial attraction to Ricci was the Jesuit's knowledge of geography, formed the opinion that here was an extraordinarily learned and virtuous man whose sense of right and wrong seemed almost infallible. At first Li resisted conversion, possibly because he did not wish to send away his concubine, as Church doctrine insisted. Only after Ricci had nursed him through a serious illness did Li finally agree to receive baptism and give up the concubine. Ricci died soon afterward, but Li became a powerful supporter of the missionaries, not least because of his strong interest in the Western scientific discoveries to which they had introduced him. The ambiguity of the title Li gave to his collection of Western works in translation suggests the complexity of his attraction to Western learning; he called it "First Collection of Writings on Learning about Heaven" (*Tianxue Chu Han*). Here "heaven" almost certainly referred to both religion and astronomy.

Under Li's influence a fellow Hangzhou scholar-official, Yang Tingyun (1557–1627), converted to Christianity in 1612 and became the third of the Three Pillars. The range of Yang's intellectual pursuits was in some respects typical of late Ming intellectual life. Earlier he had been active in promoting both orthodox Neo-Confucianism and Buddhism. But after he converted, Yang persuaded many members of his family, including his parents, to become Christians and with them formed a society in which they could together improve their grasp of Christian doctrine. Like Xu Guangqi and Li Zhizao, Yang published extensively so as to disseminate the information concerning Western science, geography, and philosophy as well as religion that he gleaned from the European missionaries. Like a number of his contemporaries, he also came to question long-cherished ideas about the distinctiveness of Chinese culture, for instance, speculating that the human race was all the same despite environmental and historical differences. Such observations did not of course endear Yang, or the Christianity he espoused, to the more traditional-minded of his contemporaries.

Yang Tingyun also devoted some effort to drawing clear distinctions between Christianity and Buddhism. To him, Christianity's strength derived from its moral rigor and humanity, in contrast with Buddhist attitudes. He noted, for example, that the man-made rules of Buddhism allowed him to keep a concubine whereas the more rigorous, immutable, God-given law of Christianity did not. (Like Li Zhizao, Yang sent away his concubine, the mother of his two sons, although, also like Li, only after personal struggles.) Moreover, Yang preferred Christianity because Buddhism focused indiscriminately on all living things, whereas Christianity elevated humans to a higher plane. It was clearly more worthwhile to devote one's energies to helping needy people than to save an animal from the butcher. Having saved a person's life, one could also try to save his or her soul. Yang Tingyun's efforts to demonstrate Christianity's superiority to Buddhism, along with his withdrawal of financial support from Buddhist institutions, provided tangible evidence that

Buddhism was losing ground to the new interloper and fueled growing Buddhist hostility to the foreign religion.

Besides the Three Pillars, Jesuits succeeded in converting almost two hundred courtiers of the Ming court prior to the dynastic transition. These included eunuchs and palace women. But Jesuits in China were unable to avoid becoming caught up in the fiery politics of the dynastic transition. After the Ming fell, some missionaries accompanied the beleaguered court as it fled south. With the help of the influential Christian loyalist eunuch Pang Tianshou (d. 1657), they converted the would-be Yongli Emperor's wife, his mother, and his eldest son, as well as his father's legal wife, who took the Christian name of Helena. Desperate to find help for the failing Ming cause, and perhaps epitomizing the sense of many converts that adherence to the foreign religion brought the promise of more than just spiritual aid, in 1650 both the eunuch Pang and the empress Helena wrote to the pope and to the Jesuit general in Rome, asking for their prayers and their help in resisting the Manchus. The empress's letter reads in part: ". . . I hope that you, in concert with the Holy One Catholic Church, will on our behalf request of God protection and assistance in restoring peace in my country. Thereby, the eighteenth ruler of Our Great Ming [the Yongli Emperor], the twelfth-generation descendant of the Great Founder, as well as his ministers, would all know to venerate the true Lord, Jesus. . . ."[3] But by the time their Jesuit emissary was able to deliver the letters, the Ming cause was beyond redemption.

For missionaries who remained in Beijing in 1644, on the other hand, it seemed only realistic to transfer the focus of their attentions to the new Qing court, which welcomed Jesuit offers of service. But to educated Han Chinese, the Manchus' willingness to employ foreigners recalled the Mongols and heightened fears that their new rulers planned to destroy first their political power and eventually their entire civilization.

Jesuit missionaries provided a whole range of services to successive Qing emperors, and their contributions undoubtedly encouraged imperial sanction for their presence, if not endorsement of their religion. But the influence their work gradually brought them at court also provoked considerable hostility from a variety of quarters. Such resentment was not surprising. In a society in which proximity to the emperor was an important key to political influence, anyone who succeeded in gaining such access was bound to acquire enemies along with it.

In the long run the Jesuits' switch of allegiance to the new regime had fatal consequences for their mission in another way: it largely discredited them among the ethnically Chinese scholarly classes. Such men had lost political power, but they remained numerically strong and socially influential. Formerly both the prime source of support for the Jesuit mission and the main target of its conversion efforts, they now regarded the foreign missionaries both as political traitors and as pawns in what they perceived as a Manchu assault on Chinese culture. Chinese scholars despised the missionaries on both counts. This gradual alienation was fueled by Qing policies deliberately restricting contact between the missionaries and the Chinese gentry. By welcoming the missionaries into the Manchu camp, the new regime consciously deprived the Chinese elite of this potentially uncontrollable source of intellectual and spiritual stimulation and kept it for themselves. The Jesuits' abandonment of their original policy of concentrating on the Chinese elite, in favor of focusing their attention on the new sources of power at the Qing court, thus turned out in the end to have been a terrible miscalculation.

In the highly charged climate surrounding the transfer of power, the role of Catholic collaborators further damaged the Jesuits' position. One such man was Zhu Zongyuan (b. 1609), baptized with the name of Cosimo at Hangzhou, Zhejiang, in 1631. In Hangzhou, which had a thriving Christian community, Zhu gathered a considerable following through his writings, which he hoped would convince people to convert to Christianity. He argued that different countries had different values but that difference did not necessarily signify inferiority. It followed, he said, that it was misguided to stigmatize foreigners as barbaric and that China had much to gain from other cultures. Christianity could serve as a pointer to the true Way. Pursuing these arguments to their logical conclusion, Zhu later threw his support to the Manchus, carrying with him many of those whom he had already persuaded to convert to Christianity. Zhu's arguments prefigured those of late-nineteenth- and early-twentieth-century thinkers who suggested that foreign influences had often revitalized Chinese culture just as it had reached a point of stagnation.

In the early Qing it happened that the new governor of Zhejiang and Fujian provinces was a northern frontiersman who had converted to Christianity along with members of his clan. He had served the

Manchus before the conquest and had encountered Christianity when the Manchus occupied Beijing. So under the political leadership of the Catholic governor, and urged on by Zhu Zongyuan and his band of Catholic converts, the formerly staunch province of Zhejiang fell to the Manchus. In this case the snowball effect of Christian conversions sought by the Jesuits led to a large-scale transfer of political allegiance. To Ming loyalists, the unexpectedly rapid fall of this prosperous coastal province to the Manchus thus seemed inseparable from the Christianity of Chinese collaborators.

After the 1630s the Jesuits rarely met with successes as spectacular as their conversion of such politically powerful men as the Three Pillars or the eunuch Pang Tianshou. But Christianity did not peter out among educated Chinese, and it persisted especially among the less elevated ranks of the scholarly. Some of the second and third generations of elite Chinese Christians assimilated the foreign religion to a greater extent than had their predecessors. By the middle to late seventeenth century, becoming a Christian was not always in itself so remarkable an event as it had once been. In fact, many of these later-seventeenth-century Chinese Catholics became Christians for the simple reason that their fathers had been Christians before them. It was, so to speak, a family matter, and many of these later converts never came into direct contact with European missionaries. But as Christianity was passed down from generation to generation, sustaining one's belief also acquired overtones of Confucian filial piety.

For these later educated converts, Christianity often became a creative force within their own culture. Their search for compatibilities between Chinese and Christian beliefs stimulated them to reexamine traditional Chinese concepts in ways that earlier scholarly converts had not. Some, for example, devoted their lives to cross-cultural studies, setting out to demonstrate the ways in which Christianity reinforced traditional Confucianism while Buddhism contradicted it. For instance, the five human relationships of Confucianism—between ruler and subject, father and son, husband and wife, older and younger brother, and friends—as well as the associated virtues of benevolence, morality, propriety, wisdom, and trust seemed entirely consonant with the law of the Christian God, while one of the perennial Chinese criticisms of Buddhism was its disregard of this ordering of society. The later converts also placed far greater emphasis than had their predecessors on expressing their Christianity through the promotion of social welfare.

Their overall approach, sometimes called inculturation, was qualitatively different from that of men such as the Three Pillars. For Yang Tingyun, for example, Christianity's strongest appeal lay in its moral firmness at a time of uncertainty, whereas for the later generations that kind of attraction, while still present, was complemented in a deeply meaningful way by the insight that Christianity could in effect do something for Confucianism. These second and third generations of elite Chinese Christians have been relatively little studied, so we do not yet know a great deal about them and their beliefs, nor are they thought to have been very numerous. We do know that although they generally lacked significant influence among their scholarly contemporaries, they sometimes acquired considerable local followings and thus contributed to the spread of Christianity in the countryside.

II: The Use of Secular Knowledge

The second distinctive mission strategy of the Jesuits in China was their use of secular knowledge as a lure. They hoped to establish a more or less equal intellectual relationship before any question arose of trying to convince Chinese of the ultimate truths of Christianity. In addition, recognizing the unusual antiquity and sophistication of Chinese civilization, they feared that an immediate challenge to fundamental Chinese values might easily prove counterproductive.

This policy was fairly successful, but it had two important consequences in China. First, the strategy of postponing any discussion of possible conversion raised doubts among some Chinese about the Europeans' true intentions. Initially it had seemed that the missionaries simply wanted to discuss science, technology, and ethics, to exchange information. Only gradually did Chinese come to understand that the Europeans hoped to persuade them to adopt Christianity. Second, many Chinese pursued the scientific and technical knowledge they acquired from missionaries with at least as much zeal as they addressed to grasping European religion and philosophy. In other words, Chinese caution about Christianity had much to do with the way in which it was introduced to them.

Once again, Ricci set the tone. His erudition and his mastery of Chinese language and culture enabled him to publish in Chinese a number of works that helped ingratiate him with his Chinese readers. *On Friendship*, for instance, published in 1595, drew on the Western classical tradition in much the same way as a Chinese scholar might draw on the Chinese classics. Popular among Ricci's learned friends, it had an uplifting message that was designed as a recommendation for some of the loftier aspects of European culture, not including its religious aspects. Ricci also made a profound impression with extraordinary feats of memory, which greatly appealed to Chinese scholars, for whom public success depended on the ability to absorb vast amounts of classical scholarship.

Ricci also began a tradition of presenting such elegant and intricate objects as prisms made of Venetian glass, elaborate clocks, mechanical toys, and engravings. Given the late Ming enthusiasm for imported luxuries, these went down very well, although their popularity prompted some Europeans to jump to the inaccurate conclusion that Chinese admired trivia above all else. Another skill Jesuits used to draw in educated Chinese was cartography. Ricci, for instance, hung on his wall a map of the world, on which he traced for visitors his itinerary from Rome to China. The map drew on existing sources, both Chinese and European, not all of which met the standards of accuracy he was striving to demonstrate. Yet many found it riveting, prompting him to make a series of world maps for the Chinese that incorporated some of the latest European discoveries. As we shall see in the next chapter, Jesuit cartography came to form an important part of the introduction of Western knowledge into China, as did Jesuit astronomy.

By their transmission of secular knowledge, Jesuit missionaries helped attract attention to some of the most exciting aspects of their native cultures. The emperors they served employed them primarily because they were all, in varying degrees, extremely interested in the information and skills these learned Europeans of multiple talents had to offer.

The Kangxi Emperor (1662–1722), in particular, was passionately interested in Western scientific knowledge and set out to learn their skills himself. Jesuits at his court instructed him in a wide range of subjects and gave lessons to some of his many sons, as we can see from the reconstruction of the old emperor's musings done by Jonathan Spence:

> In the early 1690s I often worked several hours a day with them. With Verbiest I had examined each stage of the forging of can-

> nons, and made him build a water fountain that operated in conjunction with an organ, and erect a windmill in the court; with the new group—who were later joined by Brocard and Jartoux, and worked in the Yang-hsin Palace under the general direction of my Eldest Son Yin-T'i—I worked on clocks and mechanics. Pereira taught me to play the tune "P'u Pen chou" on the harpsichord and the structure of the eight-note scale. Pedrini taught my sons musical theory, and Gherardini painted portraits at the Court. I also learned to calculate the weight and volume of spheres, cubes, and cones, and to measure distances and the angle of river banks. On inspection tours later I used these Western methods to show my officials how to make more accurate calculations when planning their river works. I myself planted the measuring device in the ground, and got my sons and bodyguards to use their spears and stakes to mark the various distances. I held the calculating tray on my knee, wrote down the figures with a stylus, then transposed them with a brush. I showed them how to calculate circumferences and assess the area of a plot of land, even if its borders were as jagged as dogs' teeth, drawing diagrams for them on the ground with an arrow; and calculated the flow of river water through a lock gate by multiplying the volume that flowed in a few seconds to get a figure for the whole day.[4]

The use of secular knowledge did not lead to large-scale Chinese conversion to Christianity. Apart from arousing suspicions among a number of Chinese about missionaries' true intentions, another major disadvantage was that Jesuits tended to make science seem rigid, unchanging, and, like religious truth, endowed with eternal value because they hoped that the revelation of scientific accuracy would lead to Chinese recognition of the perfection of the Judeo-Christian God. Yet scientific knowledge was constantly undergoing transformation. The reality was that the Jesuits used their secular knowledge only as a means to an end, and they offered no more than what they deemed necessary to achieve their conversion goals. We return in more detail to Jesuit missionaries' secular activities in China in the next chapter.

III: THE POLICY OF ACCOMMODATION

The policy of accommodation conformed with the unusual Jesuit policy of respecting the indigenous cultures of those they sought to convert. Such a policy recalled the very early days of the Church, when it had perforce adapted to Greek, Roman, and other cultures, but in the course of the medieval period this kind of cultural modesty had dissipated. To many sixteenth- and seventeenth-century Europeans, heathenness was equated with inferiority and accommodation seemed not so much pragmatic as simply inappropriate. The adoption of the policy of accommodation in China is attributed to Matteo Ricci, who believed that some degree of accommodation was essential if Jesuits were to shepherd China into the Church. This view was borne out by the extreme reluctance of otherwise receptive Chinese to abandon certain of their traditional practices.

Accommodation meant adapting to Chinese ways to the greatest extent possible without compromising the integrity of Catholicism. It was a question of reaching a balance between two sets of firmly held principles and assumptions, each of which derived from the premise that the other would eventually recognize the universal truths of the other culture. It was for this reason that Jesuits undertook the several years' study required to learn the Chinese language. They tried to understand Chinese civilization within its own context, by studying Chinese classical texts with their scholarly commentaries. They learned about Chinese religion, Chinese culture and customs, and China's political system, and most of them dedicated their whole lives to the missionary endeavor. They came to dress and live like Chinese scholars in the hope of confronting them, as nearly as possible, on equal terms.

There were three main areas in which the Jesuits found their beliefs or principles in conflict with Chinese ways: the question of Chinese "rites," or reverence for one's family ancestors and Confucius; the question of what terminology was appropriate for "God" and other Christian concepts; and the Christian insistence on monogamy versus the upper-class Chinese practice of concubinage.

The issue concerning Chinese customary practices of reverencing one's ancestors and paying homage to Confucius was as follows. If these practices were fundamentally religious, they would constitute a form of idolatry. In that case would-be converts to Christianity would have to be persuaded to abandon such practices before they could be admitted to the Church. But if they were merely civil observances of a secular nature, then Chinese converts could continue to perform them.

Jesuits grasped that outlawing the traditional forms of displaying respect for ancestors would strike at the core of Confucian values of filial piety, a linchpin of China's social and political structure. Even the most convinced Christian converts would find that hard to swallow. So accommodation emerged out of pragmatism. Jesuits themselves were sharply divided on the issue of the Chinese "rites." Some sincerely believed that because the Chinese practices did not involve the same kind of worship as the worship of the Christian God, they did not contradict Catholic theology. Others saw accommodation as a provisional but necessary expedient without which conversion would be well-nigh impossible.

Other pressures strengthened the Jesuits' commitment to the principle of accommodation. Since they had consistently portrayed Chinese people as highly civilized, in order to gain extra credit in Europe for their eventual conversion, they could hardly admit that the rituals to which such civilized people were so attached were in effect pagan in nature because pagans were by definition uncivilized. So some Chinese customs had to be clearly defined as nonreligious in order to avoid their being deemed to be pagan practices, and if they were not religious, there ought not to be any reason to require converts to abandon them. The Jesuit position became increasingly entrenched as they defended themselves against attacks from other orders.

Whatever the practical justifications, the accommodation policy caused the Jesuits many problems. In China it laid them open to charges of caprice. Some missionaries, for instance, advised their converts to worship God in the same place where they paid their respects to their ancestors, either a family temple or the main room in their homes. But to Chinese that seemed to equate the Christian God with the ancestors and hence to contradict missionaries' claims of overarching supremacy. Other recommendations Jesuits made to their Chinese converts more directly contravened Chinese laws and customs. For when Christianity placed its God and his earthly representative, the pope, above China's emperor, it plainly interfered with the proper political order. Ricci himself, in a rare moment of imprudence, had advised his Chinese followers that obeying a superior father (i.e., the Christian God) at the expense of obeying an inferior father (i.e., the emperor or one's own parent) was perfectly in accordance with the requirements of filial piety. But in Chinese terms this was tantamount to incitement to insurrection or filial disobedience, both of which the criminal codes condemned as particularly heinous crimes, punishable by the execution of the perpetrator and his or her entire family. As one commentator summarized it, "When they require people to consider the Master of Heaven as their closest relative and to abandon their fathers and mothers and place their sovereign in second place, giving the direction of the state to those who spread the doctrine of the Master of Heaven, this entails an unprecedented infringement of the most constant rules. How could their doctrine possibly be admissible in China?"[5]

In Europe accommodation laid the Jesuits open to charges of tolerating heresy. Such charges were repeatedly leveled against them in the course of the resulting debate, known as the Rites Controversy. This dispute lasted over a century and did a great deal of damage both to the Jesuit mission in China and to the Society of Jesus more generally. Critics insisted that since the Chinese "rites" involved paying respect to graven images and "worshiping" Confucius and the ancestors as though they were gods, accommodation made nonsense of at least two of the Ten Commandments of the Bible. Even if accommodation brought more converts, it thus was just as unacceptable to many European Catholics as, for different reasons, it was in China. But if they expected China to acquiesce meekly, they reckoned without the great Kangxi Emperor.

In 1692 Kangxi, against the recommendation of Chinese advisers who resented the Jesuits' influence at court, issued an Edict of Toleration, in effect allowing religious freedom to Christians in China. The edict permitted missionaries to worship in their churches, and while it did not expressly permit preaching and other evangelistic activities, neither did it explicitly forbid them. It seemed a major triumph for Christianity in China and raised the hopes of many Jesuits, who thought it a prelude to imperial conversion.

But Kangxi's formal toleration of Christianity did not signal imperial enthusiasm for the foreign religion. Kangxi raised the prohibition on Christianity partly in recompense for missionaries' technical services and partly in recognition of the Jesuits' accommodative efforts to comprehend and appreciate Chinese civilization. The Edict of Toleration appeared to suggest that the policy of using secular knowledge was working, but in reality the most it did was to acknowledge that Christianity promoted harmony and served public morality and hence differed from heterodox sects covered by the criminal law.

Papal attempts to formalize Rome's jurisdiction over Chinese Christians put an end to Kangxi's willingness to be broad-minded about the foreign religion. In 1705 the pope sent an emissary to China, seeking imperial approval for the extension of papal authority over Chinese Catholics. Kangxi rejected the proposal absolutely. In his view, the possibility that Chinese would owe allegiance to some authority other than himself posed a direct threat to his dominion over his people. A second papal legate, who reached China in 1720, was no more successful. Jesuit missionaries then looked for creative ways to circumvent the opposing views of pope and emperor. They tried, for instance, to modify some funeral practices without actually replacing them altogether, suggesting that relatives of the bereaved offer to pay for the coffin rather than to contribute silver to use in a burial sacrifice.

The papal missions and decrees heralded the end of China's toleration of evangelism by Catholic missionaries. Kangxi, already concerned that some Westerners might be passing themselves off as missionaries to disguise some darker purpose, instituted a system of signed certificates. All Westerners wishing to live in China had to make a commitment to remain for the rest of their lives, a requirement directed against spies and profiteers as much as against missionaries. Missionaries had to agree, in addition, to allow Chinese converts to reverence Confucius and the ancestors. Refusal to sign meant expulsion.

In part influenced by those within the European Church establishment who resented Jesuit successes, the pope soon decreed that ancestor worship and the sacrifices to Confucius were simply unacceptable. The first papal bull against the Jesuits' position was issued in 1707; it was confirmed in 1715 and again in 1742. In short, the Church declined to permit Chinese Christians to continue to perform their traditional reverences on the ground that these were idolatrous and incompatible with Christian practice. Any Chinese desirous of converting to Christianity must first renounce such practices. There was no middle ground.

When Kangxi read a Chinese translation of the 1715 papal decree, he commented in his own hand: "Having read this proclamation, I ask myself how these uncultivated Westerners dare to speak of the great [philosophical and moral] precepts of China . . . most of what they say and their arguments are ridiculous. Seeing this proclamation, I at last realise that their doctrine is of the same kind as the little heresies of the Buddhist and Taoist monks. . . . These are the greatest absurdities that have ever been seen. As from now I forbid the Westerners to spread their doctrine in China; that will spare us a lot of trouble."[6]

The second main area of dispute concerning Jesuit accommodation was the question of whether to use existing Chinese terminology for the Christian God or whether such terms were too confusing and too tainted with "heathen associations." Like the issue of the rites, such debates were fraught with pitfalls. Ancient Chinese had worshipped *Shangdi* ("Lord on High") and *Tian* ("Heaven"), and some Jesuits were persuaded that these were very much the same as their own all-knowing, all-powerful God. But if Europeans used the identical terms for their own God, might Chinese fail to understand that the Christian God was in fact different? Was it preferable to create some new term such as *Tianzhu*, the "Lord of Heaven," or should the missionaries devise an appropriate transliteration for the name of God? While the Jesuits themselves could not agree about this, some Chinese found it either insulting or deceptive to equate the Sovereign on High of the Chinese classics with the God of the Western religion.

In the seventeenth century these issues became more contentious when they became part of an effort to prove that ancient Chinese ideas coincided with those of the Bible. Missionaries, who believed all human history was to be found in the Bible, devised a theory according to which the Chinese had migrated eastward from the Mediterranean area after the Great Flood of biblical times. The Europeans may have sincerely believed this theory, but for the Chinese, the implications were unacceptable. To identify Chinese history with Western, Judeo-Christian history in effect deprived the Chinese of their own history. It asked them to disown their ancestors. That was just what the Jesuits were resisting in the Rites Controversy.

The issue was muddied yet further by conflicting attempts on the parts of both Europeans and Chinese converts to demonstrate that, as the Pillar Li Zhizao put it, "There are the same minds and the same principles in the Eastern and Western seas."[7] They all sought to prove that the major points of the European religion were identical to the traditional ideas of the Chinese. The underlying purpose was very similar, but the emphasis was slightly different. Chinese tried to show the inherent Chineseness of Christian beliefs, while missionaries tried to show that ancient Confucianism was largely in accord with Christianity. They suggested that the Chinese had once known about the God of the Bible but had somehow lost their intellectual compass. In both cases the motivation was to demonstrate that the new ideas from the West amounted in essence to no more than a revamping of ideas formulated in Chinese antiquity, because they thought that in that case they would be far more likely to gain acceptance.

Chinese and missionaries each compiled lists of quotations from the Chinese classics that seemed to reveal affinities with Christianity. One such work, for example, gives sixty-five occurrences of the terms *Shangdi* or *Tian* in Chinese classical texts: thirty-three from the Book of History (*Shujing*), twenty-six from the Book of Songs (*Shujing*), three from the Mencius (*Mengzi*), two from Confucius' Analects (*Lunyu*), and one from the Doctrine of the Mean (*Zhongyong*). All these texts were fundamental works of the classical Chinese canon. Such evidence was, however, open to reinterpretation by those who used it to try to discredit the Europeans by showing that Christianity was merely a later Western corruption of Chinese ideas. In the end, and not without dissenters, Catholic Christianity became known in China as *Tian Zhu Jiao*, "the Teaching of the Lord of Heaven."

The third great issue of the accommodation policy pitted Christian insistence on monogamy against the Chinese practice of concubinage. A Christian could have only one wife. Adultery was against God's law. But what was to be done when would-be converts had one or more concubines? It was a common practice among the better-off, justified by the filial need to produce male descendants to continue one's family line. Missionaries refused to convert a man who declined to send away his concubine. That was probably what had delayed the conversion of Li Zhizao in 1608. From a Christian point of view the issue was clear. But so it was for Chinese. A woman could not in all conscience simply be sent away. She was in effect used goods, whom her natal family would not necessarily take back in—that would involve terrible loss of face as well as expense—and quite likely no one else would want her. She could perhaps be given to a poor man unable to afford a wife or sold into prostitution.

The public confession made by Wang Zheng, a scholarly convert who committed suicide when he heard of the fall of the Ming, shows the traumas men as well as women sometimes suffered over the concubine question. Wang's agonizing, typical of many of his contemporaries as they considered conversion, shows one solution to which many may have resorted, whether or not in good faith: they kept their concubines within their households but no longer slept with them. When Wang was converted to Christianity, he decided never to take a concubine. But because his wife had no son, his family overruled him. Later he repented and tried to send her away:

> My wife wept and begged me to tolerate the concubine, and we nearly had a quarrel. The concubine too was so distressed that she nearly lost her life. She would on no account remarry, and she expressed her wish to become a Christian and observe chastity. . . . Throughout the whole night I reflected [saying to myself] that I am nearly seventy, and my behavior is no better than that of a youth of seventeen. . . . Now I promise before God that in future I will treat the concubine as a friend . . . and if afterward I again commit sin with her, the angels [will be my witness] and I am willing to die the penalty of death.[8]

The insistence on monogamy also raised questions about the status of concubines' children, as one outraged detractor of the missionaries observed: "My friend was old, poor and had no son. Fortunately, he had been able to buy a concubine and by her had a son who was just one year old. [The missionaries] told him that, in their country, it was believed to be virtuous not to have any concubines and thought to be of no importance not to have a line of descendants. My friend obeyed them and ejected the mother of this child. I do not know whether the child is still alive."[9]

The missionaries tried to devise ways to circumvent the concubine problem. If a male convert's principal wife refused to become a Christian, the missionaries allowed him to marry one of his concubines. But they had no authority to grant such permission; besides, such practices clearly contravened Chinese law. Sometimes Jesuits overlooked the presence of a concubine because they recognized the hardships involved. One critic charged that they did so when the would-be convert was especially influential. For good measure he also accused the missionaries of licentious behavior: "They would like all kings and sovereigns to adhere to their vicious doctrine, expel all their concubines from their women's quarters and live like common people with but a single wife. But in their residences they themselves invite ignorant women at nightfall to enter a room draped with red hangings, where they close the doors and practise unction with holy oil, give them holy water and place their hands on five places of their bodies: these are impure and secret rituals."[10]

Thus this aspect of the accommodation policy, like the Rites Controversy and the disputes over religious terminology, made it easy for critically disposed Chinese to scorn the Jesuits as inconsistent and hypocritical and their religion as hopelessly incompatible with Chinese customs.

In sum, accommodation was double-edged. It undoubtedly played a part in bringing the Jesuits their greatest conversion successes, for they sometimes had encountered resistance to Christianity specifically on the grounds that it turned Chinese away from some of their most hallowed customs. It also helped the missionaries gain the confidence of the Kangxi Emperor, under whom they attained their greatest influence in China. Ultimately, however, accommodation and the extreme rancor that surrounded it were major factors in the downturn in Jesuit political fortunes both in China and in Europe. Each side was apprehensive about a loss of control and integrity. Kangxi saw the proposal that he surrender control over Chinese subjects to the pope as a threat to his sovereignty, while churchmen feared that to surrender control over Chinese converts to an alien, secular emperor would undermine Catholicism's integrity. In China the accommodation policy fueled suspicions about doctrinal inconsistencies, prompting a loss of respect for the Jesuits, while in Europe it contributed to the suspension—at the time it was called the abolition—of the Society of Jesus in 1773. At both ends, then, the Jesuits probably lost more than they gained by their attempts at accommodation. Yet missionaries of other orders who spurned accommodation fared little better in their conversion efforts.

CHRISTIANITY, RELIGIOUS BELIEFS, AND "SUPERSTITION"

When Jesuit missionaries reintroduced Christianity into China, they had to contend with Buddhism, which by that time had sunk deep roots in Chinese soil. Both Chinese and Europeans were aware of similarities and differences between Buddhism and Christianity; they just interpreted them differently. Considerable animosity grew up between the two religions. The enmity was partly attributable to the conversion of men such as Yang Tingyun and Buddhism's consequent loss of political and financial support. But some of the reasons had to do with Jesuit policies. The first Jesuits to reach China, including Ricci, had initially dressed as Buddhist monks since Buddhism, a religion, seemed at first glance to have much in common with Christianity. Once the Jesuit missionaries grasped, however, that Chinese scholars did not accord men of religion the kind of respect priests customarily received in Europe and that Buddhism itself did not enjoy great prestige among the most influential, they adopted the garb of Confucian scholars, hoping thus to improve their opportunities of encountering Chinese scholars on equal terms. Once the Jesuits had made this shift, they turned sharply against Buddhism.

Regarding Buddhism as a potential competitor for Christianity in Chinese minds, Jesuits attacked it as mere superstition. This tactic won them the initial support of Chinese who objected to Buddhism's lack of social conscience and saw Christianity as a tool against it. But it naturally brought some antagonism, both from Buddhists themselves and from others who thought the differences between the two religions were so slight as to be illusory. Critics of Christianity's claims to originality and uniqueness drew attention to its similarities to Buddhism—for example, the prohibitions against killing, the use of religious images and ceremonies, and the belief in paradise and hell. Missionaries, regarding the similarities as traps set by the devil to delude people into following a false doctrine, only condemned Buddhist practices all the more vehemently. The point is that although missionary successes and the zeal of wealthy and influential converts such as Yang Tingyun undoubtedly attracted the hostility of Buddhist monks and their powerful supporters toward Christianity, the Jesuits' own vilification of Buddhism, despite its superficial resemblance to Christianity, also bore considerable responsibility.

Ironically, the "superstitious practices" of Buddhism, missionary denunciations of which antagonized Buddhism's supporters, played an important role in encouraging the adoption of Christianity among ordinary people, who did not necessarily draw clear distinctions between the European religion and their own popular beliefs, and judged gods on the basis of their ability to provide assistance in times of need. Because of such people's limited literacy, we know far less about their understanding of Christianity, but scattered information gives us some sense of how it spread at the grass roots level in China.

Reports of the efficacy of Christianity among the people often took place in the context of miracle tales. Such tales were already familiar to Chinese because they were widespread in the Buddhist tradition. Moreover, the resemblance of Chinese Christian miracle tales to their Buddhist counterparts probably helped spread Christianity among ordinary people, for ideas are often more readily absorbed when they seem somewhat familiar. But the Chinese Christian miracle tales contain elements that identify them as distinctively Christian. The tales were fairly remote from the exalted doctrinal debates missionaries held with their elite converts, but even the most highly educated were not always immune to such tales' persuasive power. Li Zhizao's conversion after he recovered from the illness Ricci nursed him through was a case in point.

The moral of every miracle tale was that only belief in the Christian God could bring salvation. A sampling of two such stories gives some sense of their general flavor. Both originated among the flourishing community of Chinese Christians in early-seventeenth-century Fujian province, where the Italian Jesuit Giulio Aleni (1582–1649) was sometimes called the Confucius from the West. Both stories are taken from a morality book compiled by a scholarly convert, whose quotations are all that now remains of the tales.

The first tale tells of the death of an active convert named Zhang Shi, whose baptismal name was Michael. This story was widely disseminated and had considerable influence. It was interpreted as proof of the real existence of heaven and hell and as evidence that Chinese could go to heaven and, as it were, live happily ever after—provided, of course, they had converted to Christianity. It shows the Christian God presiding over a heavenly tribunal, much as King Yama does in the Buddhist tradition, but in this case God is assisted by the apostle Matthew and by none other than Matteo Ricci himself. Michael Zhang Shi's death had been foretold in a miraculous way: as he prayed, twenty-one golden characters had appeared on his bedcurtain. The last five characters read: "Within three years, I will come and fetch you." On the day that he died, three years to the very hour after this occurrence:

> . . . he saw with his eyes wide open how the Master of Heaven [i.e., God] judged a sinner and sent him to hell; and a child was

> sent to the place of the children. At the third judgment it was Michael [Zhang Shi]'s turn. At first he was severely reprimanded. The apostle Saint Matthew and the virtuous Matteo Ricci accompanied him and earnestly implored the Master on his behalf. Thereupon, the Master called to the Heavenly Spirit [i.e., the angel] Michael: "Let him go to the bright Heaven."
>
> At that moment, the command reverberated like thunder and Michael [Zhang Shi] regained consciousness. He felt extremely hot and asked immediately to be fanned, whereupon he gave a detailed account of his vision to the whole family. When he had finished, he passed away peacefully.[11]

The second miracle tale reproduced here concerns a family prompted to convert to Christianity after a woman had miraculously recovered from demonic possession. The scholarly editor of this collection of tales suggested that the woman was partly to blame for the possession because she had encouraged the demon by expressing her dissatisfaction with her prospective husband, but the tale itself does not seem to imply that her husband or other family members faulted her:

> Zhang Qixun was a man from Sunjiang in the prefecture of Quanzhou [Fujian] whose family for generations had earned their living as boatsmen. He was married to a girl named Fu, [from] a distinguished family of Wurong, who had lost her father at an early age, and had been betrothed to [Zhang Qi]Xun when she was not yet fourteen years old. [For that reason] she was constantly discontented and unhappy, thinking "That Zhang is no match for me." Now her [future] husband kept in his home an evil image, only one [square] foot in size, of what is popularly called Lord Zhang. Whenever this demon came at night, he used to go to Fu's bedroom, and her spirit often followed him to his dwelling-place, which was all golden gate-towers and storied buildings made of jade, and all kinds of precious and rare things, and he told her "I want to take you as my wife." So it went on for three years, during which her face from day to day become more [sickly, as if she were suffering from] jaundice. Her aunt was amazed at it, and when after inquiry she had come to know the reason [of Fu's disease], she at once had her married to Zhang Qixun, expecting that in this way she would avoid being harassed by the demon. [In actual fact, the reverse proved true;] whereas previously he might come once or twice a month, now he arrived every night. Fu and her husband slept together, and the demon also shared Fu's bed.

> Her husband was so enraged that he could not stand it any longer, and privately, without Fu's knowing it, he drove a nail into [the demon's] navel on the evil image. That night he came again and showed Fu his navel and intestines, all stained with blood dripping out. Fu's disease then daily grew worse. After abstaining from food for two or three months or even more, her condition had become critical. Her husband was deeply distressed about it; he invited a magician to expel and exorcise [the demon] but whatever he undertook, nothing worked.
>
> Then the husband suddenly heard about the Sacred Doctrine of the Lord of Heaven [i.e., the Christian God]. He thereupon went to the church, humbly begged for help, and invited the Friends of Religion to come to his house, to sprinkle Holy Water, and to paste the Holy Name on [the walls of] the bedroom. That day, just when the night was falling, the demon appeared again, but he did not dare to enter the private apartment—he only went to the hall and asked her to meet him there. The Friends of Religion again brought a Holy Cross to the house, and then the demon vanished without a trace. Fu gradually recovered from her illness, and took food and drink as before. The whole family was moved by [the Lord's] grace and they all observed the holy Religion and were baptized. This happened in [February or March of 1633].[12]

For some Chinese who came into contact with missionaries it was Daoist notions about the possibility of distilling an elixir of immortality that attracted their attention to Christianity because of its promise of eternal life. Qu Rukui (fl. ca. 1605), an accomplished scientist with considerable technical knowledge, had originally been drawn to Ricci by the possibility that the Jesuit knew about alchemy, Qu's passion. Qu later converted to Christianity, finding the spiritual relief it offered more persuasive than alchemy as an antidote to death.

Alchemy and the possibility of prolonging life sometimes produced bizarre results. In the summer of 1678 Jesuits resident in Hangzhou set about removing the remains of one of their number, Martinus Martini, to their newly established Christian cemetery. Martini had already been dead for seventeen years, so it was reasonable to expect his body would have decomposed, even though Chinese coffins were famous for being airtight. But his "hair, beard, and fingernails were . . . intact, and the tomb was found to contain no unpleasant odor."[13]

The condition of Martini's body caused a sensation among the residents of Hangzhou, who became much more enthusiastic about Christianity when they thought the Jesuits might have brought a magical substance that could preserve the body forever. It was rather different from the formula for eternal life that the Jesuits were trying to convey. The extremely slow decomposition of Martini's body continued to cause excitement even as late as the mid-nineteenth century, almost two hundred years after his death, with pilgrimages to the Jesuit cemetery to trim Martini's hair and nails.

For some missionaries the temptation to exploit alchemy's seductive power was irresistible. In 1735 Dominique Parennin (1665–1741) used his knowledge of physics and chemistry to perform "magic tricks" as a preamble to bringing his scholarly audience the enlightenment of Christianity. His ploy was not terribly effective, and as we shall see, a reputation for alchemical skill was a dangerous thing, for a hostile audience might accuse such "magicians" of the most heinous acts.

Breaking the Law

The negative side to the use of miracle tales and "magic" to encourage conversion, the promise of alchemical or magical potential, and the stories missionaries spread about Jesus' power to work miracles was that Chinese tended to suspect miracle workers of being troublemakers. They knew that Jesus himself had, after all, been put to death by the state for breaking the law. In China too there were laws against those who masked subversion with religion.

China broadly tolerated such religions as Buddhism, Daoism, Islam, and Tibetan Buddhism, as well as popular folk sects such as the White Lotus, a loosely knit group of heterodox religious assemblies known for their propensity to rebellion, so long as they kept on the right side of the law. But laws against religious groups specifically included the following unacceptable transgressions: people who tampered with the imperial calendar, for to suggest one was entitled to do so implied authority even over emperors; people who deluded others by claiming magical powers, among which alchemical skills might be included; people who assembled large and potentially disorderly groups of men and women, offending public morality; and people who offered rewards in the next life for those martyred in the present one. Christianity was subject to these laws, and some of its adherents' activities seemed to skate perilously close to just these types of banned behavior. Besides, missionaries preached the brotherhood of man and the equality of all, doctrines ominously reminiscent of the White Lotus. To a society ordered on the premise that one's role depended on one's position in a complex hierarchy, such notions were hard indeed for the Chinese to accept. They completely conflicted with basic concepts of social organization.

Thus it was not hard to build a convincing case against Christianity. Missionaries and their associates operated clandestinely, gathering groups together and forming cells in many parts of the country. They failed to maintain the proper hierarchies. They had extensive overseas connections. They received foreign funding. Their organization was strong, and they appeared to obey the directives of a central authority. Perhaps they were spies; their interest in cartography certainly suggested that possibility. In this context, when Chinese recalled that among the Japanese troops fighting in Korea in the 1590s had been fifteen thousand Christian converts, the effect was chilling. Moreover, Chinese were aware that the foreign nations that had already colonized parts of Asia embraced Christianity in one form or another. So it was not altogether farfetched to argue, as did a number of Christianity's enemies, that the spread of the foreign religion might prove a sinister prelude to invasion.

These kinds of suspicions highlight a fundamental difference between Western notions of the role played by religion and those held in China. In Catholic Europe, where attempts to separate church and state were of recent origin, the Church claimed authority over the secular sphere, but in China the reverse was true: the emperor's power was all-embracing. He was the Son of Heaven and the sole mediator between heaven and earth. The head of a religious institution could not possibly have authority over him, nor could religion exist independently. In China, religion either specifically served the state, in which case it was orthodox, or did not, in which case it constituted rank heresy. It was thus virtually unthinkable that a ruler of China would formally adopt a foreign religion that acknowledged an alternative leader, far less permit such a religion to become institutionalized in China. In other words, the Chinese concept of religion's place in the order of things presented an insurmountable stumbling block to the spread of Christianity in China, for it just seemed rife with subversive potential. In these circumstances it was no wonder Christianity failed to make broad gains in China.

THE DECLINE OF CATHOLIC INFLUENCE IN CHINA

The overall number of Catholic converts in China decreased by about one-third during the course of the eighteenth century, and mission work had to go underground. The main reason Catholic influence in China fell into decline was the debacle between the Kangxi Emperor and the pope in the early eighteenth century, but there were other contributing factors, particularly Jesuit involvement on the wrong side of an extremely bitter struggle for the imperial succession. This aroused the hostility of the eventual winner, who became the Yongzheng Emperor (1723–1736). In 1724 Yongzheng banned Catholicism, ordered all Christians to renounce their faith, and expelled to Macao all foreign missionaries except those rendering technical services to the court. Yongzheng's successor, the Qianlong Emperor (1736–1795), shared his father's distaste for Christianity and barred missionaries altogether from the provinces. But enforcement remained sporadic, and groups of European missionaries managed to proselytize in the Chinese countryside throughout the eighteenth century.

Crackdowns against Christianity were prompted in part by fears about the possible consequences of large assemblies, as we can see from a criminal case dating from 1754. Just outside Beijing a group of Catholics practicing openly came to official notice. The ringleader had been punished before for proselytizing; now it seemed he was regularly preaching to large mixed assemblies. The authorities destroyed crucifixes and religious texts uncovered in a house-to-house search. Further investigation disclosed that the community had originated when Jesuits working in the imperial workshops in nearby Beijing had converted their Chinese apprentices, who had then returned to their villages and spread the word.[14]

Farther from Beijing, things were easier. In the west China province of Sichuan, for instance, the number of Catholics multiplied, especially in the second half of the century. By 1800 there were perhaps forty thousand converts in Sichuan alone. This increase was just the reverse of the national trend.

Perhaps most striking of the various Christian communities of late-eighteenth-century Sichuan was the Institute for Christian Virgins. Sponsored by the (anti-Jesuit) French Society of Foreign Missions, the institute grew out of an indigenous movement among Chinese women to avoid marriage and dedicate their lives to religion. Its members took vows of chastity and devoted their lives to social work and teaching in schools for girls. Of course they aimed to make Christians of their pupils and focused primarily on evangelism, but the mere fact of providing education for girls was so unusual as to verge on the revolutionary.

Most Christian Virgins came from well-to-do families, often Christians themselves, who were willing to support their daughters; there was no place in Chinese society for groups of celibate women living independently. Like the White Lotus sect, which often fell under suspicion of subversion, Christianity provided outlets for women's religious fervor and allowed them a degree of empowerment that was impossible within an orthodox Confucian framework. The Institute for Christian Virgins often came under attack from Confucians, who considered the Virgins' vows of chastity antisocial, if not downright subversive; marriage was a moral duty. But the group grew steadily—by the end of the nineteenth century one thousand women were affiliated—and was finally disbanded, presumably, only in 1950.

Some accounts suggest that Qing fears of missionary subversion were not wholly unfounded. In Fujian province in 1746, for example, a Chinese man, to whom the local Jesuit had refused a loan, accused the missionaries of paying people to convert, trafficking in weapons, and inciting people to revolt. Unfortunately for the missionaries, it transpired that a number of local bandits were Christians and had European weapons and money in their homes. Local missionaries managed to escape, but a Dominican bishop was put to death in the aftermath of this episode.

As missionary influence in China steadily dwindled during the eighteenth century, the Society of Jesus was rapidly losing ground in Europe as well. The Portuguese government expelled the Jesuits in 1759; by 1762 those in Macao had also been deported, and their property confiscated. Other countries followed suit. In 1773 the papal brief *Dominus Ac Redemptor* suppressed the Society of Jesus around the world. In Beijing the brief was executed two years later. Jesuits already in China remained, but there were no new arrivals.

The last quarter of the eighteenth century saw a wave of persecutions of Christians in China, particularly in the years 1784 and 1785, shortly after the second of two major Muslim uprisings. This occurred because in a curious parallel with Englishmen who sometimes wondered if China might not be a Muslim country, the foreign origin of Islam led many Chinese to confuse it with Christianity. The anti-Christian activity represented a preemptive strike against possible rebellion. At the height of Qing imperial power, Catholic influence in China reached a low point.

Christianity and Buddhism: A Comparison

Of the two great religions China received from abroad, Buddhism took root much more deeply than did Christianity. One reason for this had to do with the respective religions' institutional structure. As the last chapter showed, Buddhism filtered into China from India in the first century. It came in a piecemeal fashion, with merchants, travelers, and some priests who journeyed across Central Asia. Later Chinese traveled to India to learn more about Buddhism and to collect scriptures to bring back and translate. The transmission of Buddhism to China was never directed by a central Church in quite the way that Rome later tried to exercise control over the Christian missions in China.

By contrast, Christian missionaries of the sixteenth through eighteenth centuries labored under a fatal disability: their entire operation was under the central direction of the pope in Rome. This sharply restricted their freedom of movement and their ability to make judgments based on their experience in the field. Many of the decisions that governed their actions were made in the context of Counter-Reformation church politics and had little to do with conditions in China. This greatly limited missionaries' effectiveness. Early Buddhists had no such handicap. This distinction had much to do with Buddhism's success in implanting itself in China.

The second reason concerned political circumstances in China at the time the foreign religion was introduced, including the presence or absence of a centralized power in China. When Buddhism was putting down its roots in China, the Han empire was in decline. After its fall in 220 there followed almost four centuries of political fragmentation. When Catholic Christianity arrived in China in the late sixteenth century, China was entering a period of social and political instability, but the resemblance was only superficial, for a number of reasons. In the first place, China's late Ming political disintegration lasted only until the Qing conquest some six decades later. Second, part of the new Qing regime's program involved the imposition of strict limits on intellectual freedom; after the Qing conquest, Chinese scholars were far less willing to take intellectual risks. The late Ming atmosphere of experimentation that had so favored the missionary cause simply evaporated, while for Chinese distraught about the peril into which their civilization had fallen, the experience of foreign occupation made any belief system of foreign origin almost automatically subject to suspicion. Finally, the Jesuits' decision to serve the conquest regime lost them much of the sympathy of the Han Chinese elite, as a consequence of loyalist and protonationalist sentiments. In the climate of the times the foreign missionaries' shift of allegiance appeared treacherous indeed to Chinese undergoing the experience of alien occupation.

Third, unlike the early Buddhists, Catholic missionaries gave far greater prominence to intellectual debate than to social activism, with some exceptions. Moreover, for various reasons their economic role was not integrated into Chinese society, whereas, as we saw in the last chapter, Buddhism and international trade were closely connected. In the Ming-Qing period, the links between Christian missionaries and European traders were much looser; commerce and religion remained largely separate. Traders were confined to coastal areas, while missionaries spread out all over the country. Moreover, the English and Dutch, who came to constitute a considerable proportion of the foreign merchant community, were Protestants unlikely to form much connection with Catholic missionaries, French, Spanish, Portuguese, or Italian.

Fourth, when Buddhism arrived, its only real competitor was Daoism, to which Buddhism bore some resemblance. Like a vine that wraps itself around existing vegetation, Buddhism attached itself to the native plant of Daoism and then flourished so much that it somewhat overwhelmed it. At that time too, Confucianism was still relatively new and insecure as a set of state operating principles; more important, it made no attempt to address spiritual needs. Thus Buddhism filled a gap by offering salvation to all, doing so without regard to social position. By contrast, when Catholicism arrived, there existed choices other than Christianity: Buddhism itself and a well-entrenched Neo-Confucianism much better placed to compete for direction of China's spiritual life. Buddhism's political role also gave it an advantage. At a time of continuous competition for political authority, it offered an alternative source of legitimacy to contending rulers. By contrast, such political influence as the Jesuits achieved never attained the same scale, and ultimately it brought them more trouble than gain.

Fifth, Christianity's all-or-nothing approach was simply incompatible with Chinese customary practice. Chinese who treated religious practices as a language for petitioning unseen powers were primarily interested in their efficacy. They saw nothing strange in mixing and matching different sets of beliefs. Buddhism was able to find its place within this tradition, but Christianity's claims to exclusivity and requirement of absolute faith presented a virtually insuperable disadvantage.

In sum, the Christian mission to China of the sixteenth through eighteenth centuries, dominated by the Jesuits, failed to make the massive inroads anticipated because of a combination of cultural and political factors within China, on the one hand, and, on the other, European Church politics. The China mission was not a total disaster as a religious endeavor—two hundred thousand or so Chinese converts are a considerable number—but it was not much to show for two centuries' work in a country whose population by 1800 approached the three hundred million mark. Where the missionaries achieved much greater success was in making it possible for Chinese to find out about other branches of European knowledge and other kinds of European people and customs.

CHAPTER THREE

Foreign Goods and Foreign Knowledge in the Eighteenth Century

"We have never valued ingenious articles, nor do we have the slightest need of your country's manufactures."[1]

The Qianlong Emperor (1736–1795)

In 1792 Britain sent Lord Macartney to China in the hope of gaining the competitive edge in the China trade over other Europeans and its former American colonies. The embassy was not a success. Historians in the West have long blamed its failure on what they have surmised to be a comprehensive Chinese antagonism to trade, a rigid adherence to a hierarchical structure of foreign relations enveloped in ritual formalities, and an overall resistance to innovation and change. But when we view matters from the Chinese point of view, it immediately becomes obvious that the reality was different. Trade played a central part in the Qing empire, which represented a major political and cultural force in the region. The Qing did not wish to take a chance on allowing Europeans unlimited access to Chinese markets. In part they were anxious not to lose control of the profits, but they were also unwilling to risk the insidious effect on their overlordship that might result from the free circulation of goods emanating from altogether different cultures. In short, the Qing considered that unrestricted interchange posed a potential danger to national security.

Qing caution sprang from a much greater degree of sophistication about international affairs than has sometimes been imagined; by the eighteenth century they knew enough to be extremely wary of Europeans. They were familiar with them partly through the court missionaries, partly through periodic embassies, partly through the Canton trade, and partly as a consequence of European colonial pursuits in Asia. Macao, hard by China's shores, had for two centuries been a Portuguese enclave, Manila had been dominated by Spain for almost as long, and Batavia was the center of the Netherlands' by now formidable colonial power in Southeast Asia. Each was home to a sizable community of expatriate Chinese, to whom Europeans had on occasion shown great animosity. In the Philippines, in Batavia, and in Dutch-occupied Taiwan, for instance, Chinese had more than once been attacked and massacred, sometimes in vast numbers. British imperial expansion, by now impinging on the edges of Chinese territory, had not yet shown any such evidence of ill will. But even though the Qing clearly grasped the distinctions between the European countries, Britain was at least potentially tarred with the same brush.

This chapter examines the main aspects of the international exchange of goods and ideas in eighteenth-century Qing China, from the late Kangxi period down to the death of the Qianlong Emperor in 1799. Europeans were not the only foreigners with whom eighteenth-century China had dealings, but they were the newest on the scene, the most determined to disseminate their goods and ideas, and collectively the most powerful. For that reason they are the principal, though not exclusive, focus of the chapter. It is true that China did not always welcome the new arrivals with open arms. But its circumspect approach arose more out of pragmatism than out of the reactionary conservatism or primitive parochialism of which Europeans dismissively accused China.

War and Diplomacy in the High Qing

During the 150 or so years from the founding of the Qing empire in 1644 until the end of the eighteenth century, only four emperors reigned. These were: Shunzhi (1644–1661), Kangxi (1662–1722), Yongzheng (1723–1735), and Qianlong (1736–1795). Two ruled for more than sixty years apiece; Qianlong abdicated in 1795 in order not to appear unfilial by surpassing the sixty-one years achieved by his grandfather, Kangxi, but to all intents and purposes he continued to rule until his death four years later. These long reigns provided an era of continuity and stability after the chaotic wars of the dynastic transition. During this period the population grew to surpass three hundred million, and the Qing pursued with vigor the consolidation and expansion of their empire.

Qing emperors remained acutely conscious of their Manchu origins. At once emperors of China and khans of extensive domains in Inner and Central Asia or, to put it differently, as rulers for whom the Chinese portion of their empire constituted only a part of the whole, they represented themselves simultaneously as benevolent Confucian rulers and as martial conquerors in a newly crafted Manchu tradition. They also tried to establish their spiritual supremacy throughout the region, to compete with the threat posed to their authority by the Dalai Lama, to whom many Qing subjects in both Mongolia and Tibet looked for religious leadership. Qing rulers, in other words, employed a range of sophisticated strategies to reinforce their overlordship and to control the ways in which it was represented. They were worthy competitors for the title of imperialists with the Western powers that later all but overwhelmed them.

Until the mid-nineteenth century, with no single agency handling foreign affairs, the Qing formulated a series of policies designed to maintain control within the empire and to defend the inland and maritime frontiers. Some of these policies grew out of traditional Chinese formulations, while others were Qing innovations more attuned to the Manchus' Inner Asian origins. Different agencies handled relations with different groups. In many ways the variety of mid-Qing institutions dealing with outsiders was a great strength because it allowed for considerable flexibility. On the other hand, decentralization made consistent policy-making followed by concerted action much more difficult to achieve. In the nineteenth century the lack of centralization in the handling of foreign affairs came to be seen as a weakness by Western countries accustomed to dealing with a single Foreign Office or Ministry of Foreign Affairs.

An Office of Border Affairs (*lifan yuan*) handled Qing relations with its Asian neighbors to the north and northwest, including Russia. The *lifan yuan* was a Qing innovation that helped transform its foreign relations. With regard to China's traditional next-door-neighbor antagonists, such as the Mongols, the Tibetans, and others, the *lifan yuan* managed a series of ritual functions that, by diminishing cultural friction between China and these groups, helped incorporate them into the Qing empire. It was also charged with deterring any potential threat to Qing supremacy in continental East Asia.

In the 1680s the Qing turned their attention to the northwest frontiers of China. To settle their disputes with the Russians, they at first hoped to use either Dutch or Portuguese emissaries to carry correspondence by way of Amsterdam or Lisbon to Moscow. China had particularly high hopes of the Dutch, who had a strong commercial presence in Russia, but in the event, the Qing settled their Russian conflict themselves, concluding in 1689 the Treaty of Nerchinsk, negotiated with the aid of Jesuit interpreters using Manchu and Latin.

The Treaty of Nerchinsk and its successor, the 1727 Treaty of Kiakhta, clearly indicated Qing willingness to depart as necessary from a tributary framework in foreign relations. Together, these two treaties limited Sino-Russian trade to certain border outposts and certain times of the year. The Treaty of Kiakhta also permitted the establishment of a Russian Orthodox church to service the small Russian community living in Beijing since the termination of the Sino-Russian wars of the 1680s, the dispatch of an ecclesiastical mission every ten years, and triennial trading missions. Even though the treaties formally recognized the principle of equality between nations, China still insisted traders observe ceremonials that implied a relationship of superiority and submission.

The cessation of hostilities with Russia in the 1690s enabled the Qing to shift their attention to the task of defeating Zunghar tribes that were threatening China's northern and northwestern borders. The wars initiated against the Zunghars continued sporadically until, in the 1750s, a series of Qing military successes ended with the extermination of the Zunghar people and the incorporation into the empire of vast tracts of land in Central Asia. This elimination of the age-old nomadic threat to their northwest frontiers, which followed the effective incorporation of both Mongolia and Tibet into the empire, meant that by 1760 the Qing had gained control over the largest empire of Chinese history. The *lifan yuan*'s jurisdiction expanded in proportion.

The second main agency that dealt with foreign countries was the Board of Rites (*li bu*), traditionally the third of the six main ministries of government. The Board of Rites was responsible for relations with neighbors whose populations were non-Chinese but whose cultures bore some resemblance to China's, such as Korea, Burma, Siam, Vietnam, and Japan. From such countries the Qing expected formal acknowledgment of their predominance and in return offered limited trading rights, although unofficial trade often thrived side by side with formal exchanges. Europeans who sought trading privileges were encompassed in these arrangements primarily because they did not clearly fit into any other category and because unlike the contiguous states of Central Asia, they did not at first appear to harbor territorial ambitions.

A third organization supervised European missionaries working in China. This was the Imperial Household Department (*neiwufu*), which managed a wide range of the emperor's affairs. Its responsibility for the missionaries reflected the view that they had little relevance to the broader scheme of international relations. But in reality missionaries' role as interpreters for the handful of European embassies to reach China during this period gave them a considerable measure of influence that should not be underestimated. Court Jesuits, for example, natives of the Catholic countries perennially competing for power with Protestant Holland and England, tried more than once to stymie Dutch embassies to the Qing, by maligning the Dutch and by otherwise acting to impede their progress.

Religious differences, however, sometimes yielded to a sense of fellowship based on common European origins. For instance, in 1656 a Portuguese Jesuit expressed to a Dutch envoy to China the view that an invasion would not be all that difficult, but he suggested waiting until there were more Christian converts to act as a fifth column within China. On other occasions missionaries purporting to act solely as intermediaries in fact passed strategic information to Russian envoys, hoping to gain some advantage for themselves. In other words, the Jesuits were by no means politically neutral.

TRADE

Commerce played a huge role in eighteenth-century Qing China, an empire at the height of its power. With sustained peace and prosperity, the network of interregional markets within the country became increasingly elaborate, while international trade thrived as perhaps never before. A booming informal trade existed side by side with, and independently of, the formal exchanges that usually were treated as tributary in nature. To the north, periodic markets permitted at treaty-specified border posts were always busy. To the west, the newly conquered region of Xinjiang provided a conduit for interchange among China proper, Russia, and Central Asia, in an echo of the ancient Silk Road. Up and down the eastern seaboard, a thriving junk trade linked the coast to Taiwan (part of the empire since 1683), Japan, and Korea and to numerous Southeast Asian states: Siam, Malaya, the Philippines, Indonesia, and beyond. The junk trade brought China such necessities as pepper, coconut oil, rice, brown sugar, copper, wood, rattan, and sea slugs and took away Chinese ceramics, textiles, and other commodities.

Much of the population of the southeastern coastal provinces—at least hundreds of thousands of people—depended for a living on the maritime trade, and there was a constant flow of both commercial and personal communication between those who remained on the China coast and the burgeoning overseas communities. Qing authorities kept a sharp eye on overseas Chinese communities, for they were always on the alert for possible collusion among Chinese, the ever-present pirates, and ill-disposed foreigners; they assumed that only bad eggs would want to leave China altogether and that one could never discount the risk that they would pass information to unspecified hostile outsiders. Concerns of this kind periodically prompted temporary bans on maritime trade, a move that drove some to smuggling and piracy, but there were never any plans to put an end to overseas trade altogether.

The Southeast Asian trade's importance to the livelihood of coastal communities meant such bans were imposed only in extreme circumstances. The campaigns against the Taiwan-based Zheng forces, concluded in the 1680s, was an example of such extremity. Six decades later times were more secure. For example, in the aftermath of an episode in which Dutch colonists in Batavia had massacred more than ten thousand resident Chinese in 1740, the Qianlong Emperor resisted proposals for a complete ban on maritime trade precisely because of the hardship that it would cause Chinese in the coastal provinces.

Relations with Japan, with which China had no formal diplomatic ties, continued to be unfriendly. As we have seen, relations between the two countries during the late Ming had hardly been cordial. The indirect trade through Portuguese middlemen, begun in the mid-sixteenth century, had ceased in the 1630s, when Japan banned the Portuguese for fear of contamination with Christianity, but China's constant need for Japanese silver and copper kept trade going through Nagasaki, the only Japanese port open to foreign trade and residence. Meanwhile the Tokugawa shoguns who reunited Japan after 1600 insultingly suggested that Qing rulership, imposed by force, was illegitimate and helped furnish moral and material support to the Ming loyalist resistance. In such circumstances, even if Japan had been willing, the resumption of a tributary relationship was unthinkable.

Yet despite Japan's defiance of Chinese political overlordship, during this period Chinese Neo-Confucianism became an integral element of Japanese intellectual life. Both Korea and Vietnam had also adopted Chinese Neo-Confucianism as their ideology of state in Ming times. Hence much of East Asia, while neither politically cohesive nor culturally uniform, now operated in accordance with Neo-Confucian principles originating in China. It would be an exaggeration to describe East Asia during the Qing as a Chinese sphere of influence, but given the widespread prevalence of Neo-Confucianism, China and its culture constituted a very considerable presence in the region.

European merchants had been trading up and down the China coast since the lifting of coastal restrictions in 1683 and had gradually dropped much pretense about conforming to tributary notions. By the middle of the eighteenth century the British dominated the China trade. But they were becoming increasingly frustrated by the numerous extra exactions levied on foreign trade by local officials and by the difficulty of gaining access to higher-level authorities. In 1759, therefore, the British attempted to petition the emperor directly for redress and for the establishment of a more regularized system of foreign trade. This audacious move confirmed the already half-formed Qing view that the British were indeed a force to be reckoned with.

The Qing responded to the British initiative the following year by introducing restrictive procedures designed to safeguard the maritime frontier and to ensure that foreigners trading in China did so only on China's terms. Like the 1727 Treaty of Kiakhta between China and Russia, these procedures, known as the Canton system, were intended to enable the Qing to consolidate coastal defense as well as to monopolize commercial profits and control the interaction with Europeans.

The Canton system limited foreign trade to the single southeastern seaport of Canton. Foreigners were permitted to live in Canton only during the October to March trading season, and their women were banned altogether. Western merchants were required to deposit all weapons from their ships with Chinese authorities until their departure. They had to conduct their trade exclusively through specially licensed merchants known as the hong merchants (from the Chinese word for "company," *hang*), whom Qing authorities held responsible for the prompt payment of all customs duties and other charges and for the good conduct of foreigners. The foreigners had to use these men as their conduit to the court-appointed superintendent of the Guangdong maritime customs, known as the hoppo (from the Chinese word for the Board of Revenue, *hubu*). The hoppo represented Qing authority to the Europeans and helped the central government keep them at arm's length.

The informal junk trade was for the most part not subject to these regulations because it was conducted primarily by Chinese—both residents and migrants—and hence it was not regarded as foreign. After 1760 its identification as Chinese thus took on a new importance. In other words, much of the trade with Southeast Asia—the Nanyang trade—was unaffected by the new regulations and continued to operate out of ports other than Canton.

Superficially, the Canton system served its purpose of keeping Western traders under control and monopolizing the profits of international commerce for the government. But ultimately it backfired, for two reasons. First, it was often disastrous for the hong merchants. Many amassed huge debts they were unable to repay because of the countless bribes they were obliged to pay in order to maintain official favor and because of the practice of buying on credit from European traders. Several went bankrupt. Some were banished to the far northwest for their failure to meet their obligations. The possibility of making a fortune was just not enough to outweigh these kinds of risks. As a group the merchants were extremely unstable, but they were not normally allowed to withdraw, not least because of the difficulty of finding replacements. The fact that they were in effect compelled to continue indicates clearly that Qing authorities had no intention of altogether abolishing the trade. The second reason the Canton system ultimately failed was that many of the European merchants found it totally unsatisfactory. They did not regard their demands to be allowed to operate without limitation as anything out of the ordinary and were frequently infuriated by the restrictions and inconveniences of the system.

The Chinese justice system increasingly became a source of conflict between Chinese and Europeans. As Western merchants began to come to China in ever greater numbers, the Qing became stricter about enforcing the law. In the early Qing, when incidents were relatively few, Qing authorities had usually accepted financial compensation for cases involving the accidental killing of a Chinese by a foreigner. But from the 1750s they began to take stronger measures and to assert their jurisdiction over cases involving only Westerners on Chinese soil as well as those involving Chinese and Westerners.

A well-known case from 1784 serves as an illustration. A British ship, the *Lady Hughes*, fired a salute near Canton that accidentally killed two Chinese bystanders. The Chinese authorities demanded that the ship's captain give up the gunner, but the captain declared that he could not tell which gunner had fired the shot. Thereupon the Chinese arrested the ship's manager, or supercargo, as surety for the gunner, halted all trade with Europeans, and cut off communications between the Westerners living in Canton and the European ships at anchorage—British, Dutch, French, Danish, and American. It was as though the Qing construed the Europeans as a family, despite their many rivalries; it held them all, collectively, responsible for the *Lady Hughes* incident. Horrified at the cessation of trade, the Europeans rallied together and sailed their well-armed merchantmen into the harbor to register their protest. The Canton governor then proposed that all Westerners except the British could resume trade. All did so except, remarkably, the Americans, who within a decade of their revolution had already sent their first China-trading ship, the *Empress of China*, to Canton. Shortly thereafter the British surrendered the gunner into Chinese custody.

Traditional Chinese law codes contained very specific and detailed provisions covering homicide, which normally was punishable by death subject to imperial approval. Clemency was possible in the case of an accidental killing, such as that on the *Lady Hughes*, and on this ground the Canton governor proposed leniency. But the emperor ordered the gunner executed.

The imperial decision stemmed from domestic political considerations. As we saw in the last chapter, Chinese sometimes confused Christians with Muslims since each group followed a foreign religion. In 1784 a group of Muslims had rebelled in the interior for the second time in five years. Although Qianlong almost certainly grasped the distinction between Muslims and Christians, he could see some similarities too; both, for example, answered to a temporal authority beyond the emperor's control. He was also afraid that the Muslim uprising would soon lead to unrest among Christians. In addition, at the time of the *Lady Hughes* incident, he had recently ordered that all Christian missionaries operating in the provinces be suppressed. So far as he was concerned, he was acting entirely in accordance with Chinese law, and he saw no reason to do otherwise. But the British were scandalized. They regarded the gunner's execution as proof of an arbitrary and unusually cruel system of justice perpetrated by barbaric authorities. For some, at least, the Chinese system of justice was worthy only of human beings of very low caliber; later such an opinion made it easier to justify the opium trade.

Despite all the mutual difficulties and frustrations of the Canton system, foreign trade there flourished, in part because of a growing passion in Europe for things Chinese: porcelain, for which a growing export market developed; the perennially popular silk; and, above all, tea. Tea came to be the most important commodity that Europeans imported from China. The rapidly increasing demand was met virtually entirely from a small mountainous area of northwestern Fujian province, where extraordinary commercial stimulation marked one of the more positive impacts for China of European economic expansion.

Apart from substantial tea exports to Russia by way of the frontier trading post at Kiakhta, the primary market for Chinese tea was Britain, where it had become all the rage. The British East India Company imported tea in vast quantities, and although the Company's monopoly kept British competitors at bay, its various continental European counterparts also smuggled large amounts into Britain. The problem was how to pay for it because before the Industrial Revolution Europe produced very little it could trade with China. Only silver was marketable to China on a scale even nearly comparable to its tea imports.

By the early 1780s the East India Company faced financial ruin because of the tea trade. It had to find an alternative to silver, for it was taking out of China more than three times what it was bringing in. American independence had already deprived the Company of some of its market for tea and increased the competition. The passage, a few years later, of legislation reducing import duties in Britain, which helped the Company by making smuggling unprofitable, was insufficient to retrieve its fortunes because trade between China and Britain had continued to expand.

The alternative it seized on was opium. Opium grew in Britain's Indian colonies and could be sold in Canton for three times the initial cost. Opium had been known in China since the early seventeenth century and had begun to spread in the 1720s and 1730s. By the 1760s British merchants had begun smuggling it into China on a relatively small scale. Out of financial desperation, they now systematically stepped up the sales of Indian opium to China. Its addictiveness ensured a steady demand despite Qing efforts at prohibition.

The Company's opium policy was extraordinarily successful. The concerted effort to substitute opium for silver, to pay for the English tea-drinking habit, began in the late 1780s. In the next half century until the eve of the Anglo-Chinese Opium War, the British East India Company, through its licensees in the so-called country trade between India and China—conducted by a mixture of Britons, Indians, Armenians and Parsees—smuggled a total of almost 443,000 chests of opium into China, at a total cost of 230 million taels or Chinese ounces of silver.[2] The Company preferred to use these middlemen to conduct the trade with China in order to keep up the appearance that it was not violating the Qing ban on the opium trade, since it had no desire to jeopardize its legal trade in tea and other commodities. The British policy of using opium instead of silver to pay for Chinese tea was just beginning to take off at the time of the Macartney embassy in 1792 and 1793.

THE MACARTNEY EMBASSY

The Macartney embassy was the first concerted attempt by a West European power to establish a relationship with China based on equality and to "open up the China trade." It had two main goals. The first was to request the relaxation of restrictions on commerce, both because the British government perceived an expansion of trade to be in the national interest and because in the early stages of the Industrial Revolution newly powerful manufacturing interests in Britain, jealous of the East India Company's domination of the China trade, were extremely anxious to find new markets for their products. Thus the Company, which the government induced to finance the embassy, experienced ambivalent feelings about it, recognizing the possibility that success might mean the end of its own valuable monopoly on the China trade.

The second goal was to seek permission to establish a permanent British embassy in Beijing that would enable direct communication with the emperor instead of through the Hong merchants and officials in Canton, thereby presumably making it easier to protect British interests in China. In short, the conclusion of a commercial treaty that would, among other things, allow British trade to operate beyond just Canton, seemed a promising solution to all the problems they had encountered.

Accompanied by a substantial retinue of courtiers, scientists, linguists, and others and equipped with elaborate gifts, Macartney reached China in the summer of 1793 after a long sea voyage. Since officially his purpose was not to conduct trade but to pay official British respects to the emperor of China, his ships were exempt from the requirement that Western traders be confined to Canton. Sailing as far north as Tianjin, the port of Beijing, the embassy disembarked to complete its journey by land.

The gifts the embassy brought, including a fine planetarium accompanied by telescopes and other astronomical instruments, exact replicas of British warships, textiles, and weapons, were of the finest quality, intended to vaunt British scientific and manufacturing skills at their best. As Sir George Staunton, secretary of the embassy, put it, "Specimens of the best British manufactures, and all the late inventions for adding to the conveniences and comforts of social life, might answer the double purpose of gratifying those to whom they were to be presented, and of exciting a more general demand for the purchase of similar articles."[3] In this respect, the British resembled the Jesuit missionaries. Just as the missionaries hoped that European arts and sciences would prove to be the key that would open the door to Chinese tolerance, if not embrace, of Christianity, so the British hoped that the same key would open up the China market to much more trade.

Leaving the gifts on display at the Yuan Ming Yuan palace complex in Beijing for fear that transporting them any farther might damage their delicate mechanisms, the embassy journeyed on to Rehe (present-day Chengde), the summer residence of the Qianlong court. At Rehe the Qianlong Emperor received Macartney with considerable signs of favor, together with emissaries from some of his Inner Asian dominions who were in Rehe to pay their respects in the time-honored way. With graciousness and condescension, the emperor bestowed valuable gifts upon Macartney but denied his requests, courteously dispatched him under escort back to his ships, and sent him on his way. He instructed his officials in Canton to keep a particularly sharp eye on traders in general and on the British in particular.

Most accounts of Macartney's embassy place great emphasis on the envoy's refusal to prostrate himself as expected before the emperor as the immediate source of its failure, but the reality, not surprisingly, was more complicated. The whole episode was fraught with mutual misunderstanding. Generally Macartney assumed that diplomatic relations could be conducted in China in the same way that they were in Europe, and on the same premises, while Qianlong assumed that Macartney would fall in with Qing ritual practices surrounding the reception of foreign dignitaries. Both were simply mistaken. The exchange of gifts was similarly beset by mutual confusion. Macartney, for instance, unaware that the golden scepter Qianlong handed him was valued as a symbol of peace and prosperity, dismissed it as inadequate and of little intrinsic worth. Qianlong, on the other hand, thought the lavish presents brought by the British to lubricate diplomatic machinery were not substantially different from or better than what he had already seen of European products. Then Macartney's constant shifting of ground, intended to show a spirit of accommodation, only provoked a growing conviction that the British were concealing their true purpose. It made the Qing extremely edgy, and in the circumstances they were in no rush to make any concessions.

To the Qing, in any event, British requests seemed illogical. They wanted an embassy in Beijing, but foreigners resident in the capital would be too far away from their fellow countrymen trading in Canton to serve much purpose; they would simply be another group requiring supervision. They wanted more trade out of more ports, but Chinese authorities saw no reason for the British to be treated differently from other foreigners. The goods the British required were readily available through the hong system based in Canton, which ensured equal treatment of all Westerners. From China's point of view, Qianlong suggested, unmediated trade was just too risky; it threatened social order because too often greed led to conflict or at least to divided loyalties.

In retrospect the Macartney embassy was probably doomed from the outset. Certainly the British had an unfavorable advance billing in China as the result of their own overseas activities and from insinuations almost certainly made by Catholic missionaries at the Qianlong court, a majority of whom were French, about the untrustworthiness of their longtime national enemy, the Protestant British. In any event, whatever Qianlong's misgivings prior to the embassy's arrival, the actual encounter with Macartney further diminished Chinese confidence in British good faith and fueled British prejudices about Chinese reluctance to engage with the wider world. It was altogether an inauspicious beginning.

China and European Arts and Sciences

Notwithstanding his outward expression of uninterest in British manufactures, Qianlong and many others in China displayed considerable interest in all manner of things foreign, as is evident from a series of conversations he held in 1773 with the missionary Michel Benoist (1715–1774). Qianlong quizzed Benoist about Western science, philosophy, warfare, cartography, shipping, and navigational practices. In one such conversation he gravely asked Benoist whether "your Western philosophers have solved a problem that has much exercised our philosophers here: which came first, the chicken or the egg?"—an inquiry to which Benoist did his best to respond. Benoist was one of a number of Jesuit missionaries who lived and worked at the court of the Qianlong Emperor throughout his long reign, in the process also providing detailed information about China to Europe.

The technical skill and versatility of the Jesuit missionaries at the court of the great Qing emperors were astonishing. Missionaries built several astronomical instruments, including a quadrant, a sextant, a celestial globe, a theodolite, an azimuth, and several armillae, to equip an observatory that can still be visited in Beijing. They constructed fountains and a working windmill for the imperial palace. They designed a new summer palace near Beijing, at which they installed European-style fountains and plantings to surround elaborate structures adorned with European facades and interior decoration. They transplanted nasturtiums, bluebells, and other European plants and explained to courtiers how to cultivate them. They made elaborate clocks and mechanical toys. They built a harpsichord and gave music lessons. They provided technical advice on glassmaking and supervised its production, constructing furnaces of their own design. They taught themselves the art of enameling so as to be able to satisfy the imperial passion for this type of decoration. They built complicated hydraulic and other machinery, for the operation and function of which they provided detailed explanations in response to Chinese requests. They designed artillery pieces and supervised the foundries that produced them. They operated medical dispensaries and, with the help of traders down in Canton, supplied the emperor with rare European medicines: quinine for malaria and antimonic sulfide to counter parasitic diseases. They assembled devices for applying electroconvulsive shock treatment for nervous illness, which by the late eighteenth century they were administering with some success to Chinese ready and willing to take the risk. They surveyed the entire empire, traveling to take measurements in newly conquered areas as soon as possible after hostilities ceased. Finally, they worked as court painters, producing portraits and, in particular under Qianlong, detailed records of the triumphs of Qing rule. In short, they worked extremely hard and with considerable success to satisfy imperial demands for both aesthetic pleasure and practical science and technology.

The spheres of Western knowledge in which Qing emperors showed the greatest interest were those capable of supporting Qing efforts to reconfirm their legitimacy as rulers of China, their military exploits, their imperial aspirations, and their efforts to control the historical record. Among these areas of interest, astronomy and the associated science of mathematics had the most intimate connection to Qing efforts to justify their political authority.

ASTRONOMY AND MATHEMATICS

European astronomy was the mainstay of the secular knowledge that the Jesuits brought to China. Many Jesuits trained in astronomy before they embarked. Moreover, during the six months' sea voyage from Lisbon to Goa and the three more it took to get to Macao, they had ample opportunity to further their familiarity with the stars. Calendrical reform had been subject to extended debate in China not long before Ricci's arrival, so that Jesuit astronomers entered an existing fray; they did not initiate it.

In 1629 missionaries won a court-sponsored competition for the most accurate prediction of an eclipse, defeating existing officials, including Muslims using imported methods. As a result, and through the intercession of the Pillar Xu Guangqi, they were appointed to the Ming Imperial Bureau of Astronomy. As well as their superior eclipse prediction, their geometrical analysis of planetary motion, their concept of a spherical earth, and their ways of measuring its divisions consistently produced more accurate calculations than did the methods then in use in China.

Chinese acceptance of European astronomy's greater accuracy showed a proper caution, as the following statement, signed by ten officials of the Bureau of Astronomy in 1629, indicates:

> At first we had our doubts about the astronomy from Europe when it was used in [1629], but after having read many clear explanations our doubts diminished by half. Finally by participating in precise observations of the stars, and of the positions of the sun and moon, our hesitations were altogether overcome. Recently we received the imperial order to study these sciences, and every day we have been discussing them with the Europeans. Truth must be sought not only in books, but in making actual experiments with instruments; it is not enough to listen with one's ears, one must also carry out manipulations with one's hands. All [the new astronomy] is found to be correct.[4]

During the 1630s European Jesuits and Chinese scholars published a huge collection of translations of Western works on calendrical methods, mathematics, surveying techniques, and other broadly scientific topics.

As we saw in the last chapter, Jesuit missionaries offered their services to the new Qing regime very shortly after the transfer of power in 1644. Their skills in astronomy were particularly useful to an alien group seeking ways to legitimate their rule. One of their number was appointed director of the Imperial Bureau of Astronomy, an important office of state charged with regulating the imperial calendar. This position, held by Jesuits for the next 150 years, both brought them prestige and offered the opportunity to influence the entire direction of astronomy in China.

At the outset of the two centuries or so of the Jesuit China mission, Europe was making extraordinary scientific advances, most notably in Copernicus's theory of heliocentrism, according to which the sun was the center of the universe and the earth and other planets all revolved around it, and Galileo's invention of the telescope. Although missionaries did tell their Chinese counterparts about the telescope and eventually produced one, they kept quiet about heliocentrism because the Church had condemned it as heretical; the Church considered that if the earth and the humans who inhabited it were not the center of the universe, the theological implications would be simply too terrible to contemplate. Instead missionaries, who felt unable to oppose Rome in public, propounded the system of the Danish astronomer Tycho Brahe (1546–1601), who placed the earth at the center of the universe and the sun at the center of the other planets' circular orbit.

Jesuit missionaries were reticent for so long because they feared that belated revelation would create inexplicable contradictions. Such fears proved justified. By 1760, when the missionary Michel Benoist finally brought heliocentric theory to the Qianlong Emperor's attention, Chinese scholars had, not surprisingly, become extremely skeptical about European astronomy, because of all the inconsistencies and inaccuracies they had noticed. What they now learned about heliocentrism seemed to fit into a discernible pattern of disclosure followed by contradiction. As a result, by the late eighteenth century imperial confidence in European knowledge was somewhat shaken, and the general view among Chinese astronomers was that their European counterparts had little to offer.

Conventional wisdom in the West has attributed Chinese skepticism about European science to an ingrained hostility to foreign ideas, but this assumption thus failed to reflect the true sequence of events. Indeed, one may question whether the incomplete way in which the Jesuits relayed some of the new knowledge to China may not actually have interfered with scientific progress in China. Moreover, by fatally damaging their credibility as scientists, their reticence also cast doubt on the integrity of their religion and hence interfered with their ability to make conversions.

The theories of the universe Europeans transmitted into China required the introduction of new elements of mathematics. These included Euclidean geometry, practical astronomy, written arithmetic, and plane and spherical trigonometry. As in the case of astronomy, the Jesuits withheld information about all the new mathematical discoveries of the age. They did not refer to the creation of the calculation of probabilities, analytical geometry, infinitesimal calculus, the rebirth of numbers theory, or the evolution of symbolic algebra. They presented only such new ideas as were necessary to keep their astronomy accurate. The reality, after all, was that the Jesuits had not gone to China to spread European science but to spread Christianity.

Despite its limitations, the Jesuit introduction of Western science into China had a huge impact on Chinese scholars and on the whole tenor of Chinese mathematics and astronomy. As a distinguished historian of Chinese science has written:

> Wang Xishan (1628–1682), Mei Wending (1633–1721) and Xue Fengzuo (d. 1680) were the first scholars in China to respond to the new exact sciences and to shape their influence on their successors. They were, in short, responsible for a scientific revolution. They radically reoriented how one goes about comprehending the celestial motions. They shifted from using numerical procedures for generating successive angular orientations to using geometric models of successive locations in space. They changed the sense of which concepts, tools and methods are centrally important, so that geometry and trigonometry largely replaced numerical algebra, and such issues as the absolute sense of rotation of a planet and its relative distance from the earth became important for the first time. They convinced Chinese astronomers that mathematical models can have the power to explain the phenomena as well as to predict them.[5]

The introduction of Western science also resuscitated interest in indigenous Chinese science. The fall of the Ming demonstrated that running a government on abstract principles alone simply did not work, and it renewed scholarly interest in classical wisdom and practical statecraft. Intellectuals now turned their attention to such more utilitarian topics as astronomy, geography, and surveying, in addition to moral philosophy.

Part of this movement involved a repackaging of the sages of antiquity as initiators of Chinese technology as well as models of moral virtue. A leading example was that of the legendary king Yu, who was now praised as much for his role as "tamer of the floods"—a reference to his success in channeling China's major rivers—as for his outstanding moral caliber. At the same time, Chinese scientists such as Mei Wending asserted that scientific truth, including recent discoveries, transcended even the authority of the ancient sages. All these intellectual trends led to the growth of an important scholarly movement known as *kaozheng*, or evidentiary research—that is, a search for knowledge that could be verified empirically.

The goal of *kaozheng* scholars, at its simplest, was to seek truth from facts. They sought precision and accuracy in all aspects of scholarly enterprise, including not only the more technological subjects but also historical research, philology, and textual criticism, which enabled scholars to analyze ancient texts for authenticity and hence to rediscover true Confucian ideas at the source. In all these projects, the exact sciences, the revival of whose popularity derived from the Jesuits' introduction of Western scientific knowledge, provided fresh impetus. In other words, Western scientific knowledge, in addition to its intrinsic value, slotted into an ongoing reevaluation of the entire classical tradition and brought scientific methodology into the mainstream of intellectual endeavor.

To encourage serious attention to the new knowledge, eminent scholars created a myth that Western mathematics had evolved out of ancient Chinese ideas. This device did not spring from cultural chauvinism but from a desire to assure the acceptance of the foreign methods in China, where innovation gained quicker acceptance with the sanction of antiquity. Declaring a Chinese origin for Western science both gave the foreign knowledge legitimacy and made the study of mathematics and astronomy part of the scholarly movement to return to original Confucianism.

Chinese scholars worked systematically to recover their indigenous science. In the 1770s and 1780s, as many participated in a massive imperially sponsored project to collate all of China's most famous literary and historical works into a single anthology, they rediscovered and critically examined ancient works of Chinese mathematics and science. Scholars commented repeatedly on the importance of this work of recovery for current evidential research.

In 1799 a leading scholar published a collection of biographies of astronomers and mathematicians, thirty-seven of whom were Westerners, that brought together traditional Chinese and Western astronomy and drew attention to the latter. This work was influential because of the prominence of its principal compiler, Ruan Yuan (1764–1849), the director of an important academy where budding scholar-officials were trained to study science as part of the Confucian curriculum. Ruan encouraged students to think about such questions as the date and timing of the transmission of mathematics and astronomy to China from India and Persia, the source of most of the Muslim knowledge on which China had largely relied from the thirteenth century until the advent of the Jesuits; the relative merits of European and Chinese astronomy; and the possible Chinese origin of both European and Muslim astronomy.

The reaffirmation of mathematics and astronomy as an integral part of a proper Confucian education reached its height in the eighteenth century. Despite the skepticism to which Jesuit inconsistencies had led, Chinese scholars did not discard Western knowledge. Scholars attributed the lag in Chinese science to Song Neo-Confucianism's preference for metaphysics over mathematics; such a preference was no longer acceptable. As Qian Daxin (1728–1804), a leading mid-eighteenth-century *kaozheng* scholar, put it:

> Comparing lands of the Eastern seas with those of the Western, we note that their spoken languages are mutually unintelligible and that their written forms are each different. Nonetheless, once a computation has been completed, [no matter where,] there will not be the most minute discrepancy when it is checked. This result can be for no other reason than the identity of human minds, the identity of patterns of phenomena, and the identity of numbers [everywhere]. It is not possible that the ingenuity of Europeans surpasses that of China. It is only that Europeans have transmitted [their findings] systematically from father to son and from master to disciple for generations. Hence, after a long period [of progress] their knowledge has become increasingly precise. Confucian scholars have, on the other hand, usually denigrated those who were good mathematicians as petty technicians. . . . In ancient times, no

> one could be a Confucian who did not know mathematics. . . . Chinese methods [now] lag behind Europe's because Confucians do not know mathematics.[6]

In sum, there is no question that the introduction of Western astronomy and mathematics enormously affected the direction of intellectual activity in China. The scope of its influence extended well beyond the immediate fields of what we think of as science. To suggest that Chinese intellectuals resisted this type of Western knowledge, for whatever reason, is wrong. To the contrary. On the one hand, they paid close attention to European astronomy and mathematics to the extent that what they learned from the Jesuits made sense. On the other hand, their creative incorporation of Western scientific knowledge and its methods into preexisting scholarly debates dramatically shifted the direction and the parameters of intellectual endeavor in China.

CARTOGRAPHY

Unlike mathematics and astronomy, Jesuit cartography in China took great account of the strong Chinese tradition of cartography and geographical description. It also represented a cooperative rather than a competitive effort between Jesuits and their Chinese colleagues. Jesuits used maps to show where they had come from and to clarify Europe's geographical relationship with China. Their first major work of cartography was Ricci's world map, produced in 1584. It was a Chinese version of a European map of the world that he had brought with him from Europe and hung on his wall. This map attracted the attention of at least one of the late Ming emperors and intrigued Ricci's Chinese contacts, although not all the information it provided was as much of a revelation as Ricci supposed. In any event, he supervised the production of thousands of copies, and many more were pirated without his authority.

More Jesuit cartography followed. In 1623 Fujian-based missionary Giulio Aleni produced an illustrated geographical treatise that brought together European maps with information derived from Chinese sources; the geographer and Catholic convert Li Zhizao wrote a preface. In 1674 Ferdinand Verbiest, by then director of the Imperial Bureau of Astronomy, produced an updated world map that synthesized new knowledge, accompanied by an expanded version of Aleni's work, and in the mid-eighteenth century Michel Benoist also drew a new world map for the Qianlong Emperor.

The most extensive Jesuit cartographical work in China was a survey of the Qing empire undertaken at the behest of the Kangxi Emperor. With the steady expansion of imperial territory, the Qing required accurate maps of the empire as well as accurate maps of the heavens. At first Kangxi authorized court missionaries to carry out relatively limited surveys of the Great Wall and of the environs of Beijing; pleased with the result, he soon sponsored a Jesuit-supervised survey of the entire empire.

The Kangxi survey took ten years, from 1708 to 1718. Missionaries traveled far and wide, taking advantage of their imperially authorized journeys into the interior for evangelistic as well as cartographical purposes. They plotted points by triangulation and did their best to fix latitudes and longitudes by carefully making astronomical and geographical measurements. Whenever possible, they gathered information from local officials and studied indigenous works and maps. They often used Chinese assistants, whom they trained in Western cartographical methods. These native sources and informants were all they had to go on when they produced maps of places they never visited, such as Tibet and Korea. The great Jesuit survey's reliance on Chinese cartographical experience was played down by its Jesuit publisher in Europe, who for political reasons gave all the credit to the missionaries.

In China the resulting maps were printed in four different editions during the period 1717–1726 and later were engraved on forty-four copper plates by the missionary abbé Matteo Ripa. The survey formed the foundation for subsequent geographical study of China for more than a century, both in Europe and in China, where partial reprints appeared in encyclopedias and subsequent atlases.

Jesuit surveying for the Qing continued with little interruption after the completion of the Kangxi project. In 1759 the Qianlong Emperor selected two missionaries to survey the newly conquered expanses of Central Asia known as Xinjiang. The maps they produced were kept in the palace and apparently were not made generally available probably because, then as now, maps of frontier regions were too sensitive to circulate. But the great Qianlong atlas that appeared in 1764 undoubtedly was based on their work and on other cartographical work that Jesuits and Chinese scholars worked on together. In 1776 Qianlong sent one of the missionaries who had done the Xinjiang survey to western Sichuan, once again to survey a newly pacified region.

The Jesuits' work did gradually enter the public domain. It was almost certainly the basis for maps that appeared in published gazetteers of Xinjiang from the 1770s on and in works on Tibet of the same period. Many of the new maps were engraved in copper by the missionary Michel Benoist, a self-taught craftsman who trained Chinese in the art of copper engraving. So the results of Jesuit cartography did eventually become more generally known in China and in some cases remained for some time the most reliable sources of information available. In addition, for Chinese scholars, especially the many exponents of evidential research who collaborated in these mapmaking enterprises, Jesuit cartography represented another important way in which European knowledge contributed to their work of seeking truth from facts. It also marked a departure from the traditional wariness about giving foreigners access to cartographical information.

Art and Architecture

Jesuit missionary artists at the imperial court introduced Western artistic techniques, including perspective and the use of chiaroscuro, and learned to incorporate Chinese styles in their own work. Among the Jesuits' most famous paintings are their portraits of the emperors and their favorites and family members. In one example the Yongzheng Emperor wears a long flowing Western-style wig, while another depicts a woman, possibly the imperial concubine Xiangfei, dressed in armor in the manner of a Joan of Arc.

Artists of the Qianlong painting academy, both European and Chinese, became deeply involved in documenting the triumphs of the age, especially military victories. These pictorial records included, for instance, depictions of newly conquered areas (often based on information gleaned from the missionary surveyors), heroic action paintings, portraits of meritorious generals and officials, and highlights of military victory, as well as portraits of the emperor in numerous guises. Often such works were collaborative Jesuit-Chinese efforts. Qianlong preferred the European style of portraiture to the flatter, less subtly shaded Chinese method and had missionaries depict the most important figures, while Chinese artists painted the backgrounds and the less important figures. Most of these paintings adorned halls and pavilions within the imperial palace complex. They formed part of a comprehensive historical record, compiled on imperial orders, of Qing imperial power.

Of Jesuit court art, some of the most famous was the series of battle paintings prepared to adorn a military hall of fame newly refurbished to celebrate the conquest of Xinjiang. In 1760 Qianlong commissioned four missionary artists to produce sixteen scenes depicting important battles and events in the conquest of Xinjiang. What prompted this commission? Through the missionaries the emperor was certainly aware of European depictions of war; he once questioned Michel Benoist: "There are a number of European prints that represent military victories won by your sovereigns. Who are they defeating, what enemies have they had to fight?"[7]

Perhaps too, through the missionaries at his court, Qianlong was aware of the battle paintings produced in Europe, such as those displayed at Versailles in France and at El Escorial in Spain. Although the court limited access to the originals to a select few, Qianlong wanted to broadcast his military successes; the propaganda value was too good to squander. Spurred on by some engravings of original battle paintings done by the German painter Rugendas (1666–1742) that he saw, he decided to have mass reproductions of these war illustrations made. Since at that time no one in China recalled the techniques of engraving, the emperor decided, with strong missionary encouragement, to have the work done in France. Perhaps too Qianlong had heard enough of France's considerable power that he wished to take advantage of this opportunity to let his military might become known to the French king.

Copies of the sixteen war paintings were sent to Paris on French East India Company ships with orders for two hundred sets of copper engravings. In France the project was delegated to the celebrated printmaker Charles-Nicolas Cochin (1715–1790), who in turn arranged for eight of France's best-known artists to do the engravings. Although, in theory, the contract drawn up with the French East India Company preserved copyright for the Qing Emperor, the French made a few extra copies for their king and his ministers. As a result, a few complete sets are found today in Western collections. Qianlong had Father Benoist and his Chinese assistants produce further copies, which bedecked public buildings all over the empire and were distributed to deserving officials as a mark of official favor. Later Qianlong commissioned further portraits and battle paintings series to mark new victories, but these were drawn and engraved in China by Chinese artists and craftsmen.

Emperors also employed Europeans as architects. In 1747 Qianlong ordered the Italian missionary Giuseppe Castiglione (1688–1766) to design him an entire European palace complex, just as his grandfather Kangxi had once had missionaries build him a windmill and a fountain. In Qianlong's case this use of European architectural styles may perhaps have been intended to express a wishful mastery of the nations where these originated, as was the thinking behind the reproduction of Tibetan architecture at other Qing palaces.

The buildings of the Yuan Ming Yuan palace complex, on the northwestern outskirts of Beijing, exemplified European and Chinese collaboration in terms of both building techniques and decorative styles. Chinese-style tile roofs were combined with baroque pilasters and cornices that were European. Moreover, whereas in the West the gray stone walls of such a palace would have remained unadorned, the Beijing palace was brightly colored, with walls of vermilion; roof tiles of imperial yellow, blue, green, red, and purple; and elaborate ornamentation in porcelain or gilded bronze. The interiors were decorated with paintings, engravings, tapestries, and painted wallpaper in the European style, given by foreign embassies or acquired through the merchants in Canton. Used to display Qianlong's large collection of European scientific instruments and decorative arts, the palaces were appointed with European-style furniture, probably made by Chinese craftsmen from engravings shown them by the Jesuits. The gardens also displayed a blending of Chinese and European styles, combining rockeries and plantings in the Chinese taste with European-type fountains and topiary.

These palaces were not destined to last long. The fountains ran dry before Qianlong's death in 1799, and in 1860 the whole complex was sacked by British and French troops under Lord Elgin. Before the Qing fell from power in 1911, successive depredations had reduced the Qianlong Emperor's European-style showpiece to little more than rubble.

Even shorter-lived than the Yuan Ming Yuan were the Western-style festive pavilions, galleries, and gateways often erected for specific occasions along the processional routes between the summer palaces and the Forbidden City in the center of Beijing. On such occasions it was de rigueur for every prince and high-ranking metropolitan official to have a special structure put up at his own expense. Once the occasion was over, these structures were dismantled; we know of them now through paintings that recorded the events they were built to celebrate. For example, in 1752 several structures showing distinctly Western features were erected along the route of a procession from a palace northwest of Beijing to the empress dowager's palace on the occasion of her birthday. One had Corinthian columns and a series of enameled plaques depicting figures with wavy brown hair looking up to heaven against a background of radiant light and clouds, looking, in fact, distinctly Christian. Another had a Western clock face in its gable, set with Roman numerals at five to eleven. Whether these were actually built by Jesuits is unknown, but whoever the artisans were, they clearly were familiar with many basic features of European architecture.

Like European chinoiserie, however, which faded as Europeans became disillusioned with the partly imaginary China they had once so admired, the Qing passion for European-style architectural features had worn off by the end of the eighteenth century. Not so their interest in European artillery.

Artillery

European artillery played a part in China's many wars of the seventeenth and eighteenth centuries. Gunpowder had found its way with the Mongols from China to Europe. There, spurred by the constant warfare between the European states, the use of artillery had developed to a more advanced stage than was the case in China. However, while Western cannon was relatively lighter and more mobile, the evidence suggests that China still retained the edge in the technology of gunpowder, as distinct from that of weapons construction. In the early sixteenth century European traders had brought their armaments and their casting techniques back across the world to China by way of Japan, India, and Southeast Asia. Ming China had begun importing Dutch cannon by no later than 1604. By the 1620s Chinese workmen were casting cannon in Macao under the direction of Portuguese gun founders, whose work was already greatly in demand throughout colonial Asia. At the suggestion of high-ranking Chinese converts, Ming supporters more than once either purchased Macao-made cannon or invited Portuguese artillery technicians to bring their weapons to use against the Manchus. The Manchus also used European artillery against the Ming.

By 1642 the Ming were desperate. The missionary Adam Schall (1591–1666) had already made a large number of converts at court and shown his proficiency in astronomy, so that many people held him in great respect. His lucidity on the subject of cannon, in a discussion about defending the capital, led to an imperial order that he direct the casting of cannon for the failing dynasty. Schall's principal improvement over the indigenous cannon lay in the ability to produce smaller and less unwieldy siege guns. He reduced their size from seventy-five–pounders to forty-pounders, and produced more than five hundred pieces. With a Chinese colleague, he also wrote a work on gunnery, *Huo Gong Jie Yao* ("Essentials of Gunnery"), that is still extant.

After the Ming fall European weapons continued to find favor with the Manchus. In 1673 the Kangxi Emperor, beset by rebellion, ordered his director of the Imperial Bureau of Astronomy, Ferdinand Verbiest, to establish another cannon foundry. Reluctant to comply, as Schall had been before him, Verbiest tried to insist that priests were men of peace with little knowledge of the affairs of war. But the emperor threatened to expel all Christians from China unless Verbiest complied, so the missionary felt obliged to yield. Not surprisingly, these activities were virulently attacked by the Jesuits' critics in Europe, but the pope took the view that Jesuit arms founding in China came into the category of "using the profane sciences for the safety of the people and the advancement of the Faith."[8]

Verbiest's task, much as Schall's had been, was to cast lighter and more mobile artillery than the Manchus already had—including the cannon imported earlier—for Qing troops badly needed cannon that would be capable of traversing mountains and rivers. From his designs, Chinese craftsmen produced imported Western types and improved on Chinese cannon, chiefly by lengthening the barrel. Some were made from bronze, including recycled metal melted down from old and damaged cannon. Others were made of iron with a bronze ring around the mouth and a bronze ball at the rear, the whole being covered by painted wood. Many were beautifully decorated. There were various types, all of them front-loading.

The emperor took a personal interest in the production of cannon. Usually Verbiest would produce a blueprint and build a sample cannon with which trials would be made at the Lugouqiao (Marco Polo Bridge) testing site near Beijing. Provided these proved successful, the emperor, who sometimes personally attended test firing sessions, would order several cannon of that type to be cast. The emperor's observation of the testing led him to realize the importance of aligning the sights and the target. He then ordered that soldiers attend the experimental firings so that they could learn the principles of aiming more accurately. He was so pleased with Verbiest's work that he offered the missionary his own sable coat, a rare gesture indeed.

Over a fifteen-year period Verbiest's foundry produced over five hundred cannon, more than half the total number of cannon cast during the entire Kangxi reign (1663-1722). Chinese records give some of their names, including *shenwei* ("wonderful and terrible") and *chongtianpao* ("gun for attacking heaven," a type of trench mortar popularly called *xigua pao*, "watermelon gun," after its bulbous shape). Verbiest, as had sometimes been the practice in medieval Europe, gave each cannon the name of a saint and blessed it before sending it out. A number of these weapons are now to be found in European museums, having been captured by Western troops during the numerous conflicts of the nineteenth and early twentieth centuries.

Verbiest wrote a work on artillery, now lost, that he entitled *Shenwei Tushuo* ("Explanations and Illustrations of [the Cannon Named] Wonderful and Terrible"). In this work he wrote on the importance of uniformity in the weight of cannonballs and of knowing that weight and on the critical difference that a cannon's angle of elevation could make to its accuracy in firing. Among other things, this meant that if soldiers knew the exact distance between their targets and their guns, their cannonballs would accurately hit those targets. The unmistakable implication was that good cannon could be used to best effect only when accurate land surveys were available.

The cannon made by Schall and Verbiest remained an important part of the imperial arsenal until the end of the dynasty. Verbiest's cannon foundry continued in operation after his death in 1688, and his designs continued to be used in China at least until the Opium War (1839–1842).

Although immediate acquaintance with this work was relatively limited, news of the Westerners' skills spread. In the 1740s, when beleaguered Qing armies were fighting rebels in Sichuan province near the Tibetan border, there was some idea among the troops that a Jesuit cannon founder might come to the rescue, although there is no evidence that any such plans existed. Thirty years later Qing forces fighting a resurgence of the same groups were horrified by a rumor—unsubstantiated—that Catherine the Great of Russia had sent an army that was about to enter the fray on the rebels' side.

Although Russian troops did not materialize to fight for the insurgents in that war, the Qianlong Emperor followed his grandfather's precedent of exploiting missionaries' military knowledge to the full, as we can see from a 1772 account sent from Beijing to Rome: "By [the emperor's] order, the fathers of our tribunal are sometimes called to go and assist at artillery practice; at other times we are called to figure out the usage of the different arms brought by European merchants, that the mandarins in Canton present to his Majesty. Finally . . . our fathers were . . . questioned as to whether they could, as in the past, cast pieces of artillery, to which they replied that at present there was no one who knew how to do it."[9] In other words, by no later than the 1770s Jesuit missionaries, possibly against their will, had become accomplices not just in arms manufacture but also in arms sales to the Qing empire. Certainly the Qianlong Emperor regarded them as armaments experts, a view the missionaries appear to have done little to discourage. To judge from a contemporary account, the emperor had been interested in a missionary plan for the defense of Beijing, but it had encountered resentment on the part of Chinese and Westerners alike: "He offered to make [the plan] in relief . . . the emperor took the plan and resolved to have it explained to him, and perhaps to have it executed on the spot. But his ministers sought to find fault with it; they criticized every part of it. Moreover, we [Jesuits] were afraid that in Europe we would be accused of 'teaching the infidels the art of war.'"[10]

Nonetheless, soon after this episode a Jesuit missionary again helped the Qing cast cannon to use against insurgents in their war against indigenous peoples rebelling near the Tibetan border. The Qing, hampered by the difficulty of transporting heavy cannon along precipitous paths, were unable to destroy the rebels' stone forts, deep in the mountains. They solved this problem in part by the expedient of carrying thousands of metal ingots that artisans attached to the army forged into cannon when and where needed. With a view to building cannon mobile enough to use in the mountains but powerful and accurate enough to destroy the enemies' forts, the Qianlong Emperor ordered the Portuguese director of the Imperial Bureau of Astronomy, Father Felix da Rocha (1731–1781), to proceed to the war front in 1774 both to bring out and probably to explain designs for cannon and to take measurements, as we can see from the emperor's order: "Previously we used mortars to attack [the rebels' stone forts], thus accelerating our victory. We dispatch A-mi-ta to transport the cannonballs, cannon designs, and surveyors to the front. If their surveying is very accurate, it may help us. We think that the Westerners are expert in surveying, more so than [Chinese] surveyors. . . ."[11]

The designs most likely were those of Verbiest, which had recently been republished with detailed specifications. Shortly after da Rocha's arrival at the front, he made various measurements, relating mainly to the angle at which the cannon was fired, just as Verbiest had discussed in his treatise. It then became possible to fire the cannon with a far narrower margin of error, so that bombardment of the rebel fortresses became considerably more effective. Not long afterward Qing artisans also built a new cannon, based presumably on the designs da Rocha had brought with him and perhaps produced under his actual supervision. Like his grandfather Kangxi, then, the Qianlong Emperor had no compunction about using foreign science and technology, and when he thought it would help him win a war, he showed no hesitation whatsoever.

For we must bear in mind, as eighteenth-century Europeans sometimes did not, that imperial power—domestic control and national security—were the driving concerns of the Qing at its height. As one of the imperial princes commented to a Jesuit missionary extolling the virtues of the Montgolfiers' hot-air balloon, which had just made its first flight, "Only in war do we have no regard for expense, difficulty or danger; we are ready to try anything."[12]

Qing concern for security issues underlay their restrictions on emigration and overseas travel. But increasingly, Chinese went abroad anyway, in most cases drawn by the prospect of making a fortune but in some instances attracted to the entourage of a foreign missionary returning home.

CHINESE ABROAD

Chinese from coastal areas had long been traveling overseas for business and pleasure, and by the seventeenth century sizable communities had sprung up all over Southeast Asia, forming the nucleus of a vast diaspora. Some went even farther afield. In the 1630s, for example, Chinese barbers, having traveled to the New World on returning Manila galleons, aroused local ire in Mexico City by undercutting prices, and to this day a style of embroidered women's blouse found in central Mexico bears the name *china poblana*.

Not many Chinese visited the world beyond Asia before 1800. In the eighteenth century, a few, perhaps sailors who had found work on foreign ships, surfaced in European or American ports, where they were something of a curiosity for the local inhabitants. Some found their way to Rome, where they worked with the Chinese books and manuscripts that missionaries had brought back and deposited in the Vatican library. Some, mainly convicts shipped on from Dutch colonies in Southeast Asia, appeared in colonial Africa and Ceylon, while others were recorded at a Jesuit college in Portuguese Goa, on the west coast of India.

One of the first Chinese visitors to Europe was Michael Shen Fuzong, who in the late seventeenth century traveled with the Jesuit Father Couplet (1624–1692). Shen was received by the French king Louis XIV and the English Catholic king James II. He worked at Oxford for a few years and died on his way back to China. Not much later a Fujianese named Arcadio Huang made his way via Rome to Paris. Huang had been adopted by a Frenchman from the Society of Foreign Missions after the death of his convert father. In Paris he found employment helping to catalog the Chinese books in the royal library. Huang met the French Enlightenment philosopher Charles de Montesquieu (1689–1755), with whom he held a series of conversations that, through Montesquieu's influential writings, indirectly played a part in the formation of European views of China. Huang died in Paris, predeceased by his French wife; their young daughter did not long survive him.

One Chinese traveler who did return home was Louis Fan Shouyi (1682–1753), who himself became a priest. He accompanied the Jesuit missionary Joseph-Antoine Provana (1662–1720), whom Kangxi had sent on a mission to the pope. Provana died on the journey back to China, but Fan returned to brief the emperor on his meetings with the pope and on the customs and geography of the lands he had visited, including Portugal and Italy. Fan spent the rest of his life in missionary work in China. Another who returned, but with less éclat, was John Hu, who accompanied the Jesuit missionary Jean-François Foucquet (1663–1740) to France. Hu was confined to a French lunatic asylum—possibly because of cultural difference rather than actual insanity—before eventually returning to his native Canton.

When Abbé Matteo Ripa prepared to return home from China, the emperor officially permitted him to take four young Chinese to Europe with him, in recognition of services rendered. They enrolled at the Jesuit College in Naples, founded by Ripa in 1732 and run by the Society of the Propaganda of the Faith, based in Rome. Perhaps the most famous graduate of the Naples Jesuit College was Jacob Li, who earned his passage back to China by serving the Macartney embassy as an interpreter. Members of the embassy sometimes referred to Li as Mr. Plumb, presumably because the character *li* of his name means "plum."

A few Chinese went to France as the result of the extraordinary interest in China of the secretary of state Henri Bertin (1720–1792). Most famous of these were two young men, Stephen Yang Dewang (1733–1798?) and Aloysius Gao Leisi (1733–1790?), who lived in France from 1751 to 1766. In 1759, after a period of study, they entered the Society of Jesus. After the Society was suppressed in France in 1762, the two Chinese came under Bertin's special protection, eventually receiving a royal stipend of twelve hundred livres apiece and other official bounties. Once their Jesuit training was completed, they remained in France for another couple of years. The two Chinese formed part of a project conceived by French sinophiles such as Bertin and his colleague Anne Robert Jacques Turgot (1727–1781) to establish a special intellectual relationship with China, in part by impressing upon China France's role as Europe's cultural pacemaker. Under French auspices Gao and Yang studied physics, natural history, and chemistry with two members of the Academy of Sciences, who proclaimed themselves deeply impressed by the Chinese men's aptitude. Gao and Yang also learned the art of engraving; they visited brocade manufactures in Lyons and toured artillery factories at St.-Étienne. Eventually the two Chinese returned to China, carrying gifts to the emperor from King Louis and a host of messages for the French missionaries from Henri Bertin. The two Chinese spent the rest of their lives spreading the Christian faith in China and did little to further their foreign patrons' broader cause.

ORIGINS OF A STEREOTYPE

By the time of the Macartney embassy, the balance of European opinion had tilted against China. Westerners, earlier in the century almost uncritical in their admiration of China, were coming to the conclusion that Chinese seemed unwilling, or unable, to improve on their earlier inventions, such as gunpowder and the compass, which formed part of the foundation for Western development. The Qianlong Emperor's famous assertion, that China was self-sufficient (quoted at the beginning of this chapter), came to epitomize Chinese aloofness to the potential offered by Western knowledge, and this inference in turn became broadened to a supposition that Chinese disliked anything foreign.

When in 1793 Qianlong pretended disdain for things Western, he was not speaking the whole truth. He and many others found European arts and sciences, and just about everything Europe had to offer, fascinating and useful. Even in 1793 the emperor's response to his British visitors belied the assumption of his indifference, for he had them demonstrate several of the instruments with which they presented him. The single gift that most intrigued him was a 110-gun model of the warship *Royal Sovereign*, and he impressed his European audience with the technical knowledge his many questions revealed.

In short, Qianlong's assertion of self-sufficiency and his public diffidence to European achievements were, to say the least, disingenuous. They were primarily prompted by domestic political agendas and did not reflect objective reality. The same was true of European readiness to accept his statement at face value in spite of readily available evidence to the contrary.

The Chinese background to this misunderstanding was essentially as follows. Qianlong's public declaration was intended for a multiple audience. For a variety of reasons he preferred not to admit publicly his interest in and awareness of the potential of foreign technology. His motivation becomes clearer when we place the whole episode within the context of late-eighteenth-century Chinese politics. The Manchu Qing dynasty imposed and ultimately maintained its rule over China by military means. At the same time, it sought to present to its Chinese subjects and the world at large an image that was both thoroughly Confucian and ethnically even-handed. For the Qianlong Emperor these somewhat contradictory goals meant, among other things, that he made a virtue of his own civilian accomplishments, yet simultaneously leaned toward military culture by, for example, promoting the martial traditions of the Manchus. He awarded high civil office, normally the prize of scholars successful in a series of highly competitive examinations based on classical Chinese texts, to successful generals, almost all of whom were Manchus. He prohibited the private possession of any weapon and jealously guarded access to all information, especially any that smacked of technology, conceivably of use to would-be rebels.

No less important, it was wholly out of the question for the emperor to suggest a need for outside help. To the contrary, Qianlong realized there was considerable propaganda value, domestic and international, to be gained from declaring China's self-sufficiency to a foreign state of whose potential menace against Chinese national security China was quite conscious. This emperor, with his pretensions to universal monarchy, was hardly likely to admit openly to the representative of a foreign ruler an interest that, in Chinese minds, was susceptible of unfavorable interpretation as an intimation of inferiority. The imperial declaration may well also have been subtly intended to remind Qianlong's Chinese subjects that their Manchu rulers remained faithful to the traditional public Chinese attitude of superiority toward foreigners. The best explanation for the apparently general Chinese uninterest in the gifts the Macartney embassy brought, so disparaged at the time by the British, is that Chinese officials, schooled in caution, were simply taking their lead from the emperor.

The expression of Chinese uninterest also had to do with the intensely factionalized world of late-eighteenth-century Chinese politics. In 1793 there were two principal factions at the Qing court, one clustered around a general named Agui (1717–1797) and the other associated with the imperial favorite, Heshen (1750–1795). Agui had participated in a number of the major military campaigns of the middle and later eighteenth century, but it was the war in which the advice of the Jesuit missionary Rocha on cannon had rescued his faltering campaign that really made his reputation. Much admired by the Jesuits, Agui was said to be deeply intrigued by Western knowledge, and it is reasonable to attribute his interest at least partly to his wartime experience. His opponent, Heshen, was in charge of embassy liaison in 1793. Heshen had little experience and absolutely no aptitude for military affairs; on Heshen's only—and disastrous—military venture Agui, arriving at the crucial moment, saved his life and subsequently put in a good word for him with the emperor. Heshen offset the potential political disadvantage of lacking military qualifications, however, by his close association with one of the most successful of late-eighteenth-century generals, Fukang'an (d. 1796). In 1793 Fukang'an had recently returned from Tibet to take up the governor-generalship of Guangdong and Guangxi provinces. That is, he was in the probably unique position of having encountered the British in both places—as unruly traders on the southeast coast and, as he rightly suspected, allies of his enemies the Gurkhas in Tibet. Macartney vehemently denied any such British involvement, which he learned of only later, but Fukang'an's experience led him to consider the British troublemakers. As a result, he was not only extremely and overtly hostile toward them but also actively sought to dissuade Heshen from helping them or promoting their interests in any way. It is more than likely that Heshen and his associates hoped that by displaying disdain for the embassy's gifts, they would undermine any advantage that might accrue to Agui through his contacts with the missionaries and that they found the emperor susceptible to persuasion on this score.

On the other hand, Qianlong's statement was of course directed at the king of England through his envoy Macartney. By extension it applied to any other foreigners who might individually or collectively seek to alter the structure of China's foreign relations to the disadvantage of ultimate Qing control. In this context we can better account for the emperor's remarks when we realize that they conform to a pattern, according to which China has consistently sought to absorb Western practical technical skills while remaining inimical to Western ideologies. In the modern era this disparity originated with the attempted exploitation by Christian missionaries of their scientific and technical expertise as a means of arousing Chinese interest in their religion. Many Chinese, although they fully grasped the utility of the practical knowledge, were hesitant to adopt it because it seemed inseparable from Christianity. As we have seen, they were accustomed to a political system in which ideology specifically either served orthodox authority or opposed it, and for that reason they sensed that the foreign religion was imbued with subversive potential.

Thus in the late seventeenth century, although the Kangxi Emperor clearly recognized the actual and symbolic threat that papal authority over Chinese Christians would pose and rejected it absolutely, he was nonetheless thankful to improve his arsenal under Jesuit direction when rebels threatened his still fledgling dynasty. Almost a century later, under Qianlong, Western missionaries' efforts to proselytize in the provinces met with persecution at almost the precise moment that their colleagues' technical advice helped save Qing armies and that members of the elite vied to acquire examples of the new European technology, whether purely decorative or serving a practical purpose. Also, as we shall see, in the late nineteenth century certain Chinese reformers sought to acquire the Western technology that would bring their nation wealth and power without abandoning the indigenous intellectual tradition. The pattern is still discernible in our own time, notwithstanding the changed configurations of global power.

The point is that the Chinese and their rulers have uniformly displayed a powerful reluctance to surrender authority or autonomy to any outsider or even to take a chance on doing so. This attitude must be distinguished from the isolationism, the hostility to innovation, especially when of foreign origin, and the immutable sense of superiority for which it has often been mistaken.

Responsibility for the late-eighteenth-century miscommunication cannot, however, be laid entirely on the Chinese. Like the Chinese denial of interest in Europe and what it had to offer, the shift in European views of China, from admiration to scorn, tended to reflect internal, subjective conditions rather than any change in China itself. The eyewitnesses who made note of Chinese interest in the West and what it had to offer included, on the one hand, Jesuit missionaries, whose correspondence was published and widely read in Europe at the time and, on the other, members of Macartney's mission, who recorded it in their memoirs of the embassy. The problem was that these observations came to be superseded in Western minds by the impression, recorded in other such accounts, that found Chinese sorely deficient in the inquiring and progressive spirit that Europeans were beginning to consider one of their own culture's most enviable characteristics.

There were a number of reasons for this disparagement. One was the steady decline of the Society of Jesus, whose members had once held a virtual monopoly on the interpretation of China to Europe. The triumph of those who opposed the Jesuits, represented by the abolition of the Society of Jesus in 1773, seemed to confirm the unreliability of Jesuit accounts. At least as important an influence on changing European views of China was a series of momentous developments in Europe, in particular industrialization and the new focus on political liberty, with all the profound intellectual shifts that accompanied these metamorphoses. China's great agrarian accomplishments, once vaunted by Europeans as evidence of its most admirable characteristics, seemed less laudable in a budding industrial age. The restrictive Canton system of trade went directly against the free world market advocated by Adam Smith in 1776. Moreover, the absence of political liberty or consensus in China sat ill with the French and American revolutionaries who dominated the latter part of the century. Finally, the increasing predominance of negative Western attitudes toward other cultures at this time also partly reflected the disdain felt by Westerners when they compared the relatively class-bound societies of traditional Asia and Africa with the dynamic social changes of their own postrevolutionary, industrializing societies.

From the late sixteenth to the late eighteenth century, then, Chinese were extremely interested in Europe and all it had to offer. The evidence was readily available to Europeans who chose to grasp it. Yet when in public Chinese denied such an interest, primarily for reasons of domestic politics, Europeans, similarly influenced by developments at home, took that denial as evidence of an entire mental attitude: ingrained xenophobia and a concomitant resistance to progress. In the age of progress such an attitude led automatically to the assumption that the Chinese were inferior beings. The repercussions of this assumption have reverberated to leave a profound impact on relations between China and the West in our own time.

CHAPTER FOUR

The Turning of the Tables, 1796–1860

When two small countries have petty quarrels overseas, [we] are not concerned with them; and whether or not barbarian ships have attacked each other is their own affair. However, when their ships enter territorial waters of the Interior, they must obey and respect [Chinese] prohibitions. . . . How can [the British] expect to obtain revenge on the Americans here? The warships of their countries [should] anchor outside the inner sea and wait there until they escort their commercial ships back. If [they] disobey us, not only shall we destroy their warships but we shall also suspend their trade. . . . [China] is impartial toward all nations, but will not tolerate any nation which dares to disobey its statutes.[1]

The Jiaqing Emperor, 1796–1820

In the early nineteenth century an upsurge of piracy in Asian waters, combined with the international ramifications of the Napoleonic Wars (1793–1815), provided Europeans with a useful pretext for bending China's rules prohibiting the presence of armed foreign vessels in its territorial waters. Qing authorities could not object provided European warships kept their distance from Chinese waters; the very real threat posed by enemy and pirate vessels furnished ample justification for European men-of-war to escort merchant vessels involved in the China trade. But China took the greatest exception to British moves to land troops on Macao, undertaken, so they claimed, to protect the Portuguese from the enemy French (but in actuality more concerned about possible French efforts to disrupt Britain's own Canton trade). After the first such landing attempt, China insisted the Portuguese sign a bond agreeing to prevent the troops of any other nation from landing on Macao for whatever reason. When a few years later British warships actually did land several thousand soldiers in Macao, the Qing registered strenuous objections to this clear infringement of sovereignty, at the same time criticizing the Portuguese for not fending the British off.

Meanwhile the Portuguese, who were theoretically allied with the British—France had occupied Portugal and expelled the king—felt considerable alarm at the possibility that the British would try to usurp their trading privileges or even oust them from their offshore China base altogether. In communications with the Qing authorities, the Portuguese lost no opportunity to undermine the British, making insinuations about their territorial ambitions and generally aggressive character. The British, for their part, also hastened to fill in the Chinese on the details of the Napoleonic Wars, which they naturally described in the most partial way, all the while pleading their own benevolent intentions.

Anglo-American hostilities around 1812 also impinged upon China because of the presence of both British and American merchant shipping in Chinese waters. At least twice in 1814, for example, Her Britannic Majesty's Ship *Doris* chased American ships into Whampoa, the inner harbor area of Canton. *Doris* captured the American ship *Hunter* of Boston in Chinese waters and impressed a number of its seamen, whose release and repatriation the U.S. consul at Canton then had to arrange. In the meantime these former prisoners of war hung around Canton with time on their hands, offering the locals a glimpse of one tiny tranche of American society.

When the ramifications of the war began to affect the China trade directly, the parties tried to draw in the Chinese. The British, for instance, were furious that American ships not only captured British vessels on the high seas but sold the booty—opium and other cargo—in Canton, eating into British markets and profits. Obliquely threatening to halt trading in China altogether, they tried to convince the Chinese to ban the Americans. But much as the Qing government authorities deplored the blatant disregard by both sets of Westerners of imperial regulations against sailing into Chinese harbors, they were loftily but unambiguously discouraging, as we can see from the quotation (a composite of several pronouncements) with which this chapter opens.

In these ways, then, Qing authorities in Beijing and Canton gained a distinct sense of the Westerners' ready resort to military force and their near obsession with trade and profits, as well as not a few of the intricacies of international politics. By this time they had also received pleas for help against the British from the Gurkhas in Nepal. Although the more urgent demands of suppressing domestic rebellion made it impossible for them to provide any assistance to the Gurkhas, this was one more piece of information about European bellicosity of which they carefully took notice.

The Qing were also keeping a sharp watch on Russian activities. Although Sino-Russian trade was limited by treaty to Kiakhta, in reality the Russians were gradually opening up new commercial routes by way of Xinjiang and Tibet, about which the Qing periodically raised objections. But the Qing were not absolutely inflexible; in 1806, for example, they reluctantly permitted a convoy of Russian military vessels carrying a cargo of furs to dock and trade in Canton, after some debate about why the Russians had not simply gone overland by way of Kiakhta in the usual way. Russia was motivated by both commercial and political considerations, it wished for more trade with China, and it wished to gain a competitive edge over Britain in China more generally. Exactly how much of this the Qing grasped is unclear, although they were rightly suspicious of Russian intentions; the point is that while China at this juncture showed an understandable reluctance to get caught up in other people's wars, it was neither ignorant nor heedless of world affairs.

This chapter describes the adverse impact of China's close involvement with the world economy in the early nineteenth century and how this eventually led to war with Britain. It demonstrates that China's reaction to the war—its almost immediate construction of new ships and weapons, its use of treaty provisions as a shield as well as a sword, and its acceleration of learning about the West in order to fend it off—was both dynamic and built on earlier foundations for reform. Startling as the Opium War defeat was, in other words, Chinese were capable of deriving the best from a bad situation. Nonetheless, the six decades from the death of the Qianlong Emperor to the Convention of Beijing, covered by this chapter, marked a transition from confident autonomy to an only rather precarious independence. Perhaps more than anything, the events of this period show China's remarkable capacity to resist bullying on the part of Westerners who could not imagine a better way of doing things than their own.

CHINA IN THE EARLY NINETEENTH CENTURY

In retrospect we can see that an era came to an end when Emperor Qianlong (r. 1736–1795) died in 1799. The eighteenth century had seen Qing China reach its zenith. In 1759 the annexation of Xinjiang in Chinese Central Asia had increased the territorial extent of the empire by millions of square miles. During most of the century the empire was largely at peace. The doubling of the population within a hundred years, in part the long-term result of the introduction of such New World crops as maize, sweet potatoes, and the peanut, seemed a mark of prosperity. Cities blossomed, cultural life thrived, and the flourishing commercial interchange that had marked the late sixteenth century had by now thoroughly rebounded from the interruptions of the dynastic transition.

Among other things, this commercialization meant that more farmers began to grow cash crops, instead of food, which made them dependent on a range of outside forces beyond their control. Indeed, demographic growth was a mixed blessing, as many Chinese were aware at the time. Among the less desirable consequences were increased pressure on the land, compounded by such environmental problems as deforestation and the silting up of rivers; spreading lawlessness; the growing ineffectiveness of existing institutions; and sharply intensified competition for existing resources.

One consequence of acute competition at the level of subsistence was large-scale internal migration, in particular to areas, such as Xinjiang, newly available for settlement. It also fueled the steady migration of Chinese overseas. Many went no farther than existing settlements in Southeast Asia, while others moved on to new locations within the region, such as the East India Company's trading base of Singapore, established in 1824. By no later than the early nineteenth century Chinese emigrants were beginning to go much farther. Some found their way to the ports of the Americas on both the Atlantic and Pacific coasts. In 1810, a group of several hundred Chinese tea growers journeyed under Portuguese auspices to work in Brazil, where they formed one of the first substantial Asian communities in the New World.

While state revenues remained steady and the economy expanded, costs rose. The mid-eighteenth-century surpluses had created a false sense of financial security, prompting tax remissions to stricken areas and an ostensibly filial reluctance to increase certain assessments from the rate fixed by the Kangxi Emperor in 1713. A series of military campaigns along the imperial periphery, while they redounded to imperial glory, imposed an extremely heavy financial burden on the treasury, to which had to be added the considerable costs of postwar reconstruction and new frontier administration. The silting up of rivers blocked important transportation networks, putting many people out of work. It also, with increasing frequency, caused floods that displaced rural populations and brought famine in their wake. Mass protests became more common; between 1795 and 1840 there were at least fifteen major uprisings. The increased incidence of armed unrest, and a decline in the effectiveness of Qing armies, pushed up the costs of suppression campaigns. The White Lotus rebellion (1796–1803), for example, was said to have cost about 30 percent more than the central government's entire annual income, even though much of the regional defense was organized by local notables dismayed at the government's apparent ineptitude.

Until the early nineteenth century the balance of international trade was decisively in China's favor. Along the coast Europeans and, latterly, Americans vied to buy Chinese tea, porcelains, and textiles. The Russian demand for tea and other Chinese products continued unabated. Trade within Asia similarly continued to thrive, unaffected by restrictions placed on Western traders.

But problems caused China by rising expenditures were compounded by events around the world, underscoring the fatal significance of China's close involvement with the world economy. First, emancipation movements in Latin America, the source of the greater part of China's money supply, dramatically reduced the world's silver and gold supply. This reduction had a number of important consequences. It cut the supply of silver in China just when population growth and commercialization increased demand. It caused a worldwide depression that, among other things, reduced demand and hence prices for Chinese tea. It also spurred Westerners to export more opium to China, because for them it was the most effective alternative to silver.

The opium trade flourished despite China's prohibition of opium in 1800 and repeated attempts to block imports. Average imports of opium increased tenfold from the first to the fourth decade of the nineteenth century, providing the chiefly British importers with more than enough money to pay for their tea. They took the surplus in silver. By 1828 the balance had shifted: more silver left China than came in, further limiting supplies.

At the same time that China was suffering these economic dislocations, it also encountered stiff international competition in the production of both ceramics and textiles. Chinese silk and porcelain both now faced serious competitors in Europe and Japan, so that demand on international markets declined, although it did not disappear altogether. Demand for Chinese goods was also adversely affected by the waning of the European craze for chinoiserie from its mid-eighteenth-century peak.

Moreover, a worldwide shift in the cotton market undermined the economy of Shanghai and the surrounding cotton-growing regions. In the early nineteenth century American purchases of Chinese cotton declined, partly as the result of international sanctions against the slave trade—because much of what Americans had bought had gone to the Caribbean and Africa, where they now had less occasion to go—and partly because of revolutionary changes in the cotton industry elsewhere. In 1793, the very year of the Macartney embassy, Eli Whitney had invented the cotton gin. In wide use by the 1830s, the gin made the processing of cotton far more efficient, with the result that prices of raw cotton decreased on world markets. At much the same time industrial advances in Britain and America improved the quality of machine-made cotton fabric, which dropped in price and made Chinese cotton fabric less attractive. These developments affected a huge range of people in China, from spinners and weavers to manufacturers and shippers.

Internal factors further exacerbated those derived from abroad. Diminished production of copper coinage, a reduction of government quality control, and a resultant rise in copper counterfeiting pushed up demand for silver and made it even scarcer. By somewhat counteracting the shrinking of the copper supply, counterfeiting did help steady the prices of goods dealt with exclusively in copper currency. But the consequent deterioration of the copper-silver ratio reduced grain prices and increased the cost of taxes payable in silver. The effect on the economy and on morale, especially in the more commercialized south, was devastating.

Then, in 1834, the British government abolished the East India Company's monopoly on the China trade, in deference to the demands of free traders avid to share in potential profits. The immediate effect was to bring far more foreign traders to participate in the China trade, pushing up opium sales still further and providing greater commercial competition both among foreigners and with Chinese.

To sum up, in the first third of the nineteenth century China experienced a complete reversal of the economic prosperity of the eighteenth century. This reversal was attributable partly to demographic increase and environmental pressure on land resources in the interior and partly to China's tight integration into the world economy. An overall reduction in the silver supply resulted in a general recession, while worldwide shifts in markets for raw and finished cotton worked further to China's detriment. Opium sales increased sharply, contributing to China's economic problems, but opium was far from the sole culprit. In short, China's economic health was faltering even before the cripplingly expensive series of domestic rebellions, foreign wars, and treaty indemnities of the later nineteenth century.

Foreigners in China

In the early nineteenth century foreign trade was still limited to Canton, where the Western population was beginning to expand and diversify. Sojourning seamen were not the only white men in town. The presence of Western traders in Canton, predominantly British but also French, Dutch, Swedish, Danish, American, and a few German and Spanish, meant that Cantonese, at least, were gradually becoming accustomed to dealing with Westerners and had some idea about the ways in which they operated. The numbers were still minuscule: perhaps two hundred by the mid-1830s. Most were either traders or missionaries.

Outside Canton, in Xiamen (Amoy), Fuzhou, and Quanzhou in Fujian province, Chaozhou, Shantou, and Hainan Island of Guangdong province, and Shanghai (Jiangsu), Ningbo (Zhejiang), and Tianjin (Zhili), Siamese, Indonesians, Filipinos, Malaccans, among others, came to and fro in the course of the ever-thriving junk trade, which to Europeans' chagrin continued to dominate the trade in "Straits produce" from Southeast Asia and was not subject to the restrictions imposed on Westerners by the Canton system.

In 1807 the first Protestant missionaries, cresting the wave of a major evangelical revival that swept Britain and the United States around the turn of the century, arrived in Canton. Since Christianity was still on the list of proscribed religions—where the Yongzheng Emperor had placed it in 1724—the new arrivals mostly directed their exertions to laying the foundations for future mission work, by translating religious and other texts into Chinese, more than to proselytizing actively. Some Protestant missionaries worked as medical doctors, creating a considerable fund of goodwill on which they hoped to be able to draw in the future. Others helped smooth the passage of commerce, by interpreting or negotiating for Western traders and other visitors. But most remained in and around Canton. They also published a periodical, the *Chinese Repository*, which, while purporting to offer objective descriptions of China and its culture, in fact presented them in somewhat negative terms. They did so as a corrective to what they saw as the excessive enthusiasm of the Jesuits, their leading Christian competitors for the China soul market.

In 1816, immediately after Napoleon's defeat at Waterloo, the British sent a second embassy to China under Lord Amherst, for whom the Canton-based Protestant missionary Robert Morrison served as interpreter. This unsuccessful embassy foundered officially on the issue of the kowtow, but the truth of the matter seems to have been mutual bungling, miscommunication, and high-handedness. The Jiaqing Emperor, who a few years earlier had declined to deal with Russians unwilling to kowtow, sent the Britons away without seeing them. He could not yield to one nation on a point he had recently stood firm on with another. Too late he learned that the envoys' apparent complete lack of cooperation was at least partly due to the fact that they were unwell and to the fact that his own officials, in their nervousness, had been less than gracious in their desire to hurry things along. He decided he had acted too hastily and sent propitiatory gifts and messages to Britain by way of Canton. Some of these must have been what a Chinese ambassador in London was shown some seventy years later. They had been sitting unread for all that time in a storage room at the Foreign Office. The mutual standing on dignity of the Amherst embassy and the Jiaqing Emperor thus seems to have represented one of history's great missed opportunities.

Despite the ban on missionary activity, pockets of illicit proselytizing continued in the interior. This became abundantly clear to

Qing authorities after the discovery of a map prepared for the pope that showed the distribution of Catholic converts in China. Punishment in this case was widespread and severe, and not long afterward China briefly introduced the Japanese practice of compelling suspected Christians to apostatize by trampling on a crucifix.

Questions of Chinese jurisdiction over foreigners continued to rankle. The intensity and complexity of the Canton trade inevitably led to disputes, but Qing laws prevented Chinese from pursuing foreigners through the courts. This prohibition mainly dated from the Qianlong Emperor's strong conviction that mistreatment of foreigners had been a major cause of the overthrow of several earlier dynasties. He did not intend that he or his successors should make the same mistake.

Western and Chinese merchants usually found other ways of settling their disagreements and their debts. For example, the hong merchants collectively guaranteed the debts of individual merchants, although, as we have seen, the combination of overambitious trading and the extortion of Chinese officialdom drove many of the merchants to bankruptcy. In criminal cases, the question of Chinese jurisdiction over foreigners was a continuing challenge for Qing authorities. They now began to find themselves caught between the Europeans and Americans, who objected to Chinese law because they regarded it as arbitrary and excessively harsh, and the local populace, who saw no reason for foreigners to receive preferential treatment. In 1806, for instance, Cantonese vociferously objected to a compromise reached by Chinese and British representatives in a case involving the killing of a Chinese by British sailors. They demonstrated in the streets with "foreign devil" placards, actions that vividly belied their later characterization by Westerners as passive and politically disengaged.

While such protests were of course strongly antiforeign, they displayed as much a sense of injustice as purely jingoistic prejudice. Some such sense prompted Chinese hong merchant Pan Chang'yao, known to the Europeans as Conseequa, an accomplished entrepreneur who dealt on a large scale with all the different branches of international trade in Canton, to litigate his claims against American merchants in the American courts. Pan made a great deal of money in foreign trade. He learned to speak French from French sailors—his English was more rudimentary—and he lived at one time in a mansion adorned with French decorative objects he had received as gifts. He was known for the extraordinary amount of credit he extended to foreign traders, which attracted many of them, particularly Americans, but he also had the reputation of mixing teas of different grades and passing off the resulting blend as a top-quality product.

In the first decade of the nineteenth century Pan/Conseequa fell heavily into debt, owing vast sums to the British East India Company, which commonly advanced money to the hong merchants to keep them solvent and to enable them to buy up the tea crops to sell to the Company. He tried to call in his debts from the Americans. With the help of influential friends to whom he granted power of attorney, he launched a series of lawsuits in Philadelphia, which by a legal fiction constituted itself Canton for jurisdictional purposes. Pan recovered some money, but some of his debtors counterclaimed for poor-quality goods and attached some of his property lying at harbor, while others became genuinely bankrupt as a consequence of President Jefferson's fifteen-month embargo (December 1807–March 1809) on American shipping leaving port. In the end many of Pan's American debts remained unpaid, and at his death in 1823 this once-prosperous merchant was bankrupt.

In 1814 he had directly petitioned President Madison of the United States for redress. The petition was sent to Washington in the original Chinese, in an English approximation and in a Portuguese version. The president is thought to have seen the letter, but there is no evidence of any action being taken as a consequence. The English version reads as follows:

> The Petition of Conseequa, a Hong Merchant of the City of Canton in China
> Showeth:
>
> That your Petitioner has for many years had intensive dealings in Commerce with the subjects of the United States.
>
> That whilst Trade was flourishing he heard no Complaints from them, and many returned to China and made good their engagements, and others remitted his property to him, and his losses were no greater than he could well bear.
>
> Of late years, however, he has been able to obtain returns in a very trifling proportion to the extent of the Capital which he has thus confided to American Trading.

> Some have applied the large Sums of his property in their hands to other Branches of Commercial Speculation, in which they have been unsuccessful, and are utterly unable to pay him.
>
> Many who do not labour under the inability to pay their debts, or who do not acknowledge that they are unable, object to pay them, as he thinks, upon frivolous grounds, and involve the Claims upon them in tedious litigation.
>
> When such Debtors come to, or reside in China, he cannot claim the aid of the Laws of the Imperial Dynasty in his behalf. They prohibit such confidence, as he has placed in Subjects of the United States, and he would not presume to avow to the Chief of a great Nation that he has infringed the Laws of his own Empire, but in the full consciousness that he has been guilty of nothing disloyal, or injurious in act or intention towards it, while to honorable minds, he thinks his claims would be strengthened by the Circumstances.
>
> Some resist payment of their Debts contending inferior quality of the Goods which he has supplied. He always admitted and desired inspection of his Goods before purchases, and his Debtors being professed Merchants in the articles, ought to have possessed and exercised their skill and knowledge respecting them.
>
> He does not presume to solicit your Excellency's protection and consideration, but in so far as may accord with Justice, and the Laws of the United States, they being so far, and as greatly celebrated for their equal protection of the Rich, and of the Poor, and for their dealing equal measure to their own Citizens, and to the Alien.
>
> Your Petitioner is a Stranger of a far distant Country; he knows not what observances are enacted by the American Laws, and is too distant to be able to afford an explanation, and proofs where they are wanted, and many years must elapse before he can be heard for himself through very imperfect Channels. . . .[2]

The petition goes on to claim that without restitution, Pan will be ruined both financially and in commercial reputation and suggests that such an eventuality will also damage the Americans' reputation as honest traders. The sophisticated understanding of American legal practice shown in this letter, even if, as seems likely, it represented the joint effort of the Chinese merchant and his foreign friends, offers an indication that at least some Chinese who came into contact with foreigners were altogether ready to adopt foreign ways and indeed saw such a move as a way to beat the foreigner at his own game. But such attitudes often fell victim to intricate political wrangling of one kind or another.

THE FIRST OPIUM WAR, 1839–1842

Pan Chang'yao's petition represented one individual's effort to cope with events beyond his control. Similarly, intellectuals and policy-makers attempted to arrive at a consensus on the causes of and possible solutions to the fiscal crisis and its social ramifications.

The detrimental impact of opium importation extended far beyond the economy. Opium addiction reached into virtually every segment of Chinese society, although the Indian imports were too expensive for many ordinary people, who more often used the milder native opium. Long known in China for its medicinal and aphrodisiac attributes as well as in its narcotic capacity, opium had been in use in overseas Chinese communities connected with the Dutch in Batavia and Taiwan since the seventeenth century. The first ban on opium sales that were not for strictly medical purposes came under the Yongzheng Emperor in 1729 and was not rigorously enforced. A century later opium was so pervasive as to make enforcement of the ban virtually impossible. At court bored eunuchs and imperial family members indulged in it. Soldiers took opium to blunt their fears and perhaps as a way to avoid active service, as became apparent in 1832, after six thousand troops had proved unable to suppress a local uprising because of widespread addiction. Scholars took opium to alleviate the stresses and frustrations of life; students took it to sharpen their wits at examination time; merchants took it to hone their business acumen; women took it as a release from the tension and limitations of family life. In leisured circles it became socially acceptable; Chinese served opium to their friends after dinner in the same way that Europeans might offer a liqueur.

The more expensive imported variety, being stronger, was also more effective and more addictive. But those engaged in hard physical labor, such as the haulers who dragged shipping upriver, and farmers, particularly opium growers, used domestic opium, which worked well enough to kill pain and enhance their strength temporarily. Such impoverished addicts were exposed to double jeopardy because they imperiled their health not only through drug addiction as such but because they often spent what little money they had on opium rather than on food and became as a result severely undernourished. Opium use, then, had already spread to the Chinese lower classes by the early nineteenth century. But it became widespread only later.

By the mid-1830s growing apprehension about the ramifications of widespread drug addiction compounded anxieties among Chinese scholars and officials about the drain of silver out of the country; many identified a connection. A protracted debate, strangely familiar in the late twentieth century, ensued among Qing officials and scholars. What was the best way to deal with the drug question? Should opium be legalized? Should it be banned altogether? How aggressive a stance should the Qing take against the British? And so on. Effective prohibition would without doubt be extraordinarily difficult, not only because of British military strength but because the chain of distribution in China involved so many different vested interests. Moreover, it was not at all clear that the Qing military was capable of enforcing a complete ban or, even if it could do so, that a ban would bring about peace.

Here policy-makers drew on the rather compelling precedent of Kokand, an expansionist-minded Central Asian state bordering Xinjiang, with which China had concluded a treaty in 1835. Kokand had for some time been trying to dominate Xinjiang's foreign trade, to the detriment of the much remoter Qing. A complete Qing trade ban, intended to bring the Kokandis to heel, had proved entirely ineffective. Partly concession and partly formal recognition of existing reality, the 1835 treaty brought peace to the region more quickly and more effectively than the trade cutoff had done. The treaty gave foreigners the right to live, trade, and levy taxes within the Chinese empire; they could appoint consuls, who had jurisdiction over their fellow countrymen when in China; and China paid Kokand an indemnity. Kokandis and other foreigners were allowed to rent property and hire local servants, assistants, and interpreters. It was possible to draw a loose parallel to the much earlier Treaty of Kiakhta, in accordance with which Russians had been living and trading on the Sino-Russian border since 1732. The Kokand treaty, as it turned out, brought a peace under which the influx of opium into China overland began to intensify, and so the Qing extended their prohibition of opium and its importation to Xinjiang as well as to the coast.

In 1838 the emperor decided that the opium trade must be stopped. He canvassed opinion from a broad range of people, consulting both officials on the job and influential scholars. Many of these latter were knowledgeable but for various reasons unemployed. Typically such men came together in literary clubs, established their reputations as scholars, formed a network of connections, and then, in keeping with the revived intellectual leaning toward practical statecraft, turned their attention to matters of state and to gaining political power. In some respects these networks resembled political parties, although such an institution was unthinkable under imperial rule.

The question the Qing confronted was whether to seek an accommodation with the British or to take a firm stand and risk war. There were two main camps. One faction, primarily made up of central government bureaucrats, favored provisional accommodation with the British. They held this view for a number of reasons. First, they applied the logic of the Central Asian experience to the coastal problem. Several of these proponents of accommodation were Manchus fresh from a term of service in Xinjiang, where for security reasons few Han Chinese held senior appointments. Drawing on the recent Kokand experience, they knew there was no guarantee that a trade ban would solve either the drug problem, which they correctly assessed would simply go underground, or the monetary emergency. Second, these officials probably recognized that superior British military strength meant war would almost certainly bring humiliation.

The other main faction was made up of intellectuals of the literati coalition, who collectively exerted considerable influence. These men proposed a trade embargo against the British. They wished not only to block opium imports but also to promote their faction's involvement in governance. Backing Lin Zexu (1785–1850), whom the emperor sent to Canton with a special mandate to solve the opium problem, they were insouciant of the risk of war or at least miscalculated it, seeking only to enhance Lin's political prestige and by association their own power. In short, this literati group's support for a trade embargo, which they favored as a way to further their own political agenda, played a major part in pushing China into war with Britain in 1839. After war broke out, these men's influence continued to be powerful enough to hamper the effectiveness of central government. They did so both tactically, by failing to cooperate with or criticizing official forces, and strategically, by continuing to apply pressure to fight rather than appease the British. This political dispute colored the whole war effort.

Lin Zexu launched a comprehensive attack on opium. He targeted users as well as providers of the drug, confiscating opium, creating mutual surveillance groups to help stamp out smoking, and calling on different groups of people—students, community leaders, military forces—to turn in distributors and to come up with proposals for halting the opium trade altogether. He then turned his attention to the British suppliers. Unaware that they had been stockpiling opium in mistaken anticipation of legalization—for they had followed the internal debates—he compelled them to hand over their vast opium stores, amounting to perhaps three million pounds, offering no compensation. He had the opium destroyed as thoroughly as possible by dissolving the raw drug and flushing it out to sea along huge trenches dug for the purpose by hundreds of laborers supervised by sixty officials. He ordered the British out of Canton, so they removed to Portuguese Macao. When they refused to pledge to stop trafficking in opium, which was still prohibited by Chinese law, he had them driven out of Macao. British traders then occupied the small nearby island of Hong Kong, despite the energetic resistance of the approximately four thousand inhabitants, who poisoned wells and refused to cooperate with the British in any way. Lin encouraged this local resistance, but the British showed no inclination to abandon Hong Kong's fine deepwater harbor, which made it an ideal commercial base for them, along the lines of Macao.

Against this background, the British Parliament's abolition of the East India Company's monopoly on trade with Asia was of enormous consequence. It meant that the chief representative of British interests in China now spoke for his country rather than only for the company. An insult to the British trade superintendent was now a matter of state. But the Qing did not clearly grasp this distinction.

In 1839 war broke out between Britain and China ostensibly because of Qing efforts to put an end to opium smuggling once and for all and because of accumulated British resentment of the restrictions placed on them. British ships blockaded Canton and Ningbo, farther up the coast, and seized control of Zhoushan (Chusan) Island, at the entrance to the Yangzi delta, one of the main inland waterways. They then sailed north, unopposed, and by late summer of 1840 were threatening Tianjin, the nearest port to Beijing. Subsequent negotiations achieved British withdrawal to Canton, but the agreement reached on the spot was rejected as inadequate by both sides. After further fighting around Canton, the British bombarded and then occupied parts of the city in the spring of 1841. Popular feeling ran high, stimulated by reports of British atrocities, including rapes and the desecration of local graves and temples.

Chinese popular stereotypes about foreigners, up to now relatively neutral, began to become more extreme. In an episode that later took on epic proportions as an example of the power of an aroused populace, several thousand quickly mobilized militiamen, gentry-organized self-defense units of the villages surrounding Canton, set upon British and Indian forces at nearby Sanyuanli. With the foreigners' guns suddenly disabled by a torrential downpour, the attackers were able to wound several of the foreigners and even killed one of them. Local authorities soon called off the attack to ensure that negotiations for British withdrawal not be broken off, but the participants, convinced they could have driven off the British, strongly resented this official interference, which they regarded as akin to treachery. As had happened in 1806, when local inhabitants objected to a compromise reached by Qing authorities and British representatives over a criminal case, placards appeared in Canton warning the foreign forces not to return to the site of the engagement. Some of these placards, crudely expressed, really did represent the voice of the people, but others were phrased in more elegant language, suggesting that members of the scholars' faction backing Lin, who were chafing at continued Qing appeasement efforts, might have had a hand in them.

One such manifesto read as follows: "Proclamation Addressed to the English Barbarians . . . from the People of the Countryside Residing in Canton: . . . In our passion for revenge, all of us are alike aroused; what need have we, then, to trouble our high officials to 'raise their spears' [in our defense]? Waving our arms and giving a great shout, we certainly have the power to crush the [English] beasts without anyone else's aid."[3] It was a relatively small episode, but in blaming the government for not standing up to the enemy, it set a far-reaching precedent. It also showed that despite all the restrictions on freedom of speech and the lack of an organized opposition of the type familiar in Western democracies, there were nonetheless effective ways in which to express and mobilize public opinion.

Some accounts of looting and vandalism depicted the British as just another set of the fearsome bandits and pirates who periodically made a nuisance of themselves. This attitude is clear, for example, from an account left by a Shanghai resident who was one of the few not to flee when the British captured the city. Our informant was a literate local community leader but not a member of the upper elite. He recalled:

> Before dawn a group of British broke down the door of my house with weapons. I tried to stop them, but they grabbed me and put a knife to my throat. They ransacked the house, looking for silver, jewelry and money, taking everything, even the tiniest piece of cash. With a knife at [my] throat, they questioned me, using gestures, and wanted to know where [I] had hidden anything. [I] tried to convince them we were very poor. They went to my nephew's house [nearby] but finding only books there, they left. Then they went to my uncle's house, and then to my brother's house, but everyone there had fled.[4]

It is worth noting that this informant was not particularly xenophobic, nor did he refer to the British derogatorily as barbarians; here, at least, was no suggestion of an inveterate attitude of superiority toward foreigners.

Chinese Mobilization

Although political maneuvering bore some responsibility for China's defeat in the war and certainly influenced subsequent ways in which people thought about the war, the main reason the Qing lost the First Opium War was simply that they were overcome by superior military force. But the Chinese were no simpletons in military technology, nineteenth-century British accounts to the contrary notwithstanding. They had for centuries been fortifying entire towns with massive walls and were familiar with the concept and techniques of siege warfare. Canton itself was so well fortified that, as an astonished British eyewitness noted, a two-hour pounding administered by a seventy-four-gun British warship, including some thirty-two-pounders, had virtually no effect.

Qing officials hastened to imitate British technological power. They copied British double-decked men-of-war, complete with guns, and built armed replicas of the British paddle-wheel steamers that had so effectively operated in Canton's shallow waters; they experimented with a form of the percussion cap; they devised an iron mold for casting ordnance (in place of the old sand mold) that was at least as sophisticated as those found in the West, and they steadily cast ships' guns that exactly resembled British models. All this bore out the imperial prince's comment made sixty years earlier, to the effect that the Qing were willing to try anything when it came to warfare.[5] We shall return in more detail to the issue of military modernization in the next chapter.

Chinese ability to draw on their experience in the First Opium War went beyond adopting new technology. They observed weaknesses in the British forces that they thought might well be possible to exploit. In late 1841, for example, after two shiploads of British troops, including several hundred Indian sepoys, had been shipwrecked on Taiwan, some Chinese began to develop ideas about fissures in British imperial armor. Most of the shipwrecked sepoys were abandoned to drown by their companions, but the surviving almost 150 were captured and jailed in Taiwan along with the handful of white officers taken with them. This entire episode came to the attention of Qing authorities on Taiwan, including in particular a leading member of the literati statecraft faction, Yao Ying (1785–1853). Yao noticed racial friction among the foreign prisoners awaiting execution. He questioned one of the officers at some length about the British empire in India. Whatever he learned from his interrogations combined with his observations to persuade him that colonial overextension and racial tension might well prove to be Britain's fatal weakness.

Rumors about a looming revolt against the British in Nepal in 1841 fueled his conviction, and although he was for a time in political disgrace over the mass execution of these prisoners of war, over the next few years Yao devoted considerable effort to making his views known to other influential scholars. The goal of exploiting that vulnerability became a mantra of the statecraft party. They were not the only ones to perceive the possibility of using racial issues against the British. When hostile Cantonese attacked foreign "factories" (warehouses) after the war, in late 1842, for instance, Qing officials responded to outraged British demands for compensation by claiming that the destruction was provoked by Indian sailors' causing trouble.

Imperial Commissioner Lin Zexu and some of his statecraft associates came to the conclusion that study of the foreign countries would help overcome the threat they posed to China. Lin set up his own bureau of translation in Canton to collect and translate as much information about the West as possible. By that time, as the result of foreign trade and, to a lesser extent, the presence of missionaries, there were a number of Chinese who knew English whom Lin was able to hire to help him. In this way he gained access to histories and geographies translated by Protestant missionaries and to other Western works. Among the most famous works he acquired from Westerners in Canton was Emmerich de Vattel's *International Law*, sections of which he had translated into Chinese. Lin acquired maps and diagrams of ships and weapons and arranged for translations of numerous sections from the Protestant missionary publication *Chinese Repository*. He brought all this information together in a work he entitled *Sizhou Zhi* ("Chronicle of the Four Continents"), and later turned over his source materials to his associate Wei Yuan (1794–1856), a scholar long interested in frontier policy, so Wei could continue his project.

Wei's earlier research into the military history of the dynasty, begun in the 1820s and finally written up in 1842, had convinced him it was essential to refocus attention on the military in order to deal with rising domestic rebellion, including piracy. He proposed improvements in military training, in the organization of local militia—newly prominent since the White Lotus debacle of 1796–1803—and maritime defense. Wei was also coeditor of an influential collection of essays, *Huangchao Jingshi Wenbian* ("Collected Writings on Statecraft of this August Dynasty"), begun in 1825, on government and policy recommendations; this prominently featured work on inner and coastal frontier defense and on military affairs. The point here is simply that just as opium was an important but not the sole reason for China's social and economic problems in the early nineteenth century, so the First Opium War accelerated existing trends toward reform but did not single-handedly initiate the surging ideas for which Westerners later claimed all the credit.

After the war Wei and others began to write about world geography, politics, and the technological strength of foreign nations in ways that harked back to the tradition of the high Tang. The difference was that the nineteenth-century scholars had a much greater fund of foreign sources to draw on and an immediate motivation for acquiring information in the form of the Western presence. Citing the example of Singapore, Wei perceived a dual-pronged approach to Asia on the part of the Western nations. On the one hand, they were making inroads by way of colonialism in Southeast Asia. On the other, they were advancing by way of the Chinese coast. In both cases they would stop at nothing to achieve their presumed goals. He urged making maritime defense a top priority because he visualized the British launching attacks on China from a chain of defensive outposts stretching across Southeast Asia. Britain's seizure of Hong Kong formed part of this pattern and gave it a base uncomfortably close to China.

Wei made a number of recommendations that in the decades to come carried considerable weight. He proposed, following the argument of his friend Yao Ying, first, that China link up with Britain's enemies in Southeast Asia to exploit weaknesses in Britain's far-flung empire; second, that it consolidate its hold on all its frontiers, along the coast as well as inland; and third, that it not hesitate to adopt Western technology, particularly ships and weaponry. In this way China could suppress domestic rebellion, keep the Western powers at bay on all fronts, and begin to reassert its position at the pinnacle of maritime East Asia's traditional political order, an order that largely excluded Westerners. But by this time China had signed the Treaty of Nanjing.

THE TREATY OF NANJING, 1842

The main provisions of the Treaty of Nanjing that concluded the First Opium War in 1842 were as follows. China must open to foreign residence four coastal cities in addition to Canton: Shanghai, located where the Yangzi River empties into the sea; Xiamen (Amoy) and Fuzhou, in Fujian province, and Ningbo, in Zhejiang. It must permit British subjects and their families to live and conduct trade in these five "treaty ports" without let or hindrance. This included allowing Royal Navy warships access to Chinese ports to protect trade, as well as the establishment of consulates. It must establish a fair and fixed customs duty at the five ports and limit transit dues paid on goods transported inland. British prisoners must be released, and Chinese collaborators pardoned. Derogatory terms denoting British inferiority must be banished from official

JILIN
LIAONING
INNER MONGOLIA
Niuzhuang
Peking
Tianjin
KOREA
Dengzhou
HEBEI
NINGXIA
SHANXI
SHANDONG
GANSU
SHAANXI
Yellow R.
JIANGSU
HENAN
Zhenjiang
Nanjing
ANHUI
Shanghai
SICHUAN
HUBEI
Hankou
Ningbo
Yangtze R.
Jiujiang
ZHEJIANG
HUNAN
JIANGXI
Fuzhou
GUIZHOU
FUJIAN
Danshui
Xiamen
(Amoy)
TAIWAN
GUANGXI
GUANGDONG
Shantou
(Swatow)
Canton
Gaoxiong
Hong Kong
(Br.)
Macao
(Port.)
Hanoi
FRENCH
INDO-
CHINA
Qiungzhou
HAINAN
The
Treaty Ports
c. 1860
0
500 km
0
300 miles
Chazaud

Qing communications, which henceforth must be conducted on a basis of equality. Under the treaty, China abolished the Canton system and contributed several million dollars to settling outstanding hong merchant debts. It formally ceded already occupied Hong Kong Island. It agreed to pay a huge indemnity, some of which was to compensate the British merchants for their confiscated opium. For its part, Britain agreed that its troops would forthwith leave China, except for Zhoushan Island, near Ningbo, where it would remain until all the treaty ports had been opened and the indemnity fully paid. Opium was not mentioned.

The Treaty of Nanjing was followed in short order by additional treaties concluded with the United States and France and by supplemental treaties with the British stipulating that whatever concessions one country won from China would apply to all foreign nations. These treaties particularly covered matters of religion and matters of law. They abrogated China's anti-Christian laws and granted foreigners the right to rent land in the five treaty ports on which to build churches, hospitals, and cemeteries. They sanctioned existing practice by formally permitting Westerners to learn Chinese. They established the principle of extraterritoriality—immunity for foreigners from Chinese law on Chinese soil—a right Britain demanded on the basis of its experience trading in Ottoman Turkey and other Muslim countries, where this was standard practice. Except in matters of opium smuggling, foreigners in China now had the right to be judged by their own national law. The treaties provided for review in twelve years.

In the long term these concessions, about which the Qing did not have much choice, profoundly affected Chinese life as well as the Qing hold on political power. But at the time the Qing did not regard them as of major significance, not least because many of the treaty provisions so much resembled those granted seven years earlier to Kokand in Central Asia, even though the Kokandis had not insisted on the principle of equality between nations. Thus the provisions of the Treaty of Nanjing, although in many ways humiliating, followed existing precedents, simply extending them from the inland northwest frontier on to the maritime frontier. The Qing saw the opening of the treaty ports as a way not to enlarge the scope of Western trade but to dilute it by spreading it more thinly along the coast. It was only after 1860 that treaty concessions carried into the heart of China's interior.

The path of treaty implementation did not always run smoothly. Both sides repeatedly took refuge in the specific terms of the treaties, concerning which there were sometimes disputes arising from discrepancies between the English and Chinese versions. The Chinese, for example, wanted to be sure that having claimed the right to live in the five treaty ports, Westerners actually vacated the few tiny settlements they had established outside the treaty areas. Then it took some time to abrogate effective domestic monopolies on certain commodities, because Chinese involved in the commercial chain from production to distribution to export were slow to comply with treaty provisions, out of either recalcitrance or ignorance.

Foreign behavior also caused problems. As the foreigners searched for appropriate spots on which to build or establish cemeteries, for instance, they sometimes inadvertently interfered with traditional Chinese ideas of *fengshui*, which governed the placement of structures and the plotting of land, or they disturbed existing Chinese graves. Heedlessness of this kind, while not malevolent, occasionally provoked violence. Westerners also sometimes caused incidents when they ventured inland, to explore or to hunt. The Qing objected that such sorties contravened the terms of the treaty, which allowed a foreign presence only in the actual treaty ports. They claimed that the sight of foreigners upset the local inhabitants, "especially women," and that they could not, or would not, guarantee the foreigners' safety. The British routinely threatened to see to their own security if Chinese measures proved inadequate, a threat that implied disrespect for the Qing's right to police their own territory and hence for Qing sovereignty.

Legal issues were a constant source of dispute. One point of contention was the question of how to deal with Chinese in Hong Kong. Unlike Macao, which was leased by the Portuguese but remained Chinese property, Hong Kong became Britain's "in perpetuity" by the terms of the Treaty of Nanjing.* Britain did not want any competition from Chinese officials to undermine their authority in their new colony. But China wanted jurisdiction over

*Britain took Hong Kong Island under the Treaty of Nanjing; it took Kowloon Peninsula, on the Chinese mainland, in the Convention of Beijing (1860). In 1898 Britain insisted on extending Hong Kong's boundaries to include the New Territories north of Kowloon, on a ninety-nine-year lease, expiring in 1997.

Chinese residents of Hong Kong. Eventually it was agreed that a Qing official who would be stationed on Kowloon Peninsula, on the mainland opposite Hong Kong, would have jurisdiction in cases solely involving Chinese. For some time, however, Chinese constables continued to carry out investigations and even arrests on Hong Kong itself, in contravention of the agreement and much to the annoyance of the colonial authorities. The problems took some time to subside, partly on account of a postwar resurgence of piracy that often affected both Qing and British jurisdictions.

At first such matters were dealt with case by case through diplomatic exchange. The record shows that efforts to cooperate in such cases did not always work. In 1844, for instance, one pirate was captured by the British and then "lent" to the Qing government to help capture his confederates, apparently on the understanding he would be returned to Hong Kong for trial. But he remained on the mainland, where eventually he was executed. After a few years mutual extradition arrangements were made; in 1849, for example, the Qing agreed in principle to a British request that if they captured another pirate, wanted on murder charges in Hong Kong, they would return him for trial to Hong Kong. But if they did catch him, they do not appear to have let the British know.[6]

Cases involving foreign-born Chinese also raised complicated issues. Chen Qingzhen, for instance, was a Singapore-born Chinese working as a scribe in the British consulate in the treaty port of Xiamen. He was arrested and tortured by Qing authorities on suspicion of trying to start an offshoot of the Small Sword Society, a group of Cantonese and Fujianese rebels that for seventeen months occupied part of Shanghai, causing considerable anxiety to Qing and British alike. Chen died from his injuries. The British objected, claiming that he was under British protection because he had been born in Singapore. The Qing proposed that "hairstyle and dress" should determine whether one was a Chinese "citizen" or not, posing the question "[I]f place of birth decides one's citizenship, are all British babies born in China to be regarded as Chinese?" In Chen's case, it appeared that he was in fact a native of Xiamen, but there were some sixty other Singapore Chinese living there who claimed British protection. There was plenty of scope for disagreement.[7]

Finally, the terminology issue sometimes caused difficulties. When British representatives thought that the language of Qing communications was derogatory, they objected. Qing officials sometimes blamed these episodes on ignorant scribes or interpreters or claimed that they were simply employing standard usage. However, for the most part they had little choice but to rephrase because otherwise the British simply returned the offending document unanswered.

The British selected the ports opened by the Treaty of Nanjing because they all were existing commercial entrepôts, but results were slow. In Canton overt residual hostility to the British, combined with a resurgence of lawlessness stemming from the general disorder occasioned by the war, made it for the time being virtually impossible for Westerners to establish residences or conduct business within the city. The rose-colored memory of popular victory against the foreigners at Sanyuanli aroused patriotic defiance, while the wartime British occupation of Canton rankled so much that for years public sentiment against them remained at boiling point. The British endlessly lodged formal complaints that China was violating the terms of the Treaty of Nanjing by refusing to let them enter the walled city of Canton. In response the Qing imperial commissioner noted that entrance to the city was not a material term of the treaty, that Europeans and Americans had always conducted business outside the walled city and could continue to do so.

He displayed in fact a firm grasp of the ways in which even a humiliating unequal treaty could be used as a shield with which to protect China's rights as well as a sword with which to demolish them. Asserting that feelings in Canton against the British were running out of control, the commissioner cited as persuasive evidence the ripping up of official proclamations calling for calm, and the burning down of the prefectural offices on the basis of suspicions that the Qing prefect was fraternizing with the British. He implied, in other words, that the local populace was so aroused that Qing authorities could do little about it even had they wished to. The commissioner requested his British counterparts to restrain their nationals from trying to force an entry and suggested they refrain from further inflaming local opinion by stationing warships close in to the harbor. Threats would only make things worse; only a demonstration of British goodwill and cooperative spirit stood a chance of bringing about calm. To that end Britons should stop brawling with Chinese, and they should not roam the Canton countryside, an activity that in any case contravened their treaty rights. The issue of opening Canton city remained a major bone of contention for several years and reached its height when Cantonese proposed erecting a commemorative arch celebrating resistance to the British, a proposal from which the Qing commissioner loftily dissociated himself, claiming "gentry instigation."

By 1850 Ningbo, Xiamen, and Fuzhou still had very few European residents, not least because it took some time for all three of these ports, which were much more attuned to the requirements of Southeast Asian trade, to adjust to the demands of Europeans and Americans. But precisely because of the modest Western presence, antiforeign incidents were comparatively rare in these ports.

Only Shanghai came close to meeting British expectations about the commercial potential on the newly opened China coast. Already a leading conduit for commercial exchange as the result of its strategic location where the great Yangzi River empties into the sea, Shanghai's economy had suffered from wartime trade stoppages, from the collapse of the cotton market, and from a series of famines in its hinterland caused by Yellow River flooding. But after the war Shanghai gained from the postwar obstruction of trade in Canton, for many Cantonese, frustrated by local conditions and attracted by the promise of new wealth, moved there to do business with the foreigners. Within a few years Shanghai became a boom town, and by the end of the century it had become one of the leading commercial ports of the world.

THE RISE OF SHANGHAI

Shanghai offers a particularly good example of the contrast foreigners often experienced between their formal relations with the Qing, on the one hand, and their dealings with ordinary Chinese people, on the other. As was clear from the case of Canton, many Chinese deeply resented the foreigners. Yet a substantial number, with an eye to self-interest, found it possible to overcome their scruples. At least some of the general populace in Shanghai were much less inclined to resist the foreigners than were the Qing authorities. Thus, although Qing officials in Shanghai were not terribly helpful when the first Britons arrived to open up the treaty port and establish a consulate, it was a different story with Shanghai merchants and entrepreneurs. They were absolutely ready to rent premises and furniture to the British, with whom they probably hoped to grab a monopoly along prewar Canton lines, and they were poised to make money in any way they could, including selling tickets to local inhabitants interested in seeing the "white devils eat, drink, write, wash, rest and sleep."[8]

None of the foreigners could speak the local dialect, so their contact with ordinary Shanghainese was limited. They depended on interpreters and Chinese middlemen, whom they often imported from Canton or Hong Kong, to help them conduct business and on Chinese servants and local supplies to help them survive. Not everything was rosy, of course; there were plenty of misunderstandings, and pockets of ill feeling certainly survived aplenty.

Shanghai, which for some time remained the only treaty port with a substantial Western population, became a unique example of joint Sino-Western administration. Most conspicuous was the administrative division of the city into three main sections: the International Settlement, dominated by the British but open to all nations; the French Concession; and the Chinese city. Each operated under different administrations and different laws. At first the foreign settlements, located outside the city walls, generally excluded Chinese residents other than domestic servants and others servicing the foreign community, but during the Taiping Rebellion (1851–1864) countless refugees, rich and poor, flooded into every section of Shanghai. By 1854, within a year of the rebels' capture of Nanjing, upriver from Shanghai, there were some 8,000 Chinese households in the International Settlement in addition to the 150 foreign ones, and the numbers rose steadily.

The foreign settlements in Shanghai were in effect cities within the city; they were independent municipalities under the joint jurisdiction of the foreign consuls. Among other things this meant that they adjudicated cases involving Chinese living within the settlements; over time it also meant that Chinese fled into the foreign settlements to escape Qing and later republican authorities. Within the settlements, also, Chinese and Western merchants and businessmen soon began to cooperate in joint or mutually dependent ventures.

In Shanghai too began the institution of the Imperial Maritime Customs Service, run by Europeans, operated by Europeans and Chinese together, and ultimately answerable to the emperor. In 1853 and 1854, during the Taiping Rebellion, when the Small Sword Society occupied parts of the city, Shanghai's customshouse had stopped functioning, depriving the Qing government of the lucrative revenues from the booming trade and prompting the resurgence of irregular levies on goods inland. Neither the Qing nor the foreigners stood to gain from such a situation. Efforts on both sides to remedy matters were unsuccessful, threatening the smooth operation of the entire treaty port system. Eventually a compromise was reached, whereby a foreign-run inspectorate of customs was established in 1854 to collect customs duties from the foreign traders and turn them over to the Qing government. The institution became known for its incorruptibility and efficiency and played a significant part in the economic life of the late Qing and early republic.

Another new feature of Shanghai life was the rise of a new class of Chinese known as compradors. These served as the middlemen in foreigners' dealings with Chinese, often working as managers of foreign firms. In a number of ways they provided an essential link between the old way of doing things and the new. They provided the foreigners with access to traditional Chinese economic institutions from which they might well otherwise have been excluded, such as the Chinese banks, in which compradors often were partners. Some became extremely wealthy and, as the result of their exposure to Western enterprise, in many cases readier than more traditional-minded members of the Chinese elite to invest in new industries, which they were often well equipped to manage as well. Some compradors became powerful players in Shanghai's increasingly hybrid society.

Compradors derived their influence from their wealth and their cosmopolitanism rather than from such traditional channels as examination success. They differed from traditional merchants in an important way. In the past there had been a symbiotic relationship between the educated elite and the commercial classes despite the theoretical disdain of the Confucian scholar for trade. A scholar might well send one of his sons to engage in commerce as a means of family support while the other sons studied for the examinations; a successful merchant might well try to raise his social status by providing his son with the best education money could buy, in the hope that he would pass the official examinations and become politically powerful. But the compradors were not particularly interested in political power as a means of moving up in the social scale. In their case money alone could do the trick.

In practice, at least within the treaty ports, compradors came to constitute an important part of the local elite, and they often undertook such traditional elite functions as contributing to maintaining order and providing relief to the stricken during crises. But they were really something new, a product of treaty port culture. Although their wealth and expertise were to prove a critical component in China's recovery from Western and Japanese imperialism, as a class the compradors suffered from the taint of too close a connection with the foreigners.

Chinese Emigration

Under Qing law it was still technically illegal to leave the country permanently. But in practice many Qing officials valued emigration as a safety valve for their heavily populated provinces. From their point of view, it was clearly preferable for impoverished people to leave altogether than that such people should become vagabonds, bandits, or state dependents. Furthermore, emigrants often made good and sent home infusions of money that helped the overburdened local and national economies. So the emigration prohibitions went largely ignored, and at least from 1823 an established "credit ticket" system advanced passage money to those bound for Southeast Asia and beyond.

Right after the First Opium War, a concatenation of circumstances, closely related to one another, brought about the beginning of emigration from China on a much larger scale and over much greater distances than previously. The dislocations caused by the war itself and the continuing disorder of the Canton area; the economic shifts brought on by the expansion of foreign trade; the opening of the treaty ports; the spread of colonialism around the world, combined with the unquenchable thirst of industrializing countries for manpower to extract the raw materials they needed; the dramatic demand for fresh supplies of labor following the abolition of the African slave trade (colonial employers considered Chinese harder-working and less encumbered by the requirements of religious beliefs than Indians); the new involvement of European vessels in conveying emigrants; the relative ease of slipping into Portuguese Macao or British Hong Kong, away from Qing jurisdiction; and the rumors of gold in America and Australia, known in China respectively as the Old Gold Mountain and the New Gold Mountain—all these factors combined to draw Chinese overseas, despite the continued existence of a formal prohibition under Qing law.

Some Chinese emigrants were upwardly mobile people who left home voluntarily in search of opportunity. But others, destitute and simply looking for a way to survive, provided a rich resource for employers in need of cheap labor. The first contracted shipload of Chinese laborers went from Xiamen to the French colony of Réunion, in the Indian Ocean, in 1845; it was soon followed by ships full of Chinese bound for the gold mines and sheep farms of Australia, the sugar plantations of Cuba and other European colonies in the Caribbean; the railroads, plantations, and guano fields of Peru and Chile; and the gold mines and railroads of North America. Many more went to work in the European colonies by now distributed all across Southeast Asia.

Chinese emigration was closely connected with the rise of Hong Kong as a major commercial center. Many Chinese moved there in search of new opportunities; many more passed through on their way overseas. By 1844 Hong Kong's Chinese population had swelled to about nineteen thousand, almost five times its size five years earlier, because many people seized the opportunity to pursue work in the colony. By the 1850s Hong Kong had become a major center for the coolie traffic, which contributed to the colony's commercial growth by providing work for labor recruiters, shippers, and brokers. In the four years from 1855 to 1859 alone, more than eighty thousand Chinese embarked from Hong Kong for points around the world. More often than not, those who managed to return passed through Hong Kong on their way home.

Some Chinese emigrants were press-ganged or otherwise persuaded to leave under false pretenses, as the following account shows:

> We were induced to proceed to Macao by offers of employment abroad at high wages, and through being told that the eight foreign years specified in the contracts were equivalent to only four Chinese years, and that at the termination of the latter period we would be free. We observed also on the signboards of the foreign buildings the words "agencies for the engagement of labourers" and believed that they truthfully described the nature of the establishments, little expecting that having once entered the latter, exit would be denied us; and when on arrival at Havana, we were exposed for sale and subjected to appraisement in a most ruthless manner, it became evident that we were not to be engaged as labourers but to be sold as slaves.

The numbers quickly mounted: from 1847 to 1862 American coolie traders shipped six thousand Chinese to Cuba annually.[9] Qing authorities tried to enlist the help of Western consuls to prevent the rising kidnappings of young Chinese men and women for sale overseas, with mixed success. Among emigrant communities around the world, conditions were often appalling, and as frequently they were ill-treated by the local populations in their host countries. Many emigrants intended to get rich and return, although few did so; some remitted funds back either to their families or, in the course of time, to support the massive projects that formed part of China's recovery effort. As we shall see, by the later nineteenth century the plight of overseas Chinese and the possibility of using them as a resource to fund industrial and other projects were leading issues galvanizing Qing diplomatic activism.

The Taiping Rebellion

One reason so many Chinese began to emigrate in the mid-nineteenth century was the massive civil war known as the Taiping Rebellion (1851–1864). In part the consequence of the social and economic dislocations brought about by the First Opium War in south China, the uprising demonstrates a remarkable willingness among ordinary Chinese to adopt foreign ideas.

The Taiping movement was led by Hong Xiuquan (1813–1864), a member of the despised Hakka minority who had tried unsuccessfully to pass the civil service examinations. During an illness Hong experienced several visions in which he was called to action against "demons," first by an old man and later by a middle-aged man who described himself as "elder brother." When a few years later Hong read some Christian tracts a missionary had given him, he claimed to have found in them the explanation of his visions: the old man was God, the middle-aged man was Jesus Christ, and he, Hong, was Christ's younger brother. Hong eventually came to believe that the demons he was to extirpate were none other than the ruling Manchus and that he was destined to lead a revolution infused with Christian religious fervor, as modified by his own new, God-given interpretation.

Over the next few years Hong gathered around him a core of devoted followers whom he formed into the Society of God-Worshippers, based in the southwestern province of Guangxi. Although he himself was, for unclear reasons, denied baptism, Hong baptized thousands of people. Most of his converts were Hakka peasants and aboriginal Miao, non-Han whose social position was near the bottom of the impoverished circles they moved in; they had little stake in supporting the status quo. Their numbers were swelled by refugees from the severe famines of the late 1840s and by the ubiquitous bandits, in both cases kindred spirits who similarly had little to lose.

In 1851 Hong and his followers launched an uprising with the goal of overthrowing the Qing and establishing a puritanical, egalitarian community based on Hong's quasi-Christian beliefs. They called their new society the Heavenly Kingdom of Eternal Peace (*Taiping Tianguo*). It was to be a specially favored nation under God. The Taiping philosophy of sharing everything equally from a common treasury attracted thousands more adherents from the poorest segments of society. After a series of astonishing military successes the Taiping, by now hundreds of thousands strong, occupied the former Ming capital of Nanjing in 1853. They remained ensconced in their "Heavenly Capital" for eleven years.

Westerners in the treaty ports were at first excited about this apparently Christian group which had attracted so much popular backing, and wondered whether to throw their support behind the rebels. Certainly it was true that the Taiping had been far more successful than the Western missionaries in spreading news of Christianity to the Chinese masses. But Westerners soon came to the conclusion that Hong's particular brand of Christianity reached beyond mere fundamentalism and veered away from true Christianity altogether.

Many Westerners were attracted to the Taiping more for adventure and profit than for religious reasons; by now there were enough Westerners in China that they no longer acted in concert, as the Canton merchants had usually tried to do before the Opium War. As early as 1844, right after the Opium War, Europeans arms traders had begun plying their wares on the China coast, prompting Qing objections that weapons sales were not included in the provisions of any treaty. During the Taiping Rebellion European and American entrepreneurs vied with one another to sell weapons and powder to the rebels, sailing up the Yangzi to Nanjing for the purpose, despite efforts on the part of Qing and foreign authorities alike to prevent them. The foreigners' claims that they were trying to stop their nationals from offering arms in China were unconvincing. Before long the beleaguered Qing joined the list of customers. They began buying the latest in foreign ships and weaponry, but these often fell into Taiping hands as the rebels defeated army after army sent after them. Outside Hong Xiuquan's palace, for instance, were "two handsome brass twelve pounder shell guns, marked Massachusetts 1855, with American oak carriages," recent models that almost certainly came into the category of spoils of war.[10] In other words, the Taiping military leaders were not at all averse to making use of the most up-to-date and lethal technology they could get their hands on.

Gunrunning was not the only way in which foreigners helped the Taiping cause. A sizable number of deserters from Western armies offered their services to the Taiping cause, along with other unreliable hangers-on, left over from the war or newly arrived to seek their fortune. At the official level, all foreign nations in China endeavored to convince both sides of their neutrality, hedging their bets until it became clear who would win in the end. Their principal concern was to protect their trade interests in China, by now estimated to be worth millions in Shanghai alone.

That being so, the mistrust Qing and Taiping authorities each felt for the foreigners was perhaps justified. The Qing were greatly afraid that the foreigners' purported neutrality concealed secret backing for the rebels, that the Taipings' Christianity indicated an inclination to adopt foreign values wholesale, and that the Westerners, with their formidable military strength, would eventually form an alliance with the rebels. The Taiping, on the other hand, failed to grasp the decisive advantage Western support might have given them against the faltering Qing, who had barely had time to recover from the First Opium War. They made little effort to enlist foreign aid. In 1853, for example, when the British sent a ship upriver to find out more about the Taiping and to warn them against interfering in any way with foreign trade in China, Taiping leaders astonished and alienated them by sending a communication couched in highly condescending language. It made clear the Taiping position that the subjects of Queen Victoria, although enlightened as to their religious beliefs, owed allegiance to Hong Xiuquan, the Heavenly King of the Taiping. But the British were hardly likely to retreat from their insistence on the principle of equality between nations, a principle that they had so recently fought a war against China to establish.

French and American ships soon undertook similar exploratory missions. The Americans found the rebels' uncompromising version of Christianity, which asserted the superiority of the Taiping kingdom to all comers and rested on their special relationship with God and Christ, hopelessly deviant. French overtures to the rebels also foundered after they stiffly reminded their Taiping interlocutors of their obligations under the treaties agreed on with the emperor, for the rebels took the view that anyone who could make an agreement with the chief demon was by definition an enemy.

The Qing's inability to suppress the rebellion made them open to any fresh means of support. For already by the mid-1850s not only were substantial portions of south and southwest China in the hands of the Taiping, but a second major rebellion, the Nian, was raging in east China in parts of Shandong, Honan, Jiangsu, and Anhui provinces north of the Huai River. Less ideological than the Taiping, the Nian, whose rebellion lasted from 1851 to 1868, nonetheless fought tenaciously enough to pose a threat to Qing control in the region. Meanwhile Muslim rebels were on the march in southwestern Yunnan province, in protest against heavy taxes and over control of the gold and silver mined in the region.

From a cosmological point of view, these multiple outbreaks of rebellion did not bode at all well for the Qing. Traditional belief held that outbreaks of rebellion were an indicator of popular dissatisfaction with the ruler; the Qing could not but be aware that these massive uprisings might well begin to be interpreted as signs of their loss of mandate to rule. Suppression of the rebellions thus was imperative, for it was intimately linked to dynastic survival. At the same time, of course, internal chaos made China all the more vulnerable to external predation.

THE RUSSIANS, THE BRITISH, AND THE FRENCH, 1856–1860

With the end of the Crimean War in 1856, Russia, Britain, and France all turned their attention back to China. Russia had been following events in China closely and was aware that now might be the moment to strike. During the eighteenth century the Russian empire had expanded eastward into Siberia and was now more eager than ever to expand trade with China and to investigate the possibility of extending its political and commercial influence in the northeastern parts of Manchuria that bordered its own territory. Qing policies excluding Han Chinese settlement in the area—out of a vague intent to keep Manchuria for the Manchus—had left the area sparsely populated. Russia was also anxious to take advantage of any opportunity that would strengthen its position in relation to Britain. While the Qing were distracted from frontier affairs by the Taiping and other uprisings, with many of their Manchurian military forces diverted to the interior, Russian exploratory expeditions pushed southward, and Russian settlement in northeastern Manchuria began to spread. China was in no position to resist Russian demands. A combination of aggression and skillful diplomacy enabled Russia to achieve its aim of effectively taking over control of the region from China, by the Sino-Russian Treaty of Beijing (1860). This vastly expanded trade, allowed a Russian consular presence in strategic spots in Mongolia and Xinjiang, immunity from Chinese law for Russian nationals, and much broader channels of communication than previously.

At the same time the slow pace of progress in the treaty ports other than Shanghai, together with disillusion with the Taiping, stoked the impatience of the British and other foreigners whose area of concentration was the China coast. Their main goals were the expansion of trade, the installation of ambassadors in Beijing so as to bypass Canton altogether, and the reduction of customs duties. The Westerners were particularly annoyed by the continuing refusal or inability of Qing authorities to bring Canton to heel with regard to the issue of admitting them. China was bound to apply to Britain the provisions for treaty revision inserted into an 1844 treaty with the United States, which Britain, somewhat disingenuously, interpreted as meaning that the 1842 Treaty of Nanjing was due for revision in 1854. But in 1854 Qing officials had evaded renegotiation, not least because their main attention was focused on the state of civil war prevailing in much of the country.

In 1856 the British and French found pretexts to go to war with China again. The British claimed an insult to their flag after Chinese police, alleging piracy, had lowered a British flag on a vessel, owned by a Chinese resident in Hong Kong, that had a British captain and Chinese crew. The French claimed the judicial execution of a missionary in the interior as the ground for opening hostilities. After an initial stalemate marked by a display of Chinese truculence and Western firepower—now better equipped to bombard Canton than fifteen years earlier—followed by a delay while the British dealt with the Indian Mutiny, the Second Opium War began in earnest in late 1857. By the summer of the following year the Anglo-French forces had captured Canton and Tianjin, the port of Beijing, where they negotiated a new treaty. It contained the following provisions: the opening of ten new treaty ports, including four inland along the Yangzi River as far as Hankou (subject to the defeat of the Taiping); the establishment of permanent Western diplomatic establishments in Beijing; permission for foreigners, including missionaries, to travel throughout China, by road or by steamship; the limitation of customs duties to 5 percent and of the likin tax to 2.5 percent ad valorem, and another indemnity.* In addition, although it was still illegal to sell or take opium, the treaty imposed an import duty on the drug and required that it be transported to and sold in the interior only by Chinese.

The clause allowing the establishment of foreign legations in Beijing met with strong opposition in the capital, and after the withdrawal of Western troops from the Dagu forts near Tianjin, the Qing showed little sign of compliance. They reinforced their fortifications and beat off returning Western troops, who nonetheless headed for Beijing. But skirmishing on the way there, combined with unusual brutality shown Western prisoners, prompted the Anglo-French force to burn down the Yuan Ming Yuan, the summer palace on the northwest outskirts of the capital, part of which the Jesuits had constructed for Qianlong not much more than a century earlier. Much of the Yuan Ming Yuan's contents later found its way into affluent homes in Europe and onto the European art market, as well as into the possession of Chinese entrepreneurs from the south who had helped provision the European war effort.

The burning of the summer palace passed into Chinese folklore as a benchmark of European imperialist atrocity, and it is still

*Likin was a mercantile tax levied on goods in stock or in transit and sometimes at the place of manufacture. Previously it had varied considerably in different regions.

invoked to fuel nationalist fervor. In 1860 it led in short order to the Convention of Beijing. This provided for the opening of Tianjin as a treaty port, further indemnity, the cession of Kowloon Peninsula, on the mainland opposite Hong Kong, and the effective legalization of the transportation overseas of Chinese laborers on foreign ships. The age of European imperialism in China was well under way, but its underside was the resurgence of determination among Chinese of many different backgrounds to restore China to a position of national strength. Only then would it be possible to deal on terms of real equality with the Westerners who claimed equality by force of arms.

CHAPTER FIVE

Shields and Swords, 1860–1914

> The foreigners take advantage of our shortcomings to export their own products. . . . Our government offices have foreign personnel, our factories have foreign artisans, our schools have foreign teachers. The European influence is everywhere. . . . Wherein lies our spirit? In resisting foreign insults and cherishing our same kind. Wherein lies our lifeline? In uniting our resolve and sharpening our skills. . . . With these we can win out against the foreigners, with these we can survive in the international struggle.
>
> —Construction Workers' Guild stele inscription, early twentieth century[1]

For China the half century that followed the Convention of Beijing in 1860 was not on the whole a happy one. The Qing eventually suppressed a series of major rebellions, but only at the cost of relinquishing overall control of the military to provincial leaders and their local armies. Although those leaders did not immediately turn their new military power against the central government, the consequence of this delegation of military leadership was a permanent dilution of centralized political authority. At the same time, Chinese people became increasingly interested in political participation; by 1911 these developments were to spell the end of the imperial system. In the meantime the foreign presence, partly the cause and partly the beneficiary of internal political weakness, became ever more pervasive. Foreign trade expanded enormously, while Christian missionaries fanned out all over the country. Both challenged traditional economic and sociocultural patterns. This was also the era of gunboat diplomacy, when the powers routinely threatened war if China refused to toe the line. Even though China had not become a formal colony like India or the Dutch East Indies, its independence seemed to have become a dead letter.

But China was collectively determined not to let appearance become reality. Foreign wars brought earlier reform proposals into sharp focus; the effect was galvanizing. If it were now required to conduct international relations according to specific rules of law, China would discover and make use of those rules to its own advantage. If it were necessary to match force with force, it would buy or build the necessary technology as fast as possible, using as much foreign assistance as was compatible with retention of overall control.

From 1860 the quest for self-determination took on renewed energy at every level of Chinese society. Although not every strategy worked, disputes about the best way to proceed often hampered progress, and things got considerably worse before they got better, China had struck a new path. The chief characteristic of this period was not so much relentless hostility to foreigners as it was the creative use of foreigners, whether in the form of the adaptation of their ideas, tools, and techniques to secure Chinese wealth and power (*fuqiang*) or the tactic of playing foreigners against one another to prevent their uniting against China (*yi yi zhi yi*). In these ways China pursued with great tenacity the recovery of international standing and respect and of the self-esteem that had been devastated by those same foreigners.

This chapter covers the period from the 1860 Convention of Beijing, a turning point in China's relationship with Western nations, down to the outbreak of World War One in Europe in 1914. The chapter ends in 1914 because the war marked a shift in Chinese relations with and views of the Western world. Three factors—the political rise of Japan, the war's exceptional brutality, and the peace settlement, which China considered blatantly unfair—disillusioned Chinese who had once been enthusiastic about emulating the West. This fueled a creative effort by Chinese intellectuals to rethink Chinese civilization and China's place in the world, but we reserve this discussion for the next chapter because these events form part of a complex continuum that lasted well beyond 1914.

Decline and Fall

The treaties of 1858–1860 changed China's relationship to the Western powers, and later to Japan, considerably more than those that had followed the First Opium War, which proved to be something of a false start. Among the most important long-term consequences, direct and indirect, of the later treaties, were the spread of foreign settlements and concessions to many of China's major cities on the coast and along inland waterways; the elimination of prohibitions—in practice routinely disregarded—on Chinese emigration; virtual carte blanche for Christian missionaries in China; an enormous expansion in opium smoking, and in domestic production of opium poppies, a shift that both reduced food production and more generally damaged Chinese society; the launching of industrialization, beginning in the military sphere; and the inexorable transformation of education.

After 1860 the Qing adopted a conciliatory policy toward the foreign powers, taking the view that their own most pressing objective was to recover control of the empire from the various sets of rebels: the Taiping in south and central China, the Nian in the north, the Miao ethnic minorities in Guizhou province, and the Muslims in Yunnan and in the northwest. Large portions of China were virtually in a state of civil war. Although the foreign threat was alarming, it had to take second place to the restoration of internal peace. By the 1880s the Qing had achieved this goal. The aggressively antiforeign Xianfeng Emperor was succeeded in 1861 by his five-year-old son, whose mother, the imperial concubine Cixi (1835–1908), acted as regent together with another empress, whom she soon displaced. Cixi controlled the succession in such a way that, for the next forty-eight years, until her death in 1908, she effectively held paramount power as the empress dowager. A skillful politician, for the first half of her rule Cixi strove to achieve a balance between the reforming impulse of progressive provincial leaders, whose military success against the Taiping gave them considerable clout as well as a keen interest in foreign technology, and the largely antiforeign successors to the literati groups whose pressure had helped precipitate the first war with the Western powers. Later on, however, this quest for compromise succumbed to a reactionary conservatism that she apparently regarded as her best hope for political survival.

In foreign affairs during the 1860s, 1870s, and 1880s, China suffered a number of setbacks. Russia assumed control over part of Qing Central Asia, Britain's interest in expanding outward from its colonial bases in India and Nepal threatened Qing control over Tibet, France began moving into the area of modern Vietnam, and Japan began to infiltrate the Liuqiu Islands, Taiwan, and Korea. In 1884 China lost a war with France; this defeat was followed within little more than a decade by another, this time at the hands of Japan, which imposed the crippling Treaty of Shimonoseki (1895). This second defeat enormously heightened Chinese apprehensions, dispelling forever the notion that Japan was in effect merely a junior constellation in China's civilizational orbit. As the result of the Treaty of Shimonoseki, foreign investment snowballed to such an extent that detractors had some justification in claiming that China was half mortgaged to the powers. Many Chinese feared that their country would cease altogether to have an independent existence and would be "carved up like a melon" by the foreign powers, who openly discussed such a prospect in their treaty port newspapers.

In 1900 the empress dowager threw her support to the violently antiforeign Boxer Uprising, perceiving in its popular energy a last possible chance to save Qing power and the Chinese nation. The events of 1900 aroused widespread popular feeling, not only against the foreigners but also against the Qing's ineptitude in dealing with them. No one doubted any longer that major change was in the air. Patriotism remained a given, even a driving force, but its predominant focus became resistance to the ruling house. In their own defense, the Qing introduced sweeping institutional, educational, and military reforms during the first decade of the century. They also began to introduce representative assemblies and a constitution as in Meiji Japan, which many regarded with new respect since China's defeat. But the reforms were too little, too late, and ironically they strengthened the very opponents they were intended to mollify.

The Qing empire finally fell in 1911, succeeded by a republic still firmly in the grip of overseas interests. It took some considerable time and several wars and revolutions for China to recover its former strength and achieve a position of parity with the powers. But in retrospect we can see that the writing was on the wall for foreign imperialism in China by no later than the turn of the century, even if the ink was still barely visible. The seeds of self-determination had been planted several decades earlier.

THE FOREIGN PRESENCE

In the world of the nineteenth century China was in many ways unique. It was not a colony; the Qing government continued in power. But after 1860 it was dotted with foreign enclaves that had a significant impact on its social, political, economic, and cultural life. Although Chinese sovereignty was thus still more or less intact, the treaties made significant inroads by permitting foreign residence in China under the protection of extraterritoriality, according to which foreigners could live, conduct business, and own property in designated areas immune from Qing jurisdiction.

In the last few years of the century Japan and the Western powers greedily competed to establish spheres of influence in China. Britain claimed the middle and lower Yangzi down to Shanghai; France claimed parts of the southwest adjacent to its Indochinese colonies; Germany claimed parts of east China; Japan claimed southern Manchuria, Taiwan, and Korea, and occupied the latter two from 1895 to 1945; Russia claimed northern Manchuria. During this period the foreign powers forced China effectively to concede sovereignty in their spheres of influence by granting them leaseholds together with railroad, mining, and timber rights. Germany took a lease on parts of Shandong province for ninety-nine years; Russia took the Liaodong peninsula in southern Manchuria, including two key harbors, Port Arthur and Dalian, for twenty-five years; France took the port of Guangzhouwan, opposite Hainan Island, for ninety-nine years; and Britain took the Shandong port of Weihaiwei for however long Russia kept Port Arthur and the New Territories of Hong Kong, on the Chinese mainland beyond Kowloon, for ninety-nine years, until 1997.

As the result of this "scramble for concessions," there were nearly one hundred ports in China open to foreign trade but not necessarily residence. Some had been opened by treaty agreement; others China had opened voluntarily. Different treaty ports had different arrangements. In some, "concession" areas were leased by the Chinese government to foreign governments, whose consuls, as the chief resident officials, could sublease property within the concession to individual foreigners. Such was the case in Tianjin, Hankou, and Canton, for example. In other cities, notably Shanghai, the foreign settlements whose early days were described in the last chapter were not leased but were simply designated by treaty as areas for foreign residence and trade. In such areas Chinese theoretically were barred from owning land, but in practice many did so, sometimes through a foreign intermediary.[2]

Chinese Communist rhetoric later lambasted the treaty ports in general and the foreign concessions and settlements in particular as blights on the national landscape, in which imperialists conspired to obstruct China's advance to modernity. But recent reevaluations suggest that the rhetoric has disguised at least some of the reality. Shanghai, first the focal point of the Western presence and later, repeatedly, the fountainhead of revolutionary activism, demonstrates that the foreign enclaves also made positive contributions to some of China's key transformations.

Over the course of time considerable numbers of Chinese came to live in the foreign settlements: war refugees, would-be compradors, and scions of upper-class families. They sought the protection of foreign policing, the relative security provided by the exclusion of the Chinese military, and employment. Initially many worked for the burgeoning foreign enterprises, helping them negotiate their way into the Chinese market. International commerce expanded enormously, as did joint ownership by Chinese and foreign entrepreneurs and management by Chinese compradors of foreign-owned firms that wished to infiltrate the Chinese domestic market. Both played a significant role in introducing a whole range of new business methods into China. At the same time, a new urban middle class of Chinese entrepreneurs, merchants, and tradespeople, many of whom soon set up their own businesses, also flourished. This new bourgeoisie came into its own in the first decades of the twentieth century, stepping into the vacuum left by the weakness of the state and the retraction of foreign economic interests as the result of World War One. The influence of the new merchant elite was considerable, even though developing nationalism cast an unfavorable light on their close relationship with foreigners. At the same time, however, the creation of such civic bodies as chambers of commerce, able to interpose themselves between ordinary citizens and the state, created an intermediate sphere of public life that was neither state-controlled nor completely private in its orientation.

Some educated Chinese who sought nontraditional work in the foreign-run sectors still bore the imprint of the traditional upper-class sense of responsibility for the fate of the nation. Many gravitated in large numbers toward the new publishing and newspaper industries, whose foreign operators were relieved by extraterritoriality of the fear of retaliation should they express critical views about current events, as they often did. One such foreign-owned publication, based in Shanghai, was the Chinese-language newspaper *Shenbao*, founded in 1872, which showed how it was possible to report news and to influence public opinion—for example, on the issue of conservative obstruction of railroad development. Drawing inspiration from these kinds of publications, Chinese intellectuals began operating their own newspapers and periodicals in huge numbers.

Initially circulated among Chinese in the settlements, the new publications soon spread far beyond. They included information about foreign ideologies, such as Marxism and republicanism, as well as news reporting. The wide-scale dissemination of information and opinions that neither emanated from the government nor was subject to its control proved profoundly subversive of the old order.

Among the most active of those who sought to popularize new ideas in this way was the great reform leader Liang Qichao (1873–1929). A product of the traditional educational system, Liang founded a number of periodicals dedicated to studying China's problems and proposing reforms in education, the arts, literature, and the political structure. In time his views shifted, leading him to promote a Chinese constitution and even a parliament. As we shall see, his ideas helped lay the foundations for the May Fourth Movement of the 1910s and 1920s and for the later movements for democracy.

By the end of the century railroads, telegraphs, and the rise of a popular press all helped disseminate information about the widening foreign presence into the interior of China. Other sources of information included troops from the new armies, visiting home or demobilized into the community at large, as well as workers in the budding new industrial complex. Particularly after 1895, when foreigners could establish their own industrial enterprises and factories in the treaty ports, a stream of factory workers flowed steadily back and forth between big cities, such as Shanghai, and their home villages in the surrounding countryside, taking with them word of life among the foreigners. With information traveling in all these different ways, then, by the turn of the century Chinese virtually everywhere had some degree of knowledge about the foreigners and their impact on China.

Moreover, foreign goods reached people even in the remotest areas, as the renowned intellectual Kang Youwei (1858–1927) pointed out in 1895:

> In addition to the fifty-three million ounces of silver we spend on foreign cottons, we buy such items of ordinary use as heavy silk, satins, woolens, fine silks, gauze, and felt; umbrellas, lamps, paint, suitcases and satchels; chinaware, toothbrushes, tooth-powder, soap and lamp oil. Among comestibles we buy coffee, Philippine and Havana cigars, cigarettes and rolling paper, snuff, and liquor; ham, dried meats, cake, candy, and salt; and medicines—liquid, pills, powders—as well as dried and fresh fruit. We also buy coal, iron, lead, copper, tin, and other materials; wooden utensils, clocks, watches, sundials, thermometers, barometers, electric lamps, plumbing accessories, mirrors, photographic plates, and other amusing or ingenious gadgets. As more households get them, more people want them, so that they have reached as far as Xinjiang and Tibet.[3]

Yet foreign trade remained only a small proportion of China's overall economy, with a turnover that never exceeded 10 percent of gross domestic product, and the modern sector of industry remained relatively limited well into the twentieth century.

Attitudes toward the presence of foreigners, foreign goods, and foreign values varied widely. This is hardly surprising when we recall that the population of China was approaching half a billion. It was extremely diverse. We must bear in mind issues of local and regional difference, of firsthand or merely derivative knowledge, of different perspectives based on gender and social class, and, finally, of possibly biased representation. For "the people" did not always speak for themselves, and we are sometimes forced to rely on others for reports and interpretation of popular actions. Many such interpreters had axes to grind. Missionaries seeking to bring religious enlightenment, for example, might assert that "the Chinese people are backward"; local gentry fighting to retain their traditional position in society might claim that "the Chinese people will resist this change," while progressive reformers might declare that "the peasants are extremely enthusiastic about investing in modern enterprises in their locality." All these characterizations may have been accurate in a limited sense, but most often they tell at best only part of the story. It may well be that there were so many points of view that each opposing group could readily find one to support its own perspective.

For Chinese in Shanghai and other treaty ports, the discrimination practiced by the various imperialist powers against them was particularly galling. Until World War One, for instance, foreign-controlled racecourses banned Chinese except if they paid an entrance fee on race days. There is some debate about whether an infamous notice at a public park barring "dogs and Chinese" ever actually existed, but attitudes were such that it might as well have. Restrictions of this kind did not in general extend to nonwhite colonial subjects of the Europeans—for example, Indians and Africans. Some of these had originally been brought to patrol the British-run International Settlement and the French Concession, where Sikh and Senegalese guards and policemen were commonplace. Their presence added to the city's cosmopolitan flavor, but it also stiffened the resolve of many Chinese to hold firm in the face of foreign imperialism so as not to suffer the same fate as had India and other European colonies. One way in which it still remained possible to display firmness was in the realm of diplomacy.

NEW DIPLOMACY

In 1861 the Qing created a new office of foreign affairs, the *Zongli Yamen* (Office for the General Management of Affairs Concerning the Various Countries). A subdivision of the Grand Council, the principal agency of state, it was manned by from three to eleven senior officials who simultaneously retained their other positions, such as provincial governor. For much of its life it was headed by Prince Gong (1833–1898), uncle to the first of the several baby emperors for whom the empress dowager acted as regent. His experience negotiating the 1860 peace settlement with the British and French had favorably transformed his once-hostile attitude toward the foreigners. Prince Gong's basic policy was to deal as peaceably as possible with the powers and to concentrate on reviving China's strength by learning from the foreign example. The empress dowager sought to prevent his becoming too powerful and eventually dismissed him altogether. In any event, the *Zongli Yamen* did not have sole jurisdiction over matters affecting the coast, and its decisions were subject to her approval.

The *Zongli Yamen* endeavored to invoke international law to protect China, and it sponsored the dispatch of embassies to Europe and the Americas to investigate overseas political systems and social conditions and to speak up for overseas Chinese. By the 1870s it had identified several advantages in official representation overseas. First, stationing diplomats abroad would make it possible for China to deal directly with foreign governments instead of with foreign ministers resident in Beijing. The intransigence of some foreign diplomats posted to China made the option of circumventing the quirks of individual personalities particularly appealing. Second, diplomats could gather intelligence on foreign countries, which in the case of nearby locations could help reinforce China's defenses and could glean technological information for use in its industrialization projects. Third, an overseas diplomatic presence would better enable China to assess the international situation and possibly to gain support from one foreign power against another in times of crisis. The hope of playing the powers off against one another was a persistent thread of foreign policy. Fourth, protection of overseas Chinese communities would discourage disaffection and, on the contrary, promote support for the Qing government. With luck the better-off overseas Chinese would even offer their services and some of their wealth to the home country if it made some effort to take care of their interests. Besides, the need to protect Chinese workers overseas was urgent. The absence of consular representation was one cause of Chinese impotence in the face of the ill-treatment of Chinese "coolies" around the world. That impotence tarnished China's international image.

In the 1870s and 1880s China concluded numerous treaties allowing Chinese diplomatic representation in foreign countries. These treaties, much less discussed by historians than the notorious treaties forced on China by the bellicose Western powers and Japan, were the result of Chinese activism in the protection of its interests. They were not "unequal," although China experienced considerable difficulty in implementing them. These difficulties arose partly as the result of Qing ineptitude but more important because the Western powers and Japan knew very well China could not back up its demands with effective military power. Hence the powers were at best extremely lackadaisical about compliance. At worst they simply ignored treaty provisions, often to the great disadvantage of Chinese resident overseas.

Large-scale diplomatic expansion was hampered by a chronic shortage of funds and, at least at first, a lack of sufficient qualified personnel. Therefore some early foreign missions—in Honolulu and Singapore, for instance—were partly financed by funding raised among Chinese locally. Chinese ambassadors sometimes represented their country's interests in more than one country. The ambassador to Britain, for instance, also was accredited to France and Italy, and the envoy to the United States had responsibility for Spain as well. Apart from the financial issue, some officials urged caution in diplomacy because they feared that too rapid an outreach would appear aggressive to the Western powers and might prompt a hostile response.

China also began employing foreign nationals to represent its interests overseas, in a new pattern of Qing employment of foreigners, to which the appointment of Britons to head the Imperial Maritime Customs Service also belonged. In 1867 the *Zongli Yamen* sent an investigative mission to the United States under the former American minister to China, Anson Burlingame. Among other things, the Burlingame mission led to a treaty, concluded with the United States in 1868, which sanctioned Chinese immigration to America. But within a decade the Chinese immigration issue had become a hot topic in U.S. politics, and under subsequent treaties China agreed to try to stem the flow of emigrants bound for the United States.

Violent hostility to local Chinese communities periodically flared in the United States. Anti-Chinese riots erupted in Los Angeles in 1871 and in Denver, Colorado, in 1880. The worst episode broke out in Rock Springs, Wyoming, in 1885, when twenty-eight Chinese were killed, fifteen injured, and damage was done to thousands of dollars' worth of property. By then the United States had passed, in 1882, the first of a series of stringent Exclusion Acts aimed at halting further Chinese immigration and broadly limiting the rights of Chinese already in the United States.

The American government was reluctant to make any amends for the Rock Springs massacre. But when the governor-general of the Guangdong region threatened that Americans in China might suffer reprisals at the hands of an aroused populace, the United States agreed to pay compensation for the damaged property, although not for the lost lives. It was no triumph born of gunboat diplomacy, but it was a minor victory for China. Chinese diplomatic activism also blocked the dispatch to China of a U.S. ambassador who, as a congressman, had frequently called for ending Chinese immigration.

Chinese diplomacy won other important successes. In the 1870s China sent two investigative commissions, one to Cuba, where since the abolition of slavery the sugar industry depended on Chinese labor, and the other to Peru, where Chinese worked in such industries as guano. As a result, the coolie trade as such was abolished in 1874, and agreement was reached—although by no means always honored either in letter or in spirit—for the better treatment of Chinese in those places. The treatment of Chinese in Cuba also affected Chinese relations with Spain, whose government depended on the taxes on the profits of the sugar industry.

In Japan an 1871 diplomatic treaty gave Chinese, like other foreign nationals, the right to extraterritoriality and provided for the installation of consuls in several Japanese cities in addition to the ambassador in Tokyo. Chinese consuls also gained the right to a special cemetery for Chinese who died in Japan and to a hospital for Chinese. For some time Chinese diplomats were still able to form friendly personal relationships with Japanese intellectuals, despite the growing political differences between their nations.

Networking among diplomats also enabled Qing officials to gain a better sense of where overseas representation might be most needed. In the 1890s, for instance, the Chinese ambassador to Chile passed on information he had learned from the Chilean consul to British Columbia. Chinese immigration, he had heard, was already running into the tens of thousands; it would be desirable to establish a consulate there to take care of their interests. In the last decades of the century China appointed consuls in a number of places where there was a strong Chinese presence, including Singapore, Penang, Rangoon, and several cities in Australia, New Zealand, South Africa, and Canada, as well as in Hong Kong.

Negotiations over a Chinese consulate in Hong Kong dragged on for two decades. The British feared that the presence of a Chinese official in Hong Kong, the vast majority of whose population was Chinese, would undermine their own authority. They also took it for granted that the main function of such an office would be espionage of one kind or another. But Chinese negotiators were at pains to point out that it was untenable to deny the Chinese the right to establish a consulate, given the presence of Japanese and other diplomats in the colony. A Chinese consulate eventually opened in Hong Kong in 1891.

The diplomat Xue Fucheng (1838–1894) expressed the attitude of many of his forward-thinking colleagues when he was serving as ambassador to Britain, France, Belgium, and Italy, noting in his diary:

> We should sign contracts with Brazil and Mexico for Chinese laborers and to establish consulates there for their protection. In the contract we must clearly demand fair treatment for our people even after their work is finished, so that they will not be subjected to the humiliation of mistreatment and deportation, which the American authorities have recently imposed upon our people [under the 1882 Exclusion Act and its successors]. Under the protection of our consulates our people will not be threatened by the natives and will be able to purchase land, build houses, and raise families there. After several generations, their descendants may even invest in China on account of their heritage. In all likelihood we will be building a new China outside of Chinese territory so that our people may prosper in years to come. This move will strengthen our nation, feed our people, reduce our national deficit, increase our productivity, and change our national image. Therefore it is essential to implement such a policy as soon as possible.[4]

For their part, the overseas Chinese communities tended to support anything that would strengthen and revitalize China. They understood only too well that they could hardly expect any protection of their own rights and interests if China was too weak to protect itself at home. At the same time, rising sentiments against Chinese immigrants in many different parts of the world, the outgrowth of racism, nascent nationalism, and trade protectionism helped consolidate Chinese expatriates as a group and orient them homeward.

The hope that the overseas Chinese would prove to be a source of funding was soon realized. By as early as the 1880s annual remittances from abroad amounted to as much as twenty million dollars, perhaps half of which flowed to the Canton area, from which a majority of emigrants hailed. Actual remittances were only part of the story. Trade funneled to China as the result of connections with the overseas community was estimated at several million dollars annually. This benefit flowed in particular to Canton and Hong Kong. Although the latter remained under British rule, the livelihood of a majority of its population depended on international trade.

Moreover, overseas communities, some of which became quite wealthy, could often be counted on to send funds in time of crisis because it was an effective way of demonstrating their continued loyalty to the home country. In the Sino-French War of 1884–1885, for instance, American Chinese alone sent more than a half million dollars. Before the decade was out, they contributed tens of thousands in additional relief money, as the central government proved increasingly unable to deal with regional crises. Many such crises were the consequence of natural disasters, such as floods or famine, but not a few others resulted from the periodic outbreaks of violence prompted by hostility toward foreign missionaries.

Christian Missionaries

Christian missionaries had never stopped coming to China despite the prohibitions against them. Frustrated by the constraints under which they were compelled to operate, many became militant supporters of opening China by force and aggressively protecting the Church by means of gunboat diplomacy. The treaties of 1858–1860 were the answer to their prayers.

Many Chinese continued to regard Christianity with great suspicion. For more than a century Christianity had been banned as heterodox, a characterization full of subversive connotations that Taiping adoption of Christian belief—unacceptably reworked as far as the Westerners were concerned—seemed to confirm. Suddenly, by treaty, Christianity officially lost its heterodox label, and at the same time, it all at once gained considerable social and political power.

Upper-class Chinese were hostile to missionaries because they both challenged Confucian values and assumed certain social welfare functions that traditionally lay in the gentry's bailiwick. The missionaries established themselves in Chinese communities, building churches, orphanages, medical clinics, and schools. The Chinese elite suspected too that left to its own devices, Christianity would fatally undermine their prestige by challenging their claims to moral and cultural predominance.

As a consequence of upper-class objections, the majority of Christian converts after 1860 came from the least privileged levels of society; many were women. Like the Taiping rebels and other dissenters from the established order, such people had little to lose and potentially much to gain from aligning themselves with the representatives of an alternative source of power. The opportunity to improve one's lot in this life, rather than one's chances in the next, was thus in many cases one of the most important factors in the decision to adopt Christianity.

Missionary intervention in matters involving their converts was common, and in case of dissatisfaction at the local level they rarely hesitated to complain to their consuls. That meant the *Zongli Yamen* would be notified, and the whole thing might end with a foreign gunboat sailing upriver to register a threatening presence or an indemnity for which the funds would have to be raised locally. For a local magistrate, therefore, whatever the merits of a complaint against a Christian convert, and however tempting support for local anti-Christian elements might be, it might not be worth the trouble of deciding against converts because they had such powerful backing. The resulting sense of untouchability allowed converts to behave with great arrogance, although of course not all took advantage. Still, because of the risk of missionary interference, a disgruntled non-Christian generally thought twice before bringing suit against a convert.

At the same time, the dilemma that a disturbance involving foreigners posed to local officials offered an opening to anti-Qing agitators. In other words, an incident of violence or hostility that seemed on the surface to be directed against foreigners sometimes was motivated not so much by antiforeignism pure and simple as by a desire to cause problems for local authorities or for the Qing itself.

While the benefits of missionary backing often clinched the decision to convert, they also brought down the resentment of the rest of the community on converts and their religion. What was more, converts were exempt, on grounds of religion, from making required donations to the expenses of local festivals, and by definition they were also ineligible to contribute to reparations arising from local anti-Christian activity. This financial burden had to be borne by their non-Christian neighbors. For the many who lived at subsistence level, this represented a significant additional expense.

The distinct class element—although not so much the gender element—in missionary conversions in China contributed to the ability of Christianity's opponents to discredit it and had an adverse impact on the overall standing of the foreign religion in China. It seemed at times to appeal primarily to riffraff and those incapable of rational thinking. But there were plenty of other grounds for objection. Some Chinese, like their seventeenth-century predecessors, feared that the mission endeavor represented the subversive vanguard of wholesale foreign invasion; they were perhaps not altogether off the mark. Many suspected that missionaries were sexual perverts or sorcerers, or both, lumping Christianity together with other heterodox religions often the target of similar accusations. Why did Christian men and women worship together if not for purposes of debauchery? Why did missionaries take in unwanted children if not for pedophilia, witchcraft, or worse? What magic was in their pretended medicine? Who knew what their true intentions were when they claimed to be saving the bodies or souls of Chinese children?

These suspicions gave rise to a virulently anti-Christian literature that worked on Chinese emotions to create an atmosphere of at least latent fear of and antagonism toward foreign missionaries. Curiously, some of the claims made against the missionaries in China bore a striking resemblance to those raised against Chinese immigrants in the United States, where allegedly nefarious carryings-on in Chinatowns were a constant theme in anti-immigrant polemics. Rumor created an atmosphere of suspicion, in which the chance posting of a hostile placard or some fleeting misunderstanding might quickly lead to an explosion.

Many of the most furious acts of resistance took place against the background of specific events in the broader international context. This timing suggests that they were directed against missionaries as representatives of foreign imperialism rather than against them in their capacity as God's envoys. For example, waves of violence against foreign missionaries followed China's defeat in 1885 by France.

The Chinese state also found ways to resist foreign imperialism; their approach was less immediately violent but directly concerned the use of force. From the 1860s the state launched a series of programs to modernize its military forces both in terms of organization and training and in terms of technology.

MILITARY REFORM

Well before the First Opium War, certain statesmen had identified military modernization as of key importance. But the state had made little attempt to implement their proposals because before the conflict with the British most of the enemies that the Qing had fought were technically inferior to them, so that there had been little incentive to devote much attention or funding to military industrial reform. In this respect the situation in China was different from that in Europe, where competition between states of roughly equal power gave continual impetus to the quest for military advantage.

The foreign technology that brought about China's defeat in the First Opium War made a huge impression in China. Steam propulsion, by then well established in the West, was previously unknown in China, as were the paddle-wheel boats that came so distressingly close in to Chinese harbors. Explosive shells that used slow-burning fuses, and hence made it possible to time explosions, had been in use in the West for a few decades but only now became known in China. The percussion cap, which had already revolutionized warfare in Britain and North America by making it possible to keep powder dry even in damp conditions, was also introduced into China soon after the war.

As we saw in the last chapter, Chinese began almost at once to experiment, with some success, with techniques for building Western-style warships, guns, gunpowder, and explosives. Although it was possible to buy foreign ships and weapons, the long-range goal was autonomy. So in addition to purchasing whatever they could, leading statesmen began calling for the establishment of government shipyards and arsenals to produce Western-style vessels and weapons, and they recommended using technicians from France and America (both hostile to Britain) to teach Chinese how to make and use them to greatest effect. In the late 1840s these calls came to nothing, as did French proposals, intended to give France the edge over Britain in China, that Chinese learn to manufacture ordnance in France. For at that time the lack of coordinated central control, together with the absence of any immediate military threat, derailed any concerted attempt speedily to update military matériel and revitalize the army.

Qing mid-century defeats by the Taiping, Nian, and other rebels brought new urgency to the earlier proposals for modernizing the armed forces. Attempts to adopt foreign technology and to provide the necessary education began to take place on a national level, with state backing. From shortly after the outbreak of the Taiping Rebellion in 1851, local defense forces began ordering fresh supplies of artillery. Proposals to build local arsenals led to the establishment, in 1853, of a Gun Bureau in Hunan that became an important source of ordnance, as well as a number of other small arsenals and at least one shipyard where guns and ammunition and ships were produced. Throughout the Taiping Rebellion, which lasted until 1864, provincial leaders established a network of small-scale institutions of this kind to supply their beleaguered armies. At the same time, they steadily placed orders for foreign weaponry from the treaty ports and in some cases borrowed money from foreign merchants for the purpose. As we saw in the last chapter, foreign arms dealers of course sold to all comers, including the Taiping and other anti-Qing rebels, who themselves also became skilled weapons casters.

After the conclusion of the Convention of Beijing in 1860, the Qing could much more readily obtain Westerners' military assistance because of the cessation of hostilities between them. The state, determined to upgrade its ability to produce and use military hardware, began to sponsor arsenals staffed by foreign experts and technical education to match.

The program of improving the military proceeded on the principle that however much foreign aid was needed in drilling and training, China should not at any cost become militarily dependent on foreigners. It should rigorously guard against such a possibility. This was simply an extension of the long-hallowed principle about maintaining centralized control of the military. The new regional armies created to conquer the Taiping already marked a departure from that rule, but so far they showed no intention of threatening imperial security, instead helping preserve the Qing. Abandoning military authority to voracious foreigners was altogether another matter; it was neither necessary nor something to take a chance on.

Apart from the desire not to surrender military control, accepting foreign military aid was a delicate matter because the Qing was determined not to become unduly indebted to any single foreign power. For example, in 1860 the desperate Qing finally accepted a

Russian offer, made two years earlier, to supply them with rifles, artillery, and instructors, but they still rejected the idea that the Russians might send boats to help attack the Taiping capital at Nanjing. Nonetheless, the idea of using Western gunboats was appealing, all the more so after the Taiping had captured some coastal areas. Britain and France competed to win China's order, which was eventually placed in London for seven steamers and one storeship.

This particular attempt at international cooperation is worth examining because it clearly demonstrated that the Qing, in concert with the newly powerful provincial commanders, fully intended to and actually would abide by their most cherished principles despite their political fragility. Briefly, what happened was as follows. The British head of the Qing Customs Service, Horatio Lay, helped conduct negotiations and locate a British captain and seamen to man the flotilla. But when Lay's appointee, Captain Sherard Osborn, reached China, he insisted that the arrangements gave him overall command of the ships and that he was answerable only to the emperor (a child). Lay had probably assumed the Qing would concur in whatever they could get. But the Qing authorities had never had any intention of giving up ultimate authority and ordered him to serve under Chinese officers, in keeping with the principle of retaining control of the military and in order not to appear ready to back down. After protracted negotiations, the Lay-Osborn flotilla project was abandoned and its two namesakes were paid off and sent away. The ships themselves were converted into merchantmen under British control, in an agreement intended to allay parallel Qing and American fears that their opponents in their respective civil wars might somehow get hold of the flotilla.

Notwithstanding this particular disaster, China remained ready to use foreign troops, the best-known example of which was the Chinese mercenary force known as the Ever Victorious Army. This army of a few thousand men was effectively under Chinese control, although its officers and commanders—the most famous of whom was "Chinese" Gordon, later to die at Khartoum—came from a variety of foreign countries. As a result of the Ever Victorious Army's superior training and its state-of-the-art Western weaponry, it played a significant part in the defeat of the Taiping, both because it distracted rebel troops from defending their capital at Nanjing and because its use of artillery was so effective that it converted the formerly cautious Li Hongzhang, the man who was to play a leading role in Chinese politics and international affairs from the late 1860s until his death in 1901, to active enthusiasm for foreign fire-power and its technology, about which Li became extremely knowledgeable. Among other things, under Li's auspices China became such a good client of Krupp, the German weapons manufacturer, that Alfred Krupp hung a picture of Li above his bed.

Li Hongzhang and the leading statesmen of the self-strengthening movement were interested in building a military industrial complex that before long would enable China to reduce or even abjure altogether its reliance on foreign aid. In the new workshops and arsenals, they planned to produce China's own steamships, ammunition, and ordnance. They installed capital equipment purchased from abroad and, at considerable expense, hired foreign technicians to train Chinese workers. Of course state arsenals for the production of weapons were hardly new in China, nor was it unheard of to tap foreign military expertise. What really was new was the introduction of machinery, a direct import from the Industrial Revolution of the West.

The largest and most famous of these new institutions was the Jiangnan Arsenal, substantially funded by customs revenues levied on foreign trade, a tactic, incidentally, that helped the central government regain some of the power earlier ceded to provincial leaders. The arsenal was established in Shanghai in 1865. In addition to steamships, it machine-produced the most recent models of magazine rifles; black, brown, and smokeless powder; cartridges; breech-loading rapid-fire guns; giant coastal defense artillery; large-caliber artillery shells; and electrically detonated naval mines.[5] These products, particularly the steamships and coastal defense weapons, left little doubt that the new weapons were intended to be used against outsiders as well as against rebels.

Soon there were almost twenty new arsenals and shipyards across the country. Most were in treaty port areas, which gave them ready access to imported supplies and foreign advisers. The level of sophistication improved rapidly. China not only caught up but also kept abreast of the extraordinarily rapid development in military technology simultaneously taking place in the West. It established research facilities. Within thirty-five years the Chinese arsenals were producing up-to-date arms and ammunition of generally high standard. By 1895, the year of the Chinese defeat by the Japanese, Jiangnan alone had produced almost six hundred heavy machines;

some fifty-two thousand small arms and around twenty-seven million pieces of ammunition; almost three hundred guns of one kind or another with almost half a million pieces of ammunition; more than six hundred mines; sixteen vessels, including wooden-hulled and armor-plated propeller ships, a steel-armored vessel, and one ironclad; and several tons of powder.[6]

Besides equipping its military to compete with foreign armies, China needed to train its troops in the new methods. One early episode of foreign training gave rise in 1862 to the new Beijing Field Force, which was intended to defend the capital. It was drilled by five hundred bannermen who had themselves been trained by British officers in the new treaty port of Tianjin. By the late 1860s it had grown to about twenty thousand men, but not all were so well trained. Another program was initiated in 1864 under Gordon's supervision. It had some success in training Chinese troops in the use of foreign weapons but petered out nine years later, in part because of opium addiction among the troops. A number of other, mostly short-lived military training programs were launched as the Qing tried, in a somewhat piecemeal fashion, to streamline and update their army.

The progress of the new training programs was greatly impeded by the ambivalence of official attitudes. One fundamental problem was that many existing army officers both lacked the modern training needed to make the new weaponry truly effective and strongly resented any attempt either to instruct or to replace them. As a result, training programs might teach the use of Western weapons purchased for the purpose without going the next step and permitting systematic drilling and training. Such attitudes and the lingering fear even among progressives that too much military authority, in any form, was a dangerous thing in the hands of foreigners handicapped the foreign military training project. So the new hardware was not always able to be used to best effect.

In any event, available funding was sufficient to permit the armies only in a few important locations, such as the capital area, to acquire and learn to use the newest weaponry. It might be necessary, for example, for drilling to take place with spears instead of guns, which obviously reduced effectiveness. Moreover, it was simply not possible to coordinate the rearming of the expanding armies. At century's end it sometimes happened that not even all the troops in a single battalion necessarily had the same weapons.

Nor was it feasible to complete systematic training before the next foreign onslaughts brought serious damage to the fleet and some of the best-armed and best-trained troops. To hasten the process of military modernization, the self-strengtheners continued to purchase foreign weapons in considerable quantities, but they had continually to make strategic decisions about where to concentrate their best efforts.

Observers have traditionally dismissed the military industrialization represented by the arsenals as a failure because first France and then Japan roundly defeated China in the 1880s and 1890s, in the first practical tests of China military reforms. These defeats considerably set back China's progress toward acquiring a new army and navy. But as we have seen, these defeats did not necessarily prove that the programs of military self-strengthening had failed to make impressive advances. Attentive Westerners found that the Chinese arsenals showed an alarming capacity to produce and adapt to the changed requirements of military conflict.

INDUSTRIALIZATION

The revolutionary implications of the introduction of machine production into China reached far beyond military use, as many reformers clearly recognized:

> . . . what we have is machinery-producing machinery; no matter what type of machinery it can be reproduced step by step following the [right] method; then, it can be employed to make that type of product. There are no limits to what can be produced; all things can be mastered. At present we are unable to do everything at once; it is most important that we still produce iron ordnance to meet our military needs . . . foreign machinery can produce machinery for plowing, weaving, printing, ceramics, and tile making, which will benefit the daily needs of the people; originally it was not just for munitions. . . . I predict that in several decades there certainly will be wealthy Chinese farmers and great traders who will imitate foreign machine manufacturing for their own profit.[7]

The arsenals brought into China a far-reaching infrastructure, both conceptual and mechanical, that formed the basis on which it would later be able to create its own industrial base. The tools and techniques of military industrialization were applicable in almost every other area of the economy: in the mines, which used steam-powered pumps and modern extractive methods to supply the needs of military industrialization; in the steel refineries attached to the arsenals for making artillery; and in the all-important agricultural sector. It was in the arsenals too that the production of electrical equipment and the industrial processing of chemicals—both essential ingredients of industrial modernization—first took place. In addition, the military projects' use of such new techniques as mass production and the use of interchangeable components, as well as the creation of a new organizational mentality, helped create a framework for later industrial development.

By the last decades of the century a wide range of industrial projects had sprung up: steamships for travel on the network of inland waterways and along the coast, coal mines, railroads, telegraphs, textile manufacturing, and the minting of currency. Most used Western machinery and methods. Reformers also proposed to revolutionize agriculture by introducing Western methods, including the use of machinery, and chemical fertilizer in place of night soil. In short, once industrialization, spearheaded by modernization in the military sphere, began, it knew no bounds. The goal was modernity and independence; the means was using the foreigners' methods to break free of dependence on the foreigners.

But the path of industrialization did not run at all smoothly. Certain types of enterprise encountered particularly strong opposition. Although antiforeign sentiment often played a part in this type of resistance, the reasons were more generally social, economic, and cultural. Some Chinese opponents of mechanization feared the social repercussions of new industrial enterprises, as had Europeans earlier in the century. They expressed concern that machines would put too many people out of work and create too great a disparity between rich and poor.

Some objected to railroads, mines, and telegraphs on the ground that they would upset the geomantic balance by too much digging and destroying of the land. A few early lines were even torn up in protest by local inhabitants. Reformers drew attention to the fact that telegraph wires and railroad tracks required only laying on flat surfaces and tried to placate opponents of the new machine-operated mines by explaining that they were simply narrower and deeper than those to which Chinese were accustomed. But hostility remained. When, for example, the cosmopolitan diplomat Zeng Jize (1839–1890) took a small steamship home to Changsha from Nanjing in order to attend a family funeral, a number of influential people raised an enormous outcry that lasted several years.

The first Chinese ambassador to London, Guo Songtao (1818–1891), a man often vilified for his support of modernization projects, sought to address some of these concerns when he wrote in 1877 to Li Hongzhang about the building of railroads:

> Since my arrival here a few months ago, I have actually seen the convenience of having these trains, which can make a round trip of three to four hundred *li* [approximately 100 to 130 miles] in half a day. The local gentry here also advise us to build railways, saying that marked the beginning of the foundation of British power, though originally they too had been suspicious of these railways and tried to stop their construction, fearing that they would be detrimental to the people's livelihood. For example, thirty thousand horses were formerly used to maintain communication between the port of Southampton and London. However, with the opening of the railway, over sixty or seventy thousand horses are now used. This has happened because the convenience of the railway has led to a daily increase in trade, and since the railway only follows a [single] route, people from a distance of several dozen *li* or less, who come to take the train, must first travel by horse and get there, and do so in increasing numbers. . . .[8]

Some of the reluctance about railroads, in particular, was more directly related to the foreign threat. It stemmed from a fear that railroads would simply make it easy for the foreigners to infiltrate the whole of China. But this objection was largely overruled once the Qing discovered during the 1900 Boxer Uprising that railroads enabled them quickly to transport their own troops wherever needed and that if necessary, they could impede pursuit by tearing up the lines (a notion the Boxers also grasped). But just as the Chinese authorities realized that they could turn the foreigners' railroads and weapons to their own advantage against the foreigners, so the Boxers and other anti-Qing elements realized that they could use them against the Qing itself.

THE BOXERS

The main targets of the antiforeign Boxer movement of 1899–1900 were Chinese Christians and the missionaries who backed them. Missionary objections to the harassment of their converts only heightened Boxer resentment of the imperialist presence. Drawing their inspiration from arcane rituals that included spirit possession, the Boxers believed they were impervious to Western firepower, and like the Taiping before them, they espoused an egalitarian ideology that convinced large numbers of people to join the movement.

They began by committing acts of vandalism, theft, extortion, kidnapping, and arson, sometimes injuring or even killing their primarily Christian victims. The beleaguered Qing, in despair about empire and nation, could not decide whether to crush them (which some preliminary skirmishes proved to be by no means a foregone conclusion) or to take a gamble on legitimizing them as representatives of the people's will, in a last-ditch hope of getting rid of the foreigners. In the end they adopted the latter option. The emboldened Boxers eventually assembled a large force with which they marched on Beijing, with imperial backing, attacking missionaries and Chinese Christians as they went. Several hundred Westerners and thousands of Chinese Christians lost their lives, and property damage was considerable. In the capital the Boxers killed the German ambassador and laid siege to the foreign legations. From June till August Boxer armies and their supporters effectively blocked a multination expeditionary force trying to reach Beijing from coming to the rescue.

The failure of key military leaders to back the throne in supporting the Boxers drove the empress dowager to evacuate the capital and brought about the end of the uprising. The ensuing Boxer Protocol imposed stringent penalties on China, including indemnities of legendary proportions; a two-year ban on arms imports and permission for the foreign legations to install armed protection against further attack; execution and other punishments for highly placed Boxer supporters; and the erection of memorials in China to the Westerners killed in the uprisings. The sextant and other astronomical instruments made by European missionaries more than two hundred years before were removed from the Beijing Observatory to the palace of Sans Souci in Potsdam, Germany.

A vivid sense remained among foreigners and Chinese alike that it could always happen again. Against that fear, missionaries began very gradually to initiate a spirit more of cooperation than condescension, as the inkling dawned that ultimately they would turn their entire operations, religious, educational, and medical, over to Chinese control. Moreover, although Westerners scoffed in public at China's "primitive" efforts at military modernization, some privately acknowledged that the combined imperial and Boxer forces had almost proved more than a match for the international rescue expedition, in terms of both tactics and technology, as one captain in the German forces noted: "If we had known beforehand that our small force would have to fight with all modern weaponry, it would have been greatly imprudent to start off as we did."[9] The surprising discovery that military defeat of Chinese troops was not a foregone conclusion demonstrated the unexpected extent to which China had brought its military forces much more nearly into line with those of its foreign enemies than had been anticipated by the foreigners, who generally underestimated China and its capacity to shift gears. They found that the attention to technology and training in the military was paralleled by an intense focus on every aspect of the educational curriculum.

Changes in Education

Chinese leaders were well aware that creating new institutions and importing or copying foreign technology would serve little purpose without the transformation of education. They also knew that Japan had already been sending young men overseas to learn about foreign industry and foreign machines in order to launch its own military industry, and they were anxious not to lag behind. Hitherto the curriculum for the civil service examinations had been based on classical texts (with a smattering of questions on issues of current policy). A new curriculum would have to incorporate knowledge of technology, so that the next generations of leaders would be better informed about the new institutions the reformers hoped to build nationwide and would be less dependent on foreign aid.

Hiring foreign experts to give technical training in the arsenals was only the first step. It was also necessary to translate from foreign languages a much wider range of texts into Chinese than missionaries had already translated. Although these earlier efforts had helped provide both new information and convey new points of view and new ways of looking at things, it was not enough. Not least, a vital first step was establishing uniform terminology for the newly introduced sciences and technology, in itself no mean feat.

After 1860 the Qing established a number of translation bureaus where Chinese and Westerners worked together. One such bureau was attached to the Jiangnan Arsenal, where there was a desperate need for translations of technical works. Its rate of production was remarkable. By 1870 it had put out translations of almost 150 foreign technical works. Chinese were avid to read them; more than 130,000 volumes, many of which certainly passed through the hands of numbers of different readers, were sold during this period. In addition, the translations served as textbooks for Chinese technical workers at the arsenal and in other modern enterprises.

In time, translation work expanded well beyond the officially sponsored bureaus and well beyond pure technical works. Among the best-known translators was Yan Fu (1853–1921), a graduate of the new Fuzhou shipyard who had studied in England for several years. Yan's translations of several English works on science and sociology, including Adam Smith's *Wealth of Nations*, Thomas Huxley's *Evolution and Ethics*, and Herbert Spencer's Social Darwinist *Study of Sociology*, were extraordinarily influential, as we shall see in the next chapter. Other translation projects involved putting a work through more than one language on its way into Chinese—for example, from the original German or Russian into Japanese and thence into Chinese. The net effect, at any rate, was that knowledge of the West became far more widespread; it was no longer the limited prerogative of a privileged few.

At the same time that the translation projects were getting under way, the Qing established new schools offering a nontraditional curriculum that included, in particular, the study of Western languages. This move suggested a new awareness that knowledge of the West was coming to be of strategic significance. At the College of Foreign Languages (*Tongwen Guan*) attached to the *Zongli Yamen* in the capital, for example, French, English, Russian, and German were offered; branch schools later opened in Shanghai and Canton. These institutions were intended to provide young men, at first primarily Manchus, with language training and some degree of more general education about Western countries, so that they could prepare for newly created careers as diplomats, interpreters, or engineers. As early as 1866 three *Tongwen Guan* graduates accompanied Robert Hart, the British director of the Qing Imperial Maritime Customs Service, on an informal mission to Europe.

By the 1870s the *Tongwen Guan* had expanded its enrollment to include more Chinese students and began, against conservative objections, to offer instruction not just in foreign languages but also in international law, political economy, mathematics, physics, chemistry, physiology, medicine, and astronomy. Other government schools offered study on such topics as technology, warfare, language, shipbuilding, mining, and telegraphy, as well as agriculture, newly identified as a suitable target for modernization.

The broadest-ranging of traditional educations had always included study of the scientific and other practical knowledge of the ancients, so that in a sense these new-style schools did not mark a radical departure. But they were a far cry from the many academies that focused only on classical texts and were geared to the civil service examinations. For this reason, some traditional families declined to send their sons to the new schools. Even those students who did attend had to accept on faith that the new knowledge would lead to a good career in some nontraditional area. Some evidently had misgivings; they were found practicing essays for the civil service examinations instead of studying the mathematics and English they were paid a stipend to learn. But the very existence of the new schools helped, notwithstanding, to ensure that the new knowledge itself, and a general awareness of its importance, began to filter out into educated society more generally.

The new schools naturally aroused opposition. Conservatives, as was to be expected, deplored the innovations because they thought the absorption of traditional moral values was the essence of a classical training and believed that what was good enough for the ancestors should be good enough for present and future generations. Such claims disregarded the reality that in the past Chinese intellectuals had often shown tremendous interest in foreign practical knowledge and that the indigenous tradition they so treasured had over the centuries been hugely enriched by input from the outside, if not always under the same pressure for national survival.

Beyond the government schools and training programs, Chinese could acquire a new-style education at missionary schools. Although

Catholics and Protestants shared the common goal of inculcating Christian values, their approach varied. Catholic schools offered instruction in Chinese, primarily on subjects geared to the promotion of Christianity; they did not offer foreign languages or the study of science. They also set up schools for their converts' children; by the end of the century in the Jiangnan region surrounding Shanghai alone, more than sixteen thousand boys and girls were enrolled in Catholic-run elementary schools, while the total number of Catholics in China amounted to some seven hundred thousand people, including a few hundred Chinese priests. In adopting the values of another culture, however, the candidates for the priesthood, often social outcasts seeking to improve their lot in life, further alienated local communities by their willingness to give up such staples of Chinese life as ancestor worship and by their sanctimonious renunciation of opium.

Protestant schools were altogether different. Many Protestant missionaries were professionally trained teachers and included Chinese men and women. They operated numerous elementary and middle schools and several colleges, at which enrollment rose nearly tenfold between 1877 and 1906, from six thousand to almost sixty thousand students. Instruction was in English, and many secular subjects (including medicine) were offered in addition to religious instruction. By treaty the missionaries had gained the right to establish hospitals in China, and many such institutions had medical schools attached. By the turn of the century these had turned out more than three hundred Chinese doctors and had almost as many still in training. The hospitals also employed numerous Chinese on their staffs.

After the Boxer Uprising of 1900 Chinese enrollment in mission schools and colleges increased sharply, but at the same time the Qing government began to take more determined initiatives in education as one way of responding to the newly overt nationalism. At government schools, for instance, missionary teachers no longer taught, and their textbooks were removed from the curriculum. In 1905 the abolition of the seven-centuries-old civil service examinations around which most academic programs had revolved laid open the path to a more practical, generally more Western-oriented curriculum. Chinese schools thus became far more competitive with missionary schools, where student activists backed with strikes their calls to make coursework serve patriotic goals and to eliminate required religious observance. More generally, critics often accused mission schools of cutting students off from their own culture by failing to offer proper Chinese instruction.

Many Chinese who enrolled in missionary schools never had much interest in becoming Christians. They were primarily interested in learning English so that they could more readily find employment in the treaty ports; business profits were much more appealing than religious enlightenment. More than one school in 1880s Shanghai noted that their English-language curriculum was their greatest attraction in the eyes of many of their Chinese students; the student body changed almost completely about every eighteen months because as soon as students learned enough English to work with foreigners, they left. The schools contributed in this way to the expansion of the new urban bourgeoisie, but their impact on the numbers of Christians were less striking. In 1900 there were still only about one hundred thousand Chinese Protestants.

Missionaries were well aware of their students' priorities, but they hoped that education in one of their schools would at least incline young Chinese favorably toward foreigners and their cultural values. As a foreign-language newspaper put it, "A boy educated at the missions' school is not in after life likely to be a rabid antiforeign, antichristian zealot. His better education should raise him somewhat in intellectual status above his neighbors, and this gives him an influence which ought to be on the right side."[10] But the demands of patriotism frequently overshadowed the influence of a Westernized Christian education.

In addition to operating schools for boys, missionaries ran schools for Chinese girls, a radical innovation in a society where very few females were educated outside the home. The first missionary school for girls in China was established in the treaty port of Ningbo in 1844, although in the interior women rarely had access to education until much later. Many tried to train their Chinese students to behave like Europeans, as one young woman noted in the early twentieth century: "All the lessons were given in English . . . it was not long before I could speak a little English. I was dressed and my hair was arranged now in European fashion. . . . With my English clothes, a hat which was the first I ever had on my head, the skirts which I now wore instead of trousers, I felt very much 'in the role.' . . . I learned how to drink tea as the English take it, with sugar and milk; how to eat bread and butter and toast; how to use a knife and fork instead of chopsticks, and how to take exercise."[11] The first private Chinese school for girls was established in 1897; the first government girls' school not until 1906.

Traditionally religions such as Buddhism and Daoism had held considerable attraction for Chinese women because of the chance they offered for a better position than they were likely to find within the hierarchical confines of Confucian society. Missionary educators tried to woo women away from other religious beliefs with the promise that Christianity alone could offer them equality with men on the spiritual plane. But for many, Christianity offered the possibility of a bonus rather than an alternative in spiritual terms, and they did not necessarily abandon other beliefs to become exclusively Christian.

For young women, attendance at a mission school offered all kinds of benefits in addition to acquiring an education. It gave them a measure of independence from the stifling atmosphere of the family unit, and with it a new identity. It enabled them to make friends with their peers in ways that might not otherwise have been open to them. Some certainly found solace in religion that they found nowhere else, for the missionaries were skillful at playing on the vulnerability of the many young Chinese women who were unaccustomed to anyone's paying them much attention. But Chinese women did not necessarily find Christianity as such particularly appealing.

Although some men did not care enough about their daughters to object to their attendance at a mission school, others complained bitterly, as one American missionary woman describes in a letter written in 1895 from rural Guangdong province: "The people were hostile, i.e., the men—for they said so many of the women and girls were 'believing Jesus' already, that if they allowed us to go on, soon the whole place would be filled with disobedient wives and daughters refusing to worship the idols when told. Therefore they came nights and stoned the house and commanded us to be turned out."[12]

Following the example of their teachers, a majority of whom were women, many mission-educated Chinese women expected to work outside the home, and many decided to remain single in order to follow a vocation as a doctor, a teacher, or even a missionary. Some became the financial mainstays of their families. Many were also active in the nationalist movements of the early twentieth century, for example, saving up to buy a few shares of railroad stock during the Rights Recovery Movement, an effort to push back foreign economic advances by raising money locally to buy back tracks already mortgaged to eager foreign financiers. In the patriotic spirit of the times, they found that while their schooling enabled them to do something for their country, it also made it necessary for them to demonstrate their loyalty to their non-Christian fellows. In other words, having once broken free from the constraints of family and tradition by attending missionary schools, many young women also managed to assert their independence from missionary influence.

STUDY OVERSEAS

The new trend toward acquiring knowledge of and about the powers, with a view to learning how most effectively to compete with them, lent a new prestige to foreign travel. There was nothing like firsthand experience. As we have seen, Chinese emigration around the world, both voluntary and involuntary, began to escalate in the 1840s, spurred on by Chinese merchants' need for overseas outposts and by the intensifying coolie trade. But now in addition to the emigration of laborers, educated Chinese began to travel overseas, as students and diplomats or simply to observe the wealth and power of the Western nations and Japan for themselves. Such knowledge became a cultural commodity, most valuable in the form of eyewitness accounts, but still valued when derived more at second hand. Among some intellectuals, foreign knowledge began to compete for prestige with old-fashioned Confucian erudition even before the abolition of the examination system.

Overseas study had begun shortly after the First Opium War. In 1847, for instance, Yung Wing (Rong Hong, 1828–1912), a young Macanese who had received some education from local missionaries, spent three years in a seminary in the United States and then attended Yale College, becoming in 1854 its first Chinese graduate. After considerable debate the state decided to sponsor study in the United States. From 1872 batches of students, often the sons of men who worked in the new arsenals and shipyards, traveled under the auspices of the Chinese Educational Mission to Hartford, Connecticut, where they remained for several years. They lived with families in different towns in the Connecticut Valley, attending local high schools and playing baseball, as well as regularly studying classical Chinese texts. Back in China some commentators expressed the fear that the students were becoming too Americanized. But the main reason the mission came to an end in 1881 was American hostility to Chinese people. When the Annapolis Naval College and West Point Military Academy both refused to admit Chinese students, notwithstanding treaty provisions to the contrary, China called an end to the project and withdrew its students from the United States altogether.

Given these kinds of difficulties, many young Chinese went elsewhere to pursue their studies. In the 1880s some began to go to France and Britain. Most, including translator Yan Fu, were graduates of the Fuzhou shipyard's school, more mature and less impressionable than the young boys sent to America and better equipped to study the new scientific and technological subjects.

Even more than Europe or the United States, Chinese students preferred to pursue their education in Japan, which offered proximity and a sense of shared civilization. The preference for Japan was also to some extent a question of Asian pride. Japan had had some success in fending off the imperialists, and the Chinese felt a certain solidarity with the Japanese against the Western powers, at least until Japan defeated China in 1895. Young Chinese intellectuals hoped to use Japan as a shortcut to Western knowledge because its modernization was more advanced than China's. They also believed that anything the Japanese could do, they would soon be able to do better.

The exodus of Chinese students to Japan began in the 1870s; by 1905 as many as nine thousand were there, women as well as men. Initially most were officially sponsored, but increasingly many went privately to Japan to further their studies. It was not only the formal education that attracted them. Many were exposed to a much broader range of new ideas while in exile, since a number of Western works had already been translated into Japanese but not yet into Chinese. Moreover, in Japan Chinese students enjoyed much greater freedom of thought and expression about the Qing regime and the Chinese tradition than they would have had at home. In Japan, for instance, the future revolutionary leader Sun Yatsen formed his first anti-Qing alliances, while the intellectual and reformer Liang Qichao, in exile in Japan after 1898, was at liberty to inspire many of his fellow countrymen and women with an intense sense of nationalism.

On the whole Japan welcomed the Chinese students. From Japan's point of view, becoming an educational center for Chinese was part of a long-term project to expand Japanese interests in China. They hoped to forge links with the students, perhaps future leaders, by stressing a special relationship based on their common Asian culture. But by the turn of the century Japanese often made little secret of their personal disdain for Chinese students, with whom they had relatively little intimate contact. Hence many Chinese students, rather than become enamored of Japan, often came away disenchanted and strongly anti-Japanese. These sentiments formed part of the core of twentieth-century Chinese nationalism, as we shall see in the next chapter.

The generation that came to maturity around the turn of the century bridged the gap between those who received only a traditional Chinese-style classical education and those raised after the 1905 abolition of the examination system, whose education focused more on modern, technical subjects, foreign languages, and studies of the West. Many of this bridging generation were polymaths versed in both types of knowledge, like Cai Yuanpei (1868–1940) the radical and influential president of Beijing University in the 1910s, of whom a colleague later noted: "Before the age of twenty-nine [Cai] was totally versed in the old learning, at thirty he started to study science, at thirty-two he studied Japanese, at thirty-seven he started his study of German, taking his first trip to study philosophy and fine arts in Germany at the age of forty-one . . . at the age of forty-seven he traveled to France to study French."[13]

With the course of time, however, the balance of Chinese students' interest inclined more toward the new education and less and less toward the traditional curriculum.

Opium and Footbinding

The shift in education was accompanied by a shift in attitude toward both opium and footbinding. Chinese patriots identified opium addiction among men and footbinding among women as major sources of foreign denigration of their country. As Kang Youwei observed, ". . . all countries have international relations so that if one commits the slightest error the others ridicule and look down on it. Ours is definitely not a time of seclusion. Now China is narrow and crowded, has opium addicts and streets lined with beggars. Foreigners laugh at us for these things, and criticize us for being barbarians. There is nothing which makes us objects of ridicule so much as footbinding."[14]

Ridding the country of both opium and footbinding became a high priority among Chinese tormented by national weakness. At the same time, many foreign missionaries parted company from their more commercially minded fellow countrymen by expressing their moral opposition to the opium trade. Although arguably opium had helped make possible their own presence in China, it both sat ill with their Christian mission and hindered their conversion efforts because of addicts' unreliability.

The eradication of opium in China involved banning both its importation from overseas and the prohibition of domestic cultivation, for more opium now grew in China than was imported by the British. This posed a considerable challenge, given the complex networks of vested interests both within China and around the world and the by then massive numbers of addicts. But in 1906 an imperial edict forbade both consumption of the drug and its cultivation. The widespread determination to eliminate opium that was evident in China succeeded in favorably influencing international opinion. In Britain a changed political climate led to the gradual, if in some quarters reluctant, reduction of British opium exports to China.

Because of the difficulty of obtaining opium, many smokers soon began to switch to tobacco. The opium ban gave a tremendous boost to foreign tobacco companies seeking to make inroads into the China market, such as the British-American Tobacco Company, whose enormous success in persuading Chinese people to smoke cigarettes dated from this period. Still, opium trafficking continued to be big business, and addiction remained widespread.

At the same time that they were turning their attention to the opium problem, both Chinese patriots and Western missionaries dedicated considerable energy to campaigning against footbinding. Manchu women had been forbidden to bind their feet from the time of the conquest in the seventeenth century, and some of the scattering of male Chinese who advocated greater freedom for women in the eighteenth and earlier nineteenth centuries had written against footbinding. But toward the end of the nineteenth century a majority of Chinese women of all classes still wrapped their feet tightly from childhood, in conformity with long-standing ideals of beauty.

Footbinding caused the bones to malform, the feet to grow only a few inches altogether, and allowed women only to hobble around.

Apart from the issue of China's international image, many nationalist-minded Chinese concluded, first, that women with bound feet were a wasted resource and, second, that the crippling of Chinese women symbolized the condition of China itself. From there it was easy to imagine China the hapless victim of foreign rapists. The metaphors of a crippled nation and of violation emerged all the more starkly after the Boxer Uprising. Troops of the international force sent to relieve the siege of the Beijing legations were accused of large-scale rape. Thousands of women committed suicide, and it was easy to draw the implication, both literal and metaphorical, that they—and China—might have been saved if their feet had not been bound.

The antifootbinding movement was launched with the help of foreign missionaries, who continued to support the growing opposition to footbinding vigorously because they thought it cruel and un-Christian. They strongly discouraged it in convert families and refused to admit women with bound feet to their boarding schools. But missionary support for the movement was a mixed blessing because while it helped provide inspiration and organization, it also laid supporters open to the insidious charge of succumbing to alien influence.

The antifootbinding movement had gained momentum by the turn of the century. Tiny feet simply lost their chic and their erotic attraction. The daughters of intellectuals were the first to stop binding their feet. The government jumped on the bandwagon and came out against footbinding in 1902. Some women underwent the agony of unbinding their feet, either as a political protest or simply to be able to run in times of turmoil. By the 1920s one Chinese scholar observed that whereas in the past young women with natural feet had been unmarriageable, now those with bound feet were the unmarriageable ones. This observation was, however, truer in urban than in rural areas, where change in all aspects of life was much slower to take effect.

Progressive Chinese were particularly anxious that China not be represented abroad by women with bound feet. In 1903, when some women with bound feet were sent from Japanese-occupied Taiwan to an international exhibition in Osaka, a public outcry ensued on the mainland. Similar outrage greeted the display of women with bound feet at the world's fair in St. Louis in the following year. Chinese students in America sent written protests to Beijing, while the Chinese press fulminated against this public humiliation: "Who is so shameless as to exhibit those ugly things in a place to which a thousand nations on earth pay their attention."[15] As China struggled to stand up for itself against the world's contempt, women with bound feet were inappropriate representatives of the nation.

EARLY POPULAR ACTION AGAINST FOREIGNERS

Just as educated Chinese were becoming increasingly vocal in their resistance to the foreign powers, so ordinary men and women consistently displayed a readiness to take a stand on behalf of their country. The legacy of successful popular resistance to superior foreign power bequeathed by the 1841 stand against the British at Sanyuanli, even though the reality was rather less than the glorious triumph it became in later mythology, at least fostered a sense of possibilities. Although many instances of popular action undoubtedly were organized by members of the elite or the new bourgeoisie, ordinary Chinese participated in them with considerable vigor. Such was the case just over ten years after Sanyuanli, when Chinese in Xiamen (Amoy) rioted in protest after a British coolie merchant had attempted to retrieve his Chinese broker from the local police station. The broker had been in custody after his attempts to entrap young workers had prompted members of the community to set upon him.

Individuals sometimes acted against foreigners. In Hong Kong in 1867 a Chinese baker poisoned with arsenic the bread he supplied to European households, including the governor's mansion. Several hundred Europeans fell ill; in the aftermath indiscriminate arrests by the British acknowledged their vulnerability as a minority colonial authority. From the 1860s collective resistance in the form of labor unrest was fairly common in enterprises such as the Jiangnan Arsenal, where at least in the early days management might well be in the hands of foreigners. Such outbreaks suggested that Chinese workers had from the outset some sense both of their bargaining power and of the not necessarily benign effects of foreign influence.

One of the first major instances of mass action against foreigners took place in Hong Kong in 1884. Chinese dockworkers refused to service French ships freshly returned from destroying the newly constructed Chinese fleet that had been anchored at Fuzhou. Officials and gentry in Canton, in league with secret society members opposed to the Qing, exhorted patriotic Chinese to resist the French with all means available. They offered rewards, titles, and forgiveness of past offenses to anyone who would seize French munitions or murder a French commander. In addition, conscious that some Chinese had secretly been supplying the French with food and even working for them as spies, the Canton officials displayed placards that threatened death to traitors and dire punishment to their families. Their efforts hit home both because the families of many Hong Kong workers still lived in the Canton area, threatened with French attack, and because the warships interfered with trade and hence the people's livelihood. Hong Kong workers struck again in 1888 and 1895 against regulations imposed by the colonial authorities, who found themselves effectively powerless to overcome this type of concerted action.

A second major outbreak against foreigners took place in 1905, when deteriorating American treatment of Chinese immigrants prompted an anti-American boycott in China. The Exclusion Acts of 1882–1894 prohibited Chinese workers from entering the United States, including Hawaii and the Philippines after these fell under American control in 1898 and 1900 respectively. The treaty that had led to this legislation was due for renewal, but the Qing government bowed to popular pressure at home and refused to renew it. To support the government's stand, merchants and others called for a total boycott of American goods.

Dockworkers in Canton and workers and merchants in Wuhan, Nanjing, Tianjin, Xiamen, Hong Kong, and Shanghai all joined in the boycott, which lasted three months. Chinese students in the United States sent home funds to support the boycott. All kinds of people unexpectedly found themselves its targets; a Chinese dentist in Hong Kong, for instance, lost many patients because of his American education. But others who had direct business interests with Americans were often reluctant to jeopardize their economic well-being for patriotism's sake and declined to participate.

The boycott's geographic spread, its duration, and the evident strength of underlying feeling against the Americans took many people by surprise. In response to U.S. protests, Qing authorities posted announcements opposing the boycott, but they hung them upside down to indicate their lack of enthusiasm. The withdrawal of Chinese business from American companies gave a welcome, although often only short-lived, boost to their Chinese competitors. Moreover, the clear links to the Chinese community in America confirmed the vision of the early diplomats: that, in the overseas communities, China possessed a formidable national asset. Although the boycott eventually came to an end, it had made its point.

The third major antiforeign boycott was directed against Japan. Early in 1908 Chinese gunboats had seized a Japanese freighter, the *Tatsu Maru*, off Macao because it was smuggling weapons and ammunition into Canton. The vessel was taken to Canton, and the Japanese flag replaced by a Chinese one. Reaction was strong on both sides. The Japanese at once demanded an apology, an indemnity, the release of the freighter, the purchase of the cargo, and the punishment of the responsible officials. But influential Cantonese bombarded the Chinese Foreign Ministry with exhortations to stand firm. When the Qing caved in to the threat of Japanese gunboats, mass meetings held in Canton soon decided to stage a boycott against Japanese goods. With widespread support, the boycott spread to numerous cities where Japanese merchants were in business, including Canton itself, Hong Kong, and the overseas communities of Singapore, Manila, Honolulu, and Sydney, Australia. The boycott resulted in a considerable reduction of Japanese imports into China during its nine months. Even in British Hong Kong, where the colonial authorities severely punished leading boycotters, Japanese imports dropped by almost 24 percent over the preceding year, and anti-Japanese riots broke out.

Repeatedly humiliated by military defeat, compelled to operate internationally on Western terms, mockingly dismissed by the more powerful nations as both hopelessly corrupt and pathetically unable to pull itself out of its overwhelming inertia, China viewed the West with increasing ambivalence between the conclusion of the treaties of 1858–1860 and the outbreak of World War One in Europe. Chinese men and women ran the gamut from collective self-pity to envy of the wealth and power of the West. Yet among the large-scale mortifications were a number of less spectacular but significant triumphs: at the government level, for instance, the diplomatic successes and at the level of ordinary Chinese people, successful acts of resistance to the foreign powers.

As Chinese intellectuals began to learn about the West, there was almost always a specific focus to their studies. To be sure, they wanted to find out about the West in a general sense. But for some, part of the purpose of learning about the West was also to chart China's course into the future. They believed that the path to modernity did not carry an infinite range of possibilities but rather that they already had some sense of what "modern China" would look like. It would somehow resemble the West in Chinese guise. In this respect they differed from their counterparts in India, many of whom found objectionable any version of modernity derived from their British colonial overlords.

Some found Western values of power and domination unappealing. The prospect that a modernized China might well lose some of its peculiarly Chinese characteristics and come to resemble its oppressors too closely lay at the root of widespread Chinese attempts to draw a distinction between Western learning and Chinese values. At the same time as they wanted to learn from the West in order to imitate (and eventually to surpass) its might, in the early twentieth century even those intellectuals who avidly supported reform drew back from wholesale Westernization.

This point of view, especially widespread after 1895, gave rise to a famous formulation: "Chinese learning for the essence; Western learning for the practical knowledge"—in Chinese, *zhong xue wei ti, xi xue wei yong*, popularly known as *ti-yong*. This formulation represented a clear rejection of such Western belief systems as Christianity, in favor of a traditional Chinese worldview, at the same time as it acknowledged how beneficial foreign science and technology might be for China. Some version of *ti-yong* was raised virtually without exception whenever Chinese perceived that the precarious balance between autonomy and dependence that characterized much of this period had been thrown off kilter. The question was then, and has remained ever since, whether it was possible to separate Western ideologies from Western practical knowledge and methodologies.

CHAPTER SIX

Overcoming Habits of Mind, 1914–1949

> Throughout the world, like the voice of a prophet, has gone the word of Woodrow Wilson, strengthening the weak and giving courage to the struggling. And the Chinese have listened, and they too have heard. . . . They have been told that in the dispensation which is to be made after the war, unmilitaristic nations like China would have an opportunity to develop their culture, their industry, their civilization, unhampered. They have been told that secret covenants and forced agreements would not be recognized. They looked for the dawn of this new era; but no sun rose for China. Even the cradle of the nation [strategically critical Shandong] was stolen.
>
> Shanghai Students' Union,
> *The Students' Strike: An Explanation* (1919)[1]

In the first decade of the twentieth century nobody in China seriously thought that the Western powers and Japan would ever just "go away"; it seemed clear they were there to stay. The desire to push back imperialist encroachment was widespread, but it rarely included either any illusion that it might be possible to detach China from the rest of the world or any wish to do so. Such isolation had never existed in the past and was not now China's goal.

Nor did any question remain about the validity or desirability of using Western models; the issue was "how" rather than "whether." Opinion differed sharply about the best way to proceed. We have seen how the idea of selectively adopting such Western knowledge as seemed useful for Chinese national regeneration without also taking on Western cultural baggage, an idea referred to as *ti-yong*, gained currency in the late nineteenth century. But as China's industrialization progressed, reformers came to realize that the adoption of foreign technology came with cultural strings attached and that the two might prove inseparable. For cultural conservatives, the close links between Western practical knowledge, whose value they acknowledged, and Western culture, from which that knowledge had sprung, posed a thorny problem.

The growing number of cultural radicals, on the other hand, launched an urgent reappraisal of the Chinese tradition and its continuing relevance to modernity. Many thinkers had begun to conclude that the real origin of China's loss of power and prestige in the world lay not elsewhere, not with imperialism, but near at hand. They were haunted by the suspicion that traditional Chinese intellectual life had so stultified Chinese minds that the forces propelling Western nations into positions of wealth and power might altogether bypass China. Such suspicions were symptomatic of the enormous influence that Western disparagement of Chinese civilization had even on some defenders of the tradition. Westerners often referred to China's intellectual heritage as though it were a single, static entity but in reality, as Chinese thinkers well knew, it was rich and diverse. Yet ironically its native defenders sometimes were so unnerved by Western critiques that to some extent they acquiesced in them even when they knew them to be inaccurate.

This chapter describes some of the ways in which Chinese men and women set about overcoming diverse habits of mind—their own and those of the foreign powers—in the first half of the twentieth century. First, educated Chinese tried to overcome their own conventional mind-set about their own culture, to question their own long-held assumptions. Thinking in new ways and the struggle to find the most appropriate ways of thinking were perhaps the predominant characteristics of this period. Second, they wished to find practical means of overcoming the imperialists' patronizing derogation of their country and their effective denial of China's right to an independent voice. The powers, having bullied China for more than half a century, now took it for granted that they could continue to impose their will without too much trouble. For Chinese, the sense of possibilities had rarely been stronger. The prospect of one of those possibilities—extinction of the nation—was so excruciating that the search for a feasible alternative absorbed enormous energy.

Around the turn of the century the task of national renewal assumed a new sense of urgency. Among the most compelling ideas introduced from abroad was the theory of Social Darwinism, filtered into China through the nationalist-slanted translations of new-style intellectual Yan Fu. Social Darwinism propounded the idea of a struggle for survival among human societies, in which the "fittest" would emerge victorious. That "strong societies would survive, weak ones would perish" became pervasive as a way of thinking about China's fate. Under its influence, many people found alarmingly persuasive the view that if China did not strengthen itself, it would sooner or later succumb to stronger nations. Events already suggested that process was under way; stopping it became for many the central imperative.

All manner of Western ideologies flowed through China during its transformation from an imperial to a republican system. It was the special achievement of Chinese radical intellectuals to forge from these a creative synthesis that was distinctively Chinese despite its multifarious alien origins. The constant thread was an obsessive vision of a once more proud and respected nation. The desire to bring this dream to reality sustained China through several revolutions, pitiless political conflict, the brutalities of Japanese occupation, and protracted war, not to mention the growing ambiguities of a continued Western presence.

Empire to Republic

The foreigners' impact on China was still uneven. In the treaty ports, particularly Shanghai, the presence of a large, and growing, foreign community had introduced a whole new way of life. At least some Chinese began to adopt foreign ways in their leisure activities, for example, attending Western-style horse and dog races or theater performances where men and women mingled in the audience or dancing in the new dance halls. Also, in the treaty ports Chinese women were able to support themselves in ways unthinkable for their rural compatriots: They worked long hours in the foreigners' sweatshops or supported themselves by prostitution, a major growth industry, although some, targeted by aggressive marketing techniques, became addicted to new forms of gambling that ate into their meager earnings. In the hinterland traditional ways of life persisted, and foreign influences, while they impinged on people's consciousness, had a relatively limited impact on society, culture, and the economy. It remained possible to draw a clear distinction between a "modern," urban, mostly coastal China and a "backward," rural, interior.

Between 1895 and 1898 a nationwide coalition of young intellectuals protested to the young Guangxu Emperor, just then emerging from the seclusion enforced by his aunt Empress Dowager Cixi. The movement was led by two scholars from Guangdong province, philosopher and constitutional monarchist Kang Youwei and Liang Qichao. The protesters demanded wide-ranging reform of the military, the economy, education, industry, and government. Over the next few years they bombarded the emperor with proposals. The powers, they asserted, had first enslaved and then carved up Africa; China was next. It must learn from the methods of the West or perish. To the extent that domestic resources did not suffice to ensure national survival, China should draw as necessary on the technical skills and financial backing of the several million Chinese overseas. It should send Confucian scholars overseas to broadcast Chinese beliefs as a countermeasure to missionaries' determined efforts to convert it to Christianity.

In 1898 the Guangxu Emperor made a concerted effort to assert his independence by promulgating many of the reforms Kang, Liang, and others had been promoting over the past few years. Embracing the ideas of copying from abroad and deploying the overseas communities, he declared: "Everything is to be done after the manner of foreign countries, where the mercantile and trading classes are permitted to do as they please."[2]

But the reformers' success was short-lived. After a heady one hundred days of sweeping reform edicts, the empress dowager staged a crackdown, placing her imperial nephew under indefinite house arrest and executing those of the reformers who did not manage to escape abroad. She annulled all the reform decrees except, surprisingly, that establishing a national university (the Imperial University) along Western lines. Even then she tried to minimize its impact by installing a notoriously conservative director. He, however, appointed a well-known Western translator, the former director of the *Tongwen Guan*, as head of faculty. The curriculum they devised included the study of several foreign languages and Western science. The university gained steadily in prestige, especially after the abolition of the traditional examination system in 1905, and in 1912 it changed its name to the more modern-sounding Beijing University.

The creation of the university, along with the abolition of the examination system, transformed political culture by separating intellectuals from politicians, so that the government was no longer peopled primarily by scholars, and scholars were no longer so dependent on the government for their livelihood. But the new intellectuals, with their foreign knowledge and their imported values, were also much more alienated from ordinary Chinese people than their predecessors had been, just as critics of the new education had repeatedly charged would happen.

At the same time, continued translations of foreign literary works suggested to Chinese intellectuals literature's potential as an inspiration to all manner of people. Such translations were extremely popular both for the window on new worlds that they offered and for their power to suggest ways to transform China. The towering reformer Liang Qichao, for instance, fervently, if unrealistically, commended such works for their effectiveness as instruments of change:

> Formerly, at the start of reform or revolution in European countries, their leading scholars and men of great learning, their men of compassion and patriotism, would frequently record their personal experiences and their cherished views and ideas concerning politics in the form of fiction. Thus, among the population, teachers would read these works in their spare time, and even soldiers, businessmen, farmers, artisans, cabmen and grooms, and schoolchildren would all read them. It often happened that upon the appearance of a book a whole nation would change its views on current affairs. The political novel has been most instrumental in making the governments of America, England, Germany, France, Austria, Italy and Japan daily more progressive or enlightened.[3]

Nationalism, anarchism, liberalism, socialism, democracy, and individualism all jangled for attention in the minds of Chinese students and thinkers. Learned through translated texts or experienced at first hand by travelers overseas, these ideas meant different things to different people and changed dynamically over time. Often the Chinese language lacked the vocabulary to express the new ideas—there was, for example, no word in Chinese for "revolution"—so that new words had to be formulated to express them. These neologisms might be borrowed, for instance, from Japanese, for the process of translation and the importation of new ideas were well under way in Japan, or they might derive from European loanwords in Japanese; their meanings, however, might shift in the process of borrowing and, once adopted, did not necessarily remain fixed. Overall the most striking common denominator in intellectual life was a radically new open-mindedness and, concomitantly, a sustained surge of energy.

In the opening years of the twentieth century two main strands of political thought emerged, one bent on reform, the other on revolution. The reform movement was committed to gradual change and to exploration of a national constitution. Still spearheaded by Kang Youwei and Liang Qichao, in exile since the 1898 debacle, it drew on the example of the powerful liberal democratic nations of the West. The revolutionary movement was headed by another Cantonese, Sun Yatsen (1866–1925). Sun favored fortifying China with Western practical knowledge and immediately ridding China of the Manchus. The transformation of the political system was his first objective in a long-term nationalist agenda that would then turn its attention to the foreign presence. Raised in Hawaii, a graduate of the Hong Kong College of Medicine, and a Christian, Sun lived much of his life outside China. It was a mark of his international background that when Qing agents seized him in London, his medical school professor helped effect his release. Organizations Sun founded or ran staged a number of antidynastic uprisings throughout the last years of the Qing.

The reform movement and its revolutionary counterpart each derived considerable inspiration from abroad, and each competed for funding from overseas Chinese communities. The unprecedented mobilization of the Chinese diaspora for political movements in the home country marked a new and unanticipated tendency whose ramifications were unpredictable. It created a model that has resonated to the last decades of the twentieth century.

Intellectual ferment was intense among Chinese students in the first decade of the century. Especially in Japan, or in the relative security of the foreign concessions in Shanghai, they expressed their opinions in no uncertain terms. One of the most articulate was the Sichuanese student Zou Rong, only nineteen years old when he scathingly denounced the way in which China had degenerated from its former glory as a consequence of Manchu rule. An uncompromising revolutionary, he jeered at his fellow students for learning English "in order to enslave themselves to the foreign imperialists." Zou was soon arrested and tried in Shanghai's Mixed Court, whose jurisdiction extended to Chinese residents of the foreign settlements. Sentenced to imprisonment, he died in 1905; after the revolution he was posthumously honored by Sun Yatsen himself. Zou Rong's manifesto reads in part: "Had we not been trampled underfoot by sinister scoundrels like Nurhaci, Abahai and Fulin [respectively founder, consolidator, and first emperor of the Qing dynasty], we would long ago have thrown off the Manchu yoke, and England, Russia, Germany and France, who are now making inroads into us and dividing us up with bared teeth and flying claws, would now be cowering with bated breath, fearful of our power and terrified of our might. . . ."[4]

In the last decade of imperial rule, as we have seen, the Qing sought to jump on the bandwagon of patriotism by introducing a number of reforms, including several they had rejected in 1898. They also sought to revise the overall context of China's relations with the foreign powers. This task was made easier by the growing likelihood of conflict in Europe, which distracted the powers' attention from China. The exceptions were the United States and Japan. Neither seemed so formidably imperialistic as the other powers, Japan mainly because it was Asian, and the United States because presumably it would not impose on others the colonial experience it itself had so disliked, although recent U.S. activities in Hawaii and the Philippines undercut that presumption.

Hawaii and the Philippines were among a number of places that loomed large in Chinese intellectuals' increasingly sophisticated conceptualization of the world. A new genre of writing about nations and nationalism focused attention on various countries around the world that Chinese intellectuals referred to as "lost," in every case because of imperialist rapacity. Among others, these countries included Egypt, the prey of wily maneuvering by Britain and France; Poland and Turkey, victims of Russian expansionism; Annam (Vietnam), now in French hands; and India, Burma, and the Transvaal, devoured by British colonialism. These countries came to symbolize what China at all costs must not become. Although Chinese felt a certain solidarity with each, on the other hand, they criticized them on a number of grounds, including the failure to update their traditions, overcome political disagreements, and change their institutions.

India in particular occupied a highly ambivalent position in the minds of many Chinese. Despised for capitulating to Britain and serving as its lackey—as manifested very conspicuously by the presence of Sikh policemen and guards in the foreign settlements in China—India was also occasionally admired as the wellspring of Buddhism, which by now formed an integral part of Chinese culture. But the dominant rhetoric of the times, fueled by an element of racism, held India up as the pathetic antithesis of the West, whose ancient traditions had served it ill in the modern world.

The institution of empire, and the Qing house, fell in 1911, to be succeeded by a republic. A leading priority of the new regime was to free China from foreign domination, but this was not easily to be achieved, for foreign influences and the threat of foreign intercession in Chinese affairs were simply everywhere. Before long the republican experiment fell victim to self-seeking corruption and sheer brutality. By the mid-teens Sun Yatsen was running an opposition government based in Canton, whose presence on the national political scene remained for some time relatively insignificant. Elsewhere power was fragmented among former supporters of the discredited first president, Yuan Shikai (1859–1916), most of whom owed their standing to military force and used whatever means were available to secure their own positions. Among other things, these "warlords" competed for foreign backing without much regard to nationalist imperatives. The republican revolution seemed to have achieved little more than the overthrow of the Manchus and the destruction of any semblance of order.

The sharp deterioration of social conditions and the travesty of the new politics that marked much of the 1910s and 1920s pushed many Chinese intellectuals to near despair. Widespread political demoralization showed itself in boycotts and demonstrations. Intellectuals began to explore possible choices for more radical transformations at home even as they sought to restore China to a leading role on the world's stage. By the end of the 1910s both anarchism and Marxism-Leninism had begun to take on a new allure; in particular, for many radical Chinese, Lenin's analysis of colonialism as the overseas expansion of capitalist exploitation—the theory of imperialism—and the practical success of the Russian Revolution of 1917 both held considerable appeal.

In the meantime in 1914 Japan had stepped into the breach left by the Western powers, now fighting one another in World War One, and assumed control of Shandong, where German influence had disintegrated because of the exigencies of war at home. In 1915, in return for substantial loans to Yuan Shikai (who had already received massive foreign funding), Japan pressed its Twenty-one Demands on China. A foretaste of the future, these called for special Japanese economic privileges in China; for rights of residence, property ownership, and extraterritorial legal privileges in interior portions of southern Manchuria and eastern Inner Mongolia; and for other special rights, including the right for Japan to station its own police in parts of China historically prone to disputes between Chinese and Japanese. Despite vociferous opposition by Chinese desperate to avoid having their country join Korea and Taiwan as Japanese protectorates, Yuan capitulated. As Chinese realized that Japan's position in China was substantially strengthened by these moves, their resentment against Japan came to a simmering point from which it did not recede for decades.

China and Versailles

During World War One almost one hundred thousand Chinese laborers traveled to France to serve the Allied cause. Although the Allies, from habit, still had little confidence in Chinese fighting abilities, they used Chinese manpower for menial jobs, such as digging trenches and building hospitals, to free up more young Europeans to go to the battlefront, where so many had already perished. Like other combatants, the Chinese laborers worked in often horrendous conditions. Several thousand died in Europe, but many of the survivors learned to read and write with the help of such groups as the YMCA and were able to accumulate some savings before they returned to China. They were promising candidates for political organization; returned laborers were in fact among the first to organize labor unions in China in 1919 and 1920.

China generally expected that in return for the contributions of Chinese laborers to the Allied war effort, the recent Japanese encroachments would be abrogated in the peace treaties concluded at war's end. They took heart from the declarations of U.S. President Woodrow Wilson about the self-determination of nations. Therefore, in 1919, when in the Treaty of Versailles (in accordance with secret agreements made with Chinese warlords purporting to represent the whole nation), Britain and France confirmed Japanese control over Germany's former sphere of influence in Shandong and over its other recent Chinese acquisitions, Chinese were profoundly shaken, as we can see from the quotation with which this chapter opens. The return from Germany to the Beijing Observatory of the astronomical instruments removed in 1901 offered scant consolation.

In May 1919 thousands of students demonstrated in Beijing and in at least two hundred other locations across the country. Shanghai merchants closed their businesses for an entire week. Workers came out on strike in as many as forty factories. Many foreigners then in China shared in the sense of national betrayal and expressed great dismay at the direction of the national mood in China, evoking fears that played on international apprehensions as the result of the recent success of the Russian Revolution.

Months of unrest culminated in China's refusal to sign the peace treaty. Largely irrelevant in practical terms—for like it or not, the reality was that Japan was now firmly entrenched in Shandong—the refusal sent a clear message that Versailles would be the last of the unequal treaties. But the implications reached beyond the immediate source of contention, as the early Communist leader Qu Qiubai (1899–1935) noted in 1919:

> The patriotic movement had actually a deeper meaning than mere patriotism. The taste of colonialism in its full bitterness had never come home to the Chinese until then, even though we had already had the experience of several decades of foreign exploitation behind us. The sharp pain of imperialistic oppression then reached the marrow of our bones, and it awakened us from the nightmares of impractical democratic reforms. The issue of the former German possessions in Shandong, which started the uproar of the student movement, could not be separated from the larger problem.[5]

New Culture, New Politics

The galvanizing intellectual movement of the first third of the twentieth century, named for the demonstrations that began on May 4, 1919, sought to find a solution to the "larger problem." The May Fourth Movement took place approximately between

1916 and 1926. It was driven by a passionate desire to take concrete steps to wipe out foreign domination and to reinvigorate China, if necessary through a complete cultural and political transformation.

May Fourth, an iconoclastic attack on every aspect of the Chinese tradition, locked culture and politics together. When May Fourth activists evaluated the Chinese moral heritage by the standards of Western liberalism and by its scientific methods, they found it absolutely wanting and, as such, an insurmountable barrier to progress. Nothing was sacred anymore. The linchpins of Chinese civilization—the family, the classical texts, the accepted codes of behavior, and so on—all were subject to the most thoroughgoing examination and reassessment, undertakings whose ultimate purpose was the revival of the nation. Among the clearest indications that May Fourth divided old China from new China was a novel emphasis on youth as the key instrument of national salvation. This marked a distinct break from the classic veneration of the older generation.

This focus on youth was signaled by a clarion call issued in 1916 by Chen Duxiu (1879–1942), dean of Beijing University. In the first issue of his quickly influential periodical *New Youth*, Chen called openly for a revolution in moral values, institutions, and habits of mind. Implicit, and sometimes explicit, in Chen's writings was the desire to emulate not just the methods and the ideas but the dynamism of the West. But the often ill-defined object of desire—"the West"—was at the same time the object of tremendous resentment and often ambivalence.

This inconsistency was indeed not new, and it remained highly visible as May Fourth evolved during the late teens and twenties. As much as Chen and his May Fourth cohort were riveted by the material strength and the prosperity of the West, as their nineteenth-century forebears had been before them, many educated Chinese perceived imperfections in Western societies. Their political systems might be democratic, but their politicians were corrupt and self-seeking. Liberal democracies themselves were by no means perfect, as the Versailles betrayal revealed. The religion from which missionaries derived their sense of superiority was in fact no more than superstition. Individualism could cause tremendous ethical problems and, besides, could not be reconciled with Marxist theories about class. The extraordinary bloodbath of the Great War suggested that not all the end products of Western science and technology were so desirable. The ambivalence derived from these kinds of perceptions was sometimes submerged among radical Chinese, but it was never very far from the surface.

New Youth magazine was only the most famous of hundreds of new periodicals launched in the May Fourth period, most often by Chinese educated abroad. These served a dual purpose: first, the introduction of Western thought and culture and, second, the provision of a forum for debating the burning questions of the day. Most such publications had the word "New" or "Young" in their names. They covered a broad range of ideas—isms—imported from the West: Marxism, feminism, liberalism, anarchism, relativism, Ibsenism, utilitarianism, socialism, and so on. As a consequence of the ever-expanding number of translations—of works of Western literature, ideas, and political theory—circulating by the early to middle 1920s, familiarity with other cultures became the standard among the intelligentsia; a cosmopolitan sophistication was no longer unusual.

The nationalist origins of May Fourth led to a visible shift in attitude that pervaded all aspects of daily life. For example, whereas earlier supporters of Western-inspired change had often sported Western-style clothing, radical young men and women of the May Fourth era were much more likely to wear Chinese-style garments newly redesigned to suit the modern era. Sun Yatsen himself and his American-educated wife, Song Qingling, embodied this trend. A 1915 wedding photograph shows them dressed in European style—Song Qingling in a tailored jacket and skirt, a blouse with a lace collar, cameo jewelry, and high heels, Sun in a Western suit, but photographs from the 1920s, when Sun was leader of a Nationalist party that was growing in power, consistently show them dressed in Chinese style.

After the initial excitement of *New Youth* radicalism, the intellectual currents of the May Fourth Movement went in various directions. Chen Duxiu, the magazine's initiator, was one of several who, in the search for a theoretical basis for a new Chinese culture, eventually abandoned the Western liberal values he had originally espoused in favor of Marxism-Leninism. A split in the movement was already evident by 1918, when the views of Chen and his more radical associates were ranged against those of others who, under the leadership of Hu Shi (1891–1962), remained more liberally inclined. Hu as much as Chen supported the adoption of the most rationalistic aspects of the Western tradition, symbolized by the May Fourth slogan "Science and democracy," to help solve China's problems. But under the influence of the American educator John Dewey, Hu criticized (in a famous essay entitled "Problems versus Isms") the radicals' tendency to claim comprehensive solutions to the problems of an entire society rather than to focus attention on gradually resolving particular problems in specific areas of need.

Hu Shi and others arranged for a number of leading foreign thinkers to visit China in the early 1920s. They included John Dewey, the British pacifist philosopher Bertrand Russell, and the Nobel Prize–winning Indian poet Rabindranath Tagore. Chinese intellectuals seeking to reassess their civilization's place in world history thus were able to draw on an extraordinarily variegated range of ideas.

The range of responses to Tagore's message can serve to give us some sense of the complexity of intellectual life during the May Fourth period. Briefly, Tagore proposed that the civilizations of India and China should not abandon the distinctive characteristics of Asian civilization, especially spirituality, for the destructive materialism of the West. Instead they should put their faith in that spiritual nature as well as in the redeeming power of individual self-sacrifice, in the poetic spirit, and in the overarching desire for freedom. In the eyes of some Chinese intellectuals, Tagore's identity as an Indian—a nonwhite representative from Britain's largest overseas colony—lent him a special credibility. These admirers had become critical of Western science and scientific methodology, which they had come to regard as more of a mirage than a panacea; in that context Tagore's eloquent pleas to elevate "Asian spiritualism" over "Western materialism" in the name of patriotism seemed especially pertinent. Others took a different view and spoke up for the merits of China's own particular path of historical development. They theorized that to force China into the mold of either the materialist West or the self-negating civilization of India would be a disaster. From this perspective, China had simply developed along a different track, which was not necessarily wrong or worse. For a third group, Tagore's identity and his message were more problematic. They found it objectionable that he should lecture them about the spiritual benefits of suffering and sacrifice in the face of foreign domination when to them the ever more appealing tenets of orthodox theory made plain that armed struggle was the only true solution. Still others found that the past Tagore harked back to, while perhaps romantic, was an absolutely inadequate alternative to the progressive present, as India's subjection by the British demonstrated.

WORK-STUDY

By the late teens and early twenties it was the turn of the second and even third generations of young Chinese to study overseas. Not only did the numbers, including the numbers of young women among them, increase, but also the nature of their experience changed. For example, during those decades more than two thousand young Chinese students, many of whom had already been exposed to the new radicalism, traveled to France as part of a work-study scheme. The intention was that they would perform both mental and manual labor. Scholars such as the Beijing University president Cai Yuanpei, who organized the programs, regarded such a combination as suitable to the new China, but the pairing was also deeply iconoclastic because of the classical notion, formulated by Mencius, one of the leading classical Confucian thinkers, that those who labor with their minds rule over those who perform physical labor. Apart from thus breaking with tradition, the work-study students, it was hoped, would acquire an appropriately modern outlook by living in France, admired by many as the epicenter of modernity. From a practical point of view, they would also finance their studies by working in French factories, where labor remained in short supply as the result of the slaughter of the war.

The original intention had been that the work-study students would contribute to China's national salvation by bringing home knowledge of Western technology which they would acquire both through their studies and through their working experience. But in practice the crosscurrents of this period brought about a distinct shift. Many of the Chinese students had links to the Chinese Communist Party, founded in 1921, and what they learned in the factories of Europe were not only manual skills but new forms of political ideology and organization. In the wake of the disillusion with Western liberalism occasioned by Versailles, and in parallel with May Fourth developments back home, then, they began to explore in more depth a range of foreign ideologies, including Marxism and Leninism, as a means of articulating their still embryonic notions of how to resuscitate China.

Chinese students in France and elsewhere could hardly help being affected by political developments in their host countries, some of which they had the opportunity to assess at first hand. Some gained their first experience of labor strikes while abroad; a few even formed Communist cells simultaneously with but independent of developments back home. For many, it was a time when they began to translate into action their growing sense of political commitment. This could take many forms. One Chinese student, for instance, expressed his growing radicalism by taking time out from his studies at the Paris Conservatory to attend meetings of Chinese workers, where he played the socialist anthem, "the Internationale," on his violin.

Once back in China, a majority of returned students entered politics. A number of leading figures of twentieth-century Chinese politics emerged from their numbers, including Zhou Enlai (1898–1976), who studied in Japan, France, and Germany between 1918 and 1924, and Deng Xiaoping (1904–1997), who studied in France and briefly in the Soviet Union in the early 1920s. Often their common overseas experience and the reality that linguistic and cultural problems threw them on one anothers' company created lifelong bonds between future national leaders. But although some regarded a study sojourn overseas as a prized revolutionary credential, future Communist leader Mao Zedong (1893–1976), who spent the 1920s gaining experience as a political organizer in China, claimed his very lack of any such experience was a special virtue.

In any event, political skills learned abroad stood students in good stead back in China. For the anti-imperialist impetus of May Fourth reached well beyond Chinese students and began to show signs of a class-based orientation. Many workers participated in the demonstrations and boycotts of 1919, and before long a distinctive labor movement was under way. Both economic and nationalist motivations underlay the new labor activism, which was strongest in Shanghai and Canton, where industry and foreign enterprises were the most extensive.

The first major evidence of the new labor organization was the Hong Kong seamen's strike of 1922. Although the strikers' grievances against their shipper employers were primarily economic, the strike's nationalist overtones were unmistakable. Within a few weeks it had spread to most other sectors of the Hong Kong work force, including domestic servants, rickshaw pullers, tramway workers, vegetable sellers, waiters, dockworkers, and others. When British shippers tried to bypass the strikers by buying in Canton, dockworkers refused to load their vessels. More widespread and better organized than its nineteenth-century antecedents, the strike spread rapidly to other ports in Guangzhou province, while in Shanghai the new Communist Labor Secretariat worked to block the recruitment of replacement workers. Overseas Chinese as well as men and women still in China sent funds and otherwise provided material aid to the strikers. The strike ended with the capitulation of the Hong Kong government, leaving Chinese workers to savor their newfound political power.

Patriotism permeated much of Chinese society, revealing itself in different ways. By the early 1920s, for instance, the more than one million Chinese troops under arms occasionally showed signs of latent hostility to foreign domination. For the most part they fought one another in a series of warlord wars and did not turn their weapons against foreigners. Nonetheless, they timed their annual military maneuvers to coincide with the anniversary of the eight-nation expedition against the Boxers in 1900, a choice that suggested a willingness to exploit an opportunity to display their fundamental antagonism toward foreigners.

After the summer of 1925 hostility to foreigners became overt. On May 30 of that year British-led Sikh and Chinese police in Shanghai fired into a crowd of Chinese demonstrators protesting the killing of a Chinese worker in a labor dispute at a Japanese factory. Labor unrest had proliferated, despite the energetic attempts of both warlords and employers to suppress it. Dozens died in Shanghai and in related demonstrations in Canton. The immediate aftermath was a marked swing against the foreigners, as almost all those resident in China noted in their letters home. In what became known as the May Thirtieth Movement, waves of strikes and demonstrations swept the country, while in Hong Kong another general boycott and strike against the British lasted a full fifteen months. Students withdrew from foreign schools and colleges, which they assailed as a creation of cultural imperialism intended to lure Chinese students away from proper nationalist sentiment. Christian endeavors of all kinds became once again the object of attack.

Above all, the preoccupation with the West, however complicated, provided Chinese with a new perspective on China itself. The function of the West for China in the May Fourth era was primarily to make it possible for Chinese to stand back from their own culture and see it from an outsider's point of view. But although the purpose was the salvation of the nation, embracing an alien perspective naturally laid the process all the more open to criticism on the part of both cultural conservatives and nationalist revolutionaries, who each accused the new iconoclasts of in effect betraying their own heritage.

May Fourth was full of contradictions. For instance, while foreign imperialism provoked activists' rancor, at the same time it provided rich sources of opposition to Western domination. Chinese activists also derived from the West much of their intellectual ammunition against the prevalent beliefs of the indigenous tradition. Moreover, the Japanese model was as galling as it was inspiring. The truly radical realization was that the Chinese Revolution had to transcend both the modern West and traditional China, but its full articulation came only later.

When May Fourth radicals turned abroad to arm themselves against the powerful ruling Confucian ideology, they ran the risk of inadvertently replacing one form of domination by another. For example, many May Fourth men championed issues of women's emancipation and equality, seeking to replace Chinese attitudes toward women with "modern" Western ones. But the reality was that this quest, while it may have been politically liberating for its male advocates, did not necessarily bring Chinese women the complete liberation from patriarchy they desired. To the contrary, even after they were freed, along with their male counterparts, from the oppressive weight of the Chinese past, Chinese women's newfound release from the burdens of their own tradition often liberated them only to be subjugated in new, Western-style ways. As a result, some Chinese women sought to draw a distinction between the liberation of women and the liberation of China that nationalism aimed to achieve. They rejected the symbolism that equated the fate of Chinese women with the fate of China itself because its practical consequence seemed to be deferral of the woman question in favor of the national question. These issues became even more acute during the war against Japan and World War Two.

THE GUOMINDANG, THE CHINESE COMMUNISTS, AND THE SOVIET UNION

The experience of Versailles discredited the northern warlords who had purported to make agreements with the powers about former German territories in China. It also gave tremendous impetus to Sun Yatsen and the Nationalists as the revolutionary alternative. The Nationalists' standing was further boosted by attention from the brand-new Soviet Union, where the successful Bolshevik Revolution of 1917 offered a possible source of inspiration.

Within a year of that revolution, the Soviet government contacted Sun Yatsen. It planned to use his influence to muster popular support in China for its own territorial ambitions, although publicly it expressed the hope of creating an international revolutionary alliance against Western and Japanese imperialism. For Sun, the advantage of an alliance with the Russians was that it might help compel the other foreign powers to recognize as China's legitimate ruling authority his government based in the south, rather than the northern warlord regime. His support for democratic socialist principles made such an alliance seem only natural, despite the fact that most of his supporters found Soviet views on issues such as class struggle unpalatable. Besides, the Soviet Union provided funding and military aid and training to the Guomindang (GMD), without which it was unlikely to make much progress.

The Russians also contacted radical sympathizers such as Chen Duxiu. The enormous prestige that their own credentials as leaders of the Bolshevik Revolution gave them among budding Communist movements worldwide was a compelling reason for the early Chinese Communist Party, founded in 1921 by Chen and others in Shanghai's French Concession, to acknowledge the authority of the Soviet-controlled Communist International (Comintern). At the same time, they had no intention of becoming mere satellites of either the Comintern or the Soviet Union.

At Comintern urging, the Chinese Communist Party agreed in the first place to form an alliance with Sun Yatsen's Nationalists and then to remain in the alliance despite deepening misgivings. It did so partly because it was desperate for Comintern funding and partly because it was not sufficiently well established to have the confidence to break free of domination by the acknowledged leaders of world communism. While the situation in China was showing no signs of improvement, any moves toward revolution were sure to meet vigorous resistance on the part of an alliance forming between the reinvigorated imperialists and indigenous Chinese capitalists, whose economic interests tended to override any nationalist concerns. That made the need for external support all the more pressing. Chinese Communists felt therefore that on the whole the expediency of alignment with the Soviet Union transcended considerations of autonomy, even though they were well conscious of the anomaly of forming an alliance with foreigners while proclaiming an explicitly nationalist agenda.

From the Comintern's point of view, what was good for the Chinese Communists, who might never amount to much nationally, was less important than what suited Soviet purposes. It preferred to remain allied with Sun's Guomindang, which it thought had a better chance of achieving national power in China or certainly of doing so before the still-fledgling Communists did. Soviet and Comintern insistence on an alliance between the Chinese Communists and the Nationalists also had to do with the growing rift in the Soviet Union between Stalin and Trotsky. Trotsky had denounced the CCP's cooperation with the bourgeois Nationalists; his support for a Communist breakaway thus made such a split, by definition, anathema to Stalin, irrespective of any inherent merits.

Chinese radicals felt all the more attracted to the Bolshevik model after the new Soviet Union publicly announced in 1920 its unilateral cancellation of the rights claimed by its imperial predecessors under the unequal treaties. But the Soviet Union was playing a tricky game. The 1920 announcement was effective propaganda, but in a series of almost simultaneous secret agreements made with the northern warlords, the Soviet Union ensured that for some time Russia's earlier treaty privileges did not in fact disappear. For all their rhetoric against imperialism, in other words, the new Soviet authorities entertained ambitions of empire in East Asia not vastly different from those of the czars or from those of the Western powers and Japan. They had no intention of abandoning Russian claims to territory in Mongolia and Manchuria. They pursued this policy both to strengthen the Soviet Union against hostile foreign powers and because they wanted a firm foothold from which to train native leaders for the next wave of socialist revolutions, which they thought most likely to take place in Asia.

In partial furtherance of these aims, the Soviet Union also concluded a series of secret agreements with Japan in 1925, upholding Japan's Twenty-one Demands, even as they encouraged the Chinese Nationalists and Communists to step up their agitation against Western and Japanese imperialism in the context of the May Thirtieth Movement. This agitation served a number of purposes. On the one hand, it helped divert international attention from Russian activities on China's northern frontiers. The deception was important because the Western powers, wary that the USSR might be creating a special relationship with China by virtue of its apparent abrogation of its treaty rights, were inclined to take steps so as not to propel China into the Bolshevik camp. On the other hand, the agitation contributed significantly to a resurgence of Guomindang power, as its politicians vied with one another to demonstrate their patriotism by displaying ever-greater resolution in the face of foreign domination. By injecting nationalistic fervor into the ranks of the working classes, it also gave a vigorous leg up to the still embryonic Communist Party, whose membership began to swell dramatically. The USSR's supposed support of the Chinese Communists also helped the latter gain legitimacy at a critical moment in its development.

Chinese Communist misgivings about the united front with the Guomindang proved well founded. In 1927 Sun Yatsen's successor as leader of the Guomindang, Tokyo- and Moscow-educated Chiang Kaishek, concluded that Communist gains in the wake of the May Thirtieth Movement ran counter to his goals for personal power and national reconstruction. He decided to take dramatic action to consolidate his own position and eliminate the threat of a Communist takeover altogether. In the ensuing crackdown tens of thousands of people, Communist Party members and sympathizers and worker and peasant activists, perished at the hands of Guomindang troops. This purge received an influx of funding from contributions, part voluntary, part forced, made by Shanghai capitalists who feared the impact that Communist labor organization would have on the profitability of their businesses. It marked the beginning of two decades in which Chiang Kaishek repeatedly sought ways to eliminate communism in China, at virtually any cost.

For Communist survivors of this cataclysm, which an earlier severance of the GMD-CCP alliance would surely have mitigated, if not avoided altogether, the disaster demonstrated the perils of trying to transcend national differences in the cause of international solidarity against Western and Japanese imperialism. The CCP had stayed in the alliance only at Soviet insistence; its subsequent quest to create specifically Chinese versions of socialism and communism were in part the consequence of their deep mistrust of Soviet and Comintern authority after 1927. In sum, the Soviet Union's complex and sometimes paradoxical role in Chinese politics during the 1920s spawned a legacy of profound mistrust on the part of the Chinese Communists.

Chiang's decision to part company with the Communists must be set against the turn of events in relation to the foreign presence in China. Since early in the century the foreign powers had promised in principle to rescind at least the most objectionable portions of the unequal treaties: extraterritoriality and foreign control of various tariffs. But progress had been slow. Germany had involuntarily lost the right to extraterritoriality in China following World War One; the Russians had voluntarily abandoned it in 1924. The United States, by remitting the Boxer indemnity, had at least shown evidence of good intentions. During the 1920s China made considerable further advances toward abrogating foreign rights and privileges. By now the powers, shaken in their moral and military certitudes by the devastation of the Great War, were ready to recognize, at least in principle, the claims of Chinese nationalism. At the 1922 Washington Conference they made arrangements intended gradually to restore full sovereignty to China, but for various reasons these were never fully implemented. The delay only contributed to Chinese resentment.

This resentment was no longer something the foreign powers could laughingly disregard. Gunboat diplomacy was no longer an option. Not only were they themselves unwilling to enter lightly into a China war, but also the evidence showed that Chinese armies now were a force to be reckoned with. Thirty years after the end of the First Sino-Japanese War, Chinese strategy and tactics had had time to catch up with military industrialization. Moreover, a flood of World War One surplus matériel had found its way to China despite attempted Western bans. In an era of warlordism the military had become a much more powerful force in Chinese society. Chinese had also gained a lot of experience in fighting. Among the foreign powers, only Japan was at all likely to risk armed engagement in China.

Western willingness to make concessions gathered momentum after the blossoming of Chinese hostility to imperialism in 1925. Feelings ran especially high in Shanghai, not just because of the strong foreign presence or because the May Thirtieth incident had taken place there but because the city had become a hotbed of vice of all kinds, with the connivance and support of the Westerners who controlled part of the city. Although some attempts were made to clean up Shanghai, it offered countless jurisdictional loopholes, as the result of its multiplicity of municipal authorities and the elaborate network of corrupt collaboration between gangsters and the various police forces and municipal councils. Chinese newspapers accused the foreign authorities of indifference to the corruption of Chinese society, citing the kidnapping and sale of women and children, the destitution of the already impoverished through casino and racetrack gambling, and a flourishing sex industry found at every level of society. It seemed that if the foreigners could not extinguish the nation by military force, they would do their best to do so by steadily destroying its social fabric.

By 1930 China had recovered tariff autonomy from the powers, one of the most irksome of the rights yielded by treaty. It had reclaimed control of some of the foreign concessions, sometimes by mutual agreement and sometimes de facto after spontaneous outbreaks of violence. It was also negotiating the termination of extraterritoriality, although objections from some members of the foreign community stalled negotiations, which then were shelved indefinitely by the 1931 Japanese invasion of Manchuria.

Supporters of the Guomindang were less antagonistic toward the foreigners than were the Chinese Communists, although they regarded the Communists, dominated as they seemed to be by the Soviet-based Comintern, as themselves little more than instruments of expansion-minded foreigners. A number of influential Chinese saw some advantage to the presence of Western establishments in China, either because they hoped that they might prove a desirable counterweight to Japanese aggression or because they preferred the idea of obtaining financial aid from the Western powers and Japan to obtaining it from the Soviet Union. They feared the spread of bolshevism in China much more than they feared foreign capitalism, from which they thought it might be possible to derive some advantage. At the same time, Chiang Kaishek still thought it expedient to keep open the lines of communication with the Soviet

Union, for he aimed to use Moscow as a lever against the Chinese Communists, whom they appeared to control.

FLIRTING WITH FASCISM UNDER NATIONALIST RULE, 1927–1937

Once Chiang Kaishek had ruptured relations with the Communists, he was forced to look beyond the Soviet Union for his principal overseas support. German advisers soon stepped into the breach. If nothing else, China and Germany had in common their ill-treatment by the Allied powers after World War One. Each saw in the other a long-term means to recoup some of their losses. German aid to China began with military supplies and advice, as Chiang began to reorganize and reequip his army on the basis of principles that had proved successful both in Prussia and in Japan, which had itself followed the Prussian model. During the course of the 1930s Chiang's government reached a series of secret agreements with Germany to exchange German military and industrial supplies for Chinese raw materials that the Germans would use for rearmament. But this lasted only until German fears of the Soviet Union prompted an alliance with Japan, already well established as China's enemy. The program came to a definitive end as the Germans began to move in the direction of war.

Chiang Kaishek derived inspiration for some of his most notorious programs of the 1930s from abroad, particularly from the totalitarian regimes gaining power in Italy and Germany; he also admired some aspects of Stalin's Soviet Union. Some of their techniques conformed to Chiang's basic military orientation; he had formerly directed the Whampoa Military Academy, from which many of the leaders of both the Guomindang and the Communist Party emerged. In 1934 he launched a New Life Movement, using as his advance guard an often brutal organization known as the Blue Shirts (whose name recalled Mussolini's Black Shirts). The New Life Movement exhorted Chinese to stand up straight, not to spit, to be punctual, to button up their clothes, not to eat noisily, and to wash their faces in icy water. Chiang intended such regimentation would get China back on its feet:

> [The New Life Movement] is to thoroughly militarize the lives of the citizens of the entire nation so that they will cultivate courage

> and swiftness, the endurance of suffering and a tolerance for hard work, and especially the habit and ability of unified action, so that they will at any time sacrifice for the nation . . . in the home, the factory, and the government office, everyone's activities must be the same as in the army . . . in other words, there must be obedience, sacrifice, strictness, cleanliness, accuracy, diligence, secrecy . . . and everyone together must firmly and bravely sacrifice for the group and for the nation. . . .

Although fascism later fell into discredit, in the 1930s many people around the world saw it as a possible solution to mounting social and political problems. But the tilt toward fascism did not bode well for the democratic institutions towards which the Nationalist Party had once claimed to aspire. Chiang's calls for a "sense of national superiority and faith in the leader" were of course tailor-made for an authoritarian, nationalistic party headed by an autocratic and ambitious leader.[6]

The Guomindang was not, then, wholly opposed to foreign ideas and ideologies, but it sought to be selective about which foreign ideas should be allowed to enter China. The Blue Shirts, for instance, frowned on "cultural decadence" imported from abroad, both because they considered it unconducive to effective regimentation and because Nationalist propaganda drew a clear connection between such permissiveness and the leftist political views they regarded as anathema. Such decadence could be deemed to manifest itself, for example, in wearing Western clothing—sartorial patriotism again—or in dancing to modern music. Under the Blue Shirt reign of terror, offenders were liable to physical violence inflicted without warning, while arrests and political assassinations became commonplace. Ironically, a significant percentage of the Guomindang's revenues and police support came from Shanghai vice in its various manifestations, the most egregious examples of just the kind of activity the New Life Movement claimed to find so abhorrent.

Nationalist goals sometimes made for strange bedfellows. Collaboration with foreigners played a part in the many campaigns against decadence and political dissidence that punctuated the Nationalist era. Under the Qing, foreign settlements in the treaty ports, such as Shanghai's French Concession and the International Settlement, had once offered a safe haven from imperial authority. But French and British authorities now lagged only slightly behind

Chiang Kaishek in their aversion to communism. In the areas under their jurisdiction, they were ready to cooperate in enforcing laws against Communists and other naysayers.

Irony too dogged the flirtation with foreign ideologies. Germany's alliance with Japan eventually forced Chiang into the Allied camp, so that in World War Two China was on the opposite side from the fascist countries he had once sought to emulate. Despite Guomindang links first with the Soviet Union and then with early Nazi Germany, China provided an important haven for refugees—White Russians and Jews—from both these totalitarian regimes, at least until the Japanese occupation.

Rural Reconstruction

The foreign-inspired New Life Movement and the Blue Shirts were only one aspect of the pervasive and complex foreign influences circulating in China during the "nationalist decade" from 1927 to 1937. A completely different example was epitomized by the work of rural reconstruction associated with James Yen, a Sichuanese who had studied in Hong Kong and the United States. He worked for the YMCA among the Chinese laborers in France in World War One, teaching them to read and write and writing letters home for them. After he returned to China, he played a major role in setting up and operating an experimental project to bring basic literacy and hygiene as well as agricultural technology and some degree of self-government to a group of villages in Ding County, in north China. Yen also made good use of his American contacts to raise funds for the project.

The Dingxian (Ding County) project was part of a hybrid movement of rural reconstruction known as the Mass Education Movement. Partly Confucian and partly Christian in its inspiration, it was foreign in its funding—for American philanthropic organizations in particular responded to Yen's call for help—and it was run by Chinese. With its mix of patriotic means with imported ends, the Dingxian experiment and others resembling it eventually became politically unacceptable, despite their considerable successes, because of the taint of Western religion and Western money. But notwithstanding what might be called Dingxian's defiant disregard of conspicuous nationalism, the reality was that programs later espoused by the Chinese Communists often aimed to achieve the same overall goals as did the Mass Education Movement.

THE GUOMINDANG, THE COMMUNISTS, AND JAPAN

By the late 1920s the Japanese presence in Manchuria, in the form of immigrants, railroads, and commercial and industrial enterprises under the authority of a South Manchuria Railway Company, a Foreign Ministry, and a militant army, was already considerable. The Japanese were only one of several foreign powers with armies in China. Among them more than twenty thousand foreign troops were stationed in Shanghai alone, and almost fifty warships were anchored in the vicinity. But Japan took the most aggressive stance in defense of its interests in China. In 1927, when Chiang Kaishek led an army northward in an attempt to reunify China, for example, Japan responded to outbreaks of violence against Japanese in Hankou with machine-gun fire and warships and sent troops to Shandong, its prized sphere of influence, to try to block the advance of the revolutionary army. Chiang bypassed Shandong to try to avoid fighting the Japanese, infuriating his patriotically inclined Chinese troops, who were unkindly disposed to the presence of Japanese soldiers.

In 1931 Japanese troops in Manchuria took advantage of a pretext to mount a brisk military campaign that wiped out Chinese armies stationed in the region. Chiang, awash in political infighting and garnering all available support, ordered the local warlord, Zhang Xueliang (b. 1898), not to fight and held back his own armies because he was conserving them to crush the Communists. The assault culminated in a complete Japanese takeover of Manchuria, where in 1932 the Japanese installed Pu Yi (1906–1967), the last Qing emperor, who as a small child had been deposed in 1912, as puppet ruler of Manchuguo ("Land of the Manchus"). The Japanese thus effectively denied Chinese sovereignty over the whole of the three northeastern provinces, stretching from not far north of Beijing to the Soviet border.

In China outraged nationalist sentiment gave rise to protests and boycotts. In Shanghai the depth of anti-Japanese feeling led to first an exchange of fire between Chinese troops and Japanese marines and then, in early 1932, a full-scale Japanese bombing of the Chinese sections of the city. Chinese fought back with a tenacity few expected, but many civilians as well as soldiers died. The Western allies in effect wrung their hands and declared their indignation at Japanese actions. They refused to recognize Japanese sovereignty in Manchuria but took little concrete action to expel or discourage them. Two years later, when the Japanese fought their way south across the passes to the vicinity of Tianjin, they were able to consolidate their control over the area south of the Great Wall without too much trouble and concluded the grossly advantageous Tanggu Truce.

Japanese expansion in China was fueled partly by its growing need for China's natural resources during the spreading global economic depression and partly as the result of the Tokyo government's feeble authority over militaristically inclined adventurers stationed in China. In addition, Japan's considerable political turmoil during the years leading up to the war resulted among other things in a strong Japanese aversion for communism. At the same time, a new goal was evolving: the establishment of a Greater East Asia Co-Prosperity Sphere, a Japanese empire in Asia that would match and eventually drive out white imperialism.

By the mid-1930s the global situation was steadily deteriorating. It was still unclear whether Chiang Kaishek's enormous antipathy to the Communists would eventually push him to accept Japanese offers of aid against them. Late in 1935 Chiang Kaishek dismayed the whole gamut of anti-Japanese forces by reorganizing his cabinet to include several Japanese-educated men more favorably inclined toward Japan. Whether he intended actually to ally with Japan seems unlikely; he hoped in this way, however, at least to gain time to maneuver as negotiations with Japan continued.

But China, however beset, was not willing to exchange one overlord for another. A letter written from occupied Manchuria in 1936 gives some sense of life under Japanese occupation and particularly of the animosity many felt toward collaborators, or "Chinese traitors." The author was a male college student returning home to care for a sick father:

> . . . On the train I discovered I was being followed by a Chinese-traitor plainclothes detective. He sat next to me and, posing as an

> ordinary passenger, periodically looked over and spoke to me. At first we chatted casually about everyday matters, but then we gradually shifted to the situation in China proper and recent student movements. He blabbed on and on throughout the whole trip. I disliked him very much but I had to pretend to be interested. When the train arrived in Yingkou, I was immediately grabbed by the [Japanese] military police, who took me to the . . . Police Station. . . . Besides myself, a young, husky ricksha puller was there, having been brought in before I was. He was on his knees crouching like a mouse listening to a Chinese traitor tongue-lash him. At first I thought that he had committed a major crime as serious as murder. Later I learned that he had delivered a [Japanese] woman to the wrong address. Before they let him go, they beat him severely and fined him two dollars.
>
> My interrogator was typical of the "people from the friendly power"[i.e., Japanese]. He spoke beautiful Chinese, asking questions more or less similar to the ones that the detective had asked on the . . . train. But this time I had to write down in detail my native place, my address, and the names of my ancestors for three generations. In the end his face became more serious and he said to me: "You are a student. We have universities in Manzhouguo and they are free of charge. Why must you go to China to study? Hey, it's all right if you go to China as long as you report monthly on the situation concerning the Chinese student movement. Otherwise, I will consider you a member of the group that opposes Manzhouguo and resists [Japan]."[7]

Within China, the Communists were under siege. Driven by Nationalist encirclement from their bases in Jiangxi province, in 1934 and 1935 they undertook the Long March, a yearlong, zigzagging flight that decimated their numbers and, for survivors, came to constitute almost unimpeachable revolutionary credentials. Journeying through extraordinarily difficult terrain, the Communists for a time lost all contact with the outside world, including Moscow. This isolation suggested that any alliance the Communists could achieve, however out of sync with their ideological preferences, might be necessary if they were to avoid becoming altogether irrelevant. At the same time, it encouraged the formation of an independent ideology and strategy more geared to specifically Chinese circumstances. At the end of the Long March, the Communists reestablished their headquarters in Yan'an, in northwest China, where they remained until the end of World War Two.

In 1936 an upsurge of nationalist activism compelled Chiang to shelve the Communist question for the time being because of the growing Japanese threat. That activism manifested itself, first, in widespread student demonstrations and, second, in the Xi'an Incident. In this crisis Chiang's own officers helped the Manchurian warlord Zhang Xueliang kidnap Chiang, whom they refused to release until he swore to form an alliance with the Communists against Japan. Chiang's extreme reluctance to fight the Japanese until he had destroyed the Communists enabled the latter to accuse the Nationalists of a lack of patriotism. It was an assertion that set them off to considerable moral advantage in the subsequent struggle for control of China.

In the meantime the Soviet Union had become extremely concerned about Japan's aggressive intentions toward itself and sought a strong China that could help fend off any Japanese attack on Soviet territory. In November 1936 Soviet apprehensions intensified when Germany and Japan signed an anti-Comintern pact, which Stalin feared Chiang might join. During the Xi'an Incident Soviet fears that if Chiang were killed, his replacement might well be even more pro-Japanese prompted them to push the Chinese Communists into an anti-Japanese united front with the Guomindang. Mao and the Chinese Communists agreed to this second united front despite their detestation of Chiang mainly because of their ongoing desperate need for Soviet support and because they calculated—correctly, as it turned out—that the long-term domestic political gain would be theirs. At the same time, Moscow convinced Chiang it would use its influence with the Chinese Communists to restrain them from subverting the Nationalist government.

In 1937 Japan openly declared war on China. The Japanese assault on Chiang Kaishek's former capital at Nanjing in December 1937 left hundreds of thousands of Chinese dead in an attack of notorious savagery. The Nanjing massacre launched a brutal period of warfare and occupation that affects Chinese attitudes toward Japan to this day.

With the declaration of war on China, in 1937 the Japanese rapidly took Beijing, Tianjin, Shanghai, and Nanjing. Within the year they also controlled Wuhan, in central China; Canton, in the southeast; and most major industrial cities. China suffered massive losses, particularly in Nanjing, and was divided into occupied zones run by puppet governments and "free China," based in Chongqing, far up the

Yangzi River in Sichuan province. Japanese control of the coastline cut off inland China from this line of communication to the outside world. Free China itself was split between Nationalist and Communist control; fragmentation became once more the order of the day.

The rapidity of the Japanese advance was profoundly demoralizing. But out of the darkness came occasional rays of hope. The Nanjing massacre, horrendous as it was, bolstered the Chinese will to resist, while occasional Chinese victories against the apparently invincible Japanese, such as that won at Taierzhuang, Shandong, in April 1938, suggested the enemy might after all be vulnerable. For despite Japan's impressive military power, in China it found it had bitten off more than it could chew. Added to Japanese overextension, the vastness of the terrain and the dogged tenacity of the Chinese people made China ultimately unconquerable even by Japan's far superior technological power.

Politically the war was fought three ways, between the Japanese and the Nationalists, the Japanese and the Communists, and the Communists and the Nationalists. The theoretical alliance between the Nationalists and Communists lasted only until 1941, when in a notorious incident Nationalist forces unexpectedly turned on their supposed allies and destroyed an entire Communist army.

Intellectuals, whatever their political persuasion, were fairly uniformly opposed to the Japanese. But some people were more ambivalent. Despite prohibitions issued on both sides, illicit trade flourished between free and occupied areas, with Japanese exchanging cotton and other imports for food and the raw materials needed to supply their military machine. Chinese Nationalist military personnel were among the most active traders with the Japanese, an involvement that often compromised their willingness to serve their country. For example, in 1944 the commander of the Chinese Nationalist forces in Guangdong province negotiated an agreement with the occupying Japanese not to attack nearby coal mines in which he had a financial interest. In return, he apparently agreed not to attack Japanese-occupied Canton, for when he was ordered to do so by Chiang Kaishek, he refused. There were many similar examples in which economic benefit eroded patriotic fervor. Both sides rationalized their dealings with the enemy: the Chinese on the ground of economic need, and the Japanese on the assumption, apparently justified, that commerce with the enemy helped neutralize Chinese military effectiveness.

Substantial numbers of Nationalist Chinese troops defected to the Japanese. Many were incorporated into the armies of occupation in the puppet zones and given garrison and patrol work, so as to free the more certainly reliable Japanese troops for active combat duty. Some defectors effectively continued to serve Chiang Kaishek by fighting the Communists from the Japanese side. Even at the height of the war Chiang remained in contact with puppet army commanders and with the Japanese. Thus at war's end it was hardly surprising that some Chinese troops who had fought on the Japanese side used their strategic position to receive the Japanese surrender. In this way they helped the Nationalist cause by preventing occupied areas from falling at once into the hands of the Communists, whom they feared even more than the Japanese.

Among ordinary Chinese there was great animosity toward the Japanese, but it was not as universal as patriotic propaganda might lead one to suppose. Some who experienced Japanese brutality at first hand may well have been aroused to nationalist sentiment, but many merely wished to survive the depredations of all comers. Political consciousness was surprisingly limited in some areas. Even in 1948, after the Japanese war was over and only a year before the establishment of the People's Republic, peasants in a village just forty miles from the Nationalists' wartime capital in Chongqing had only the vaguest idea about the leaders of the two sides of the civil war, of which they were barely aware, or about the different ideological positions of the two sides.

China and the Western Allies in World War Two

By tying down perhaps 40 percent of Japan's military forces, China contributed importantly to the Allied war effort in World War Two. But it seemed to gain little in return. The German and Italian advisers, ubiquitous a decade earlier, were gone; commerce with the European Axis countries and joint industrial development projects had atrophied or simply dried up. Britain and France, once the leading imperialist powers in Asia, were too beleaguered at home to resist Japanese demands in Asia. Any lingering Chinese respect for the power of the leading European imperialists withered away as Britain lost Singapore, Malaya, Hong Kong, and Burma, one after the other, to Japanese control, while France underwent German occupation. After 1941 the Soviet Union was fully occupied with fending off Nazi invasion. The United States watched developments in China closely and sent money but for the time being concentrated most of its wartime aid on Europe.

Only after the Japanese bombed the U.S. fleet at Pearl Harbor in late 1941 did America and China effectively become allies. The United States unconditionally granted billions of dollars of lend-lease aid, loans, and supplies to Nationalist China. The unusual grant of aid without specific strings attached arose both from America's need, for its own strategic purposes, to shore up China's defenses against Japan, and from a disinclination among powerfully placed men in Washington to believe the spreading tales of the misappropriations of American aid by the Chinese Nationalist government. The change from the situation during World War One was palpable. Chiang Kaishek needed foreign funds and supplies, but unlike Yuan Shikai and other earlier recipients of foreign loans, he absolutely refused to agree to any conditions. Because the Western Allies needed Chinese support, they had little choice in the matter.

Chiang's relations with the three main American military advisers in China in many ways epitomized China's awareness that it was now in a position to call the shots. Claire Chennault, formerly of the U.S. Army Air Force, had been an adviser to Chiang since 1937. Convinced of the benefits of airpower, he arranged for China to acquire some of the few American planes that could be spared from the European Allies' pressing needs. His Flying Tigers, a fighting and training force made up of American fliers, won some impressive victories against the Japanese, although their efforts to train Chinese pilots had only mixed success. Less favored by Chiang was General Joseph Stilwell, President Roosevelt's appointee to command American troops in the China-Burma-India theater and liaise with Chiang on strategy and supplies. Stilwell disagreed with Chennault about the relative merits of an air or ground war in China and insisted that Chiang cooperate with Allied forces by committing his best troops to fight the Japanese. Chiang, ever mindful of the Communists, showed great reluctance to do this. Stilwell's independence of mind and his willingness to speak truth to power, in contrast with Chennault's greater amenability and the dashing exploits of the Flying Tigers, alienated Chiang. He denied Roosevelt's request that he place Stilwell in command of all Chinese troops and demanded Stilwell be replaced. Acceding after acrimonious exchanges to this demand, Roosevelt sent as Stilwell's successor General Albert Wedemeyer, whom Chiang much preferred, appreciating his early military training in Germany and his less acidic temperament. Appeasing Chiang Kaishek and the Chinese Nationalists became an American habit of mind that affected the whole tenor of global politics in the postwar decades.

Although at their meeting in Cairo in late 1943 British Prime Minister Churchill and American President Roosevelt agreed with Chiang to return Manchuguo and Taiwan to China after the war, the prospect of actually implementing this agreement was diminished by the Soviet-Japanese neutrality pact, signed two years earlier. Among other things, the pact effectively recognized Manchuguo as an independent state. It took Germany's invasion of Russia to shift Soviet allegiances. Only at the Yalta summit in early 1945 did the USSR agree to enter the war in the Pacific within three months of Germany's by then imminent defeat. Until then the Soviet Union's main contribution to the war in China was to urge the Communists to submerge their differences with the Nationalists, in order the more effectively to distract the Japanese from attacking the USSR.

Wartime Culture

The goal of uniting all Chinese people in resistance to Japan dramatically affected cultural life during the war. Men and women earlier fired by May Fourth ideals but demoralized by the authoritarian turn of political events during the 1930s found that for all the attendant suffering, war was the answer to at least some of the complex cultural problems they had so far proved unable to solve. Resistance propaganda was a key weapon both against the occupying Japanese and in the rethinking of modern culture. Creating works of propaganda gave many intellectuals a specifically patriotic context for their work, while disseminating them brought them into a close relationship with ordinary people, from whom their acquisition of foreign knowledge and values had tended to separate them.

Wartime propaganda drew its inspiration from both the Chinese tradition and foreign sources. Of the various forms it took, didactic spoken drama was particularly successful. Even before the war such programs as the Mass Education Movement, led by James Yen, had begun to use drama as a means to foster social change. They used peasant actors to stage specially devised plays for rural audiences, for which the more sophisticated fare urban theatergoers enjoyed held little meaning. After war broke out, propagandists took over these tried-and-true techniques and added refinements of their own. Most effective were dramatized versions of newspaper reports, which provided both entertainment and information on current events from a patriotic point of view. Imported models also loomed large.

The other most effective form of Chinese wartime propaganda was cartoons, which often drew their original inspiration from Western models. Satirical art had been known in Chinese painting for several hundred years; the eighteenth-century "eccentric" artist Luo Ping (1733–1799) was a well-known exponent. From the late nineteenth century, with the spread of newspapers and a periodical press, cartoons reemerged as a potentially influential art form. They derived inspiration both in terms of artistic style and in terms of subject matter from Japanese artists, such as Katsushika Hokusai (1760–1849), and from such Western artists of war as Francisco de Goya (1746–1828), depicter of the splendors and miseries of the Napoleonic Wars in Spain; George Grosz (1893–1959), chronicler of the rise of nazism; Käthe Kollwitz (1867–1945), whose radically socially conscious woodcuts an admiring Lu Xun helped disseminate in China; and David Low (1891–1963), well known as a commentator on world affairs in general and on conditions in East Asia in particular.

Chinese wartime cartoonists suffered very consciously from the usual dilemma: some of their best techniques owed much to foreign influence, but since their main purpose was to stimulate nationalist sentiment, they needed to evolve an unadulteratedly Chinese style. They were aware of the need not to imitate the West slavishly but merely to adapt Western ideas, for instance, by incorporating indigenous folk arts into their work.

Like the cartoonists, Chinese musicians and composers now found a new role. Earlier in the century European music had offered young Chinese an appealing alternative to the classic tradition, with its emphasis on the close relationship between music and politics. But within a few decades of this May Fourth trend, musicians were devoting their energies to producing and performing patriotic songs that drew on both Western and Chinese musical cultures, combining, for instance, the martial style of Christian hymns with elements from traditional Chinese folk songs.

In short, the war effort gave a new impetus to politically committed writers. The trend toward deploying culture as a weapon was co-opted by the Communist leader Mao Zedong, whose 1942 "Talks at the Yan'an Forum on Art and Literature" declared that from then on culture must serve the nationalist revolution. The implication that the heyday of foreign cultural influences must now draw to a close was even clearer than it had been in the 1930s.

Aftermath of War

Japan's very persuasive propaganda against white imperialism hastened the demise of Western power and prestige all over Asia. In China in 1943 the Japanese interned foreigners resident in occupied areas, terminating their privileged treatment in no uncertain terms. Extraterritoriality in the rest of China finally came to a formal end by mutual agreement in 1943, although for Americans it continued de facto until the end of the war. After the war the foreign powers never fully recovered control of their spheres of influence, although colonial Hong Kong and Macao reverted to British and Portuguese control respectively for another half century. After 1945 Korea and Taiwan ceased to be under Japanese control, while for the European colonies in Southeast Asia, freedom from Japanese occupation paved the way for the fight for full independence.

The opening salvos of the Cold War were fired in the Chinese civil war between the Guomindang and the Chinese Communists, which broke out soon after the Japanese surrender in 1945. Supported respectively by the United States and the Soviet Union, each accused the other of being the tool of foreign imperialists. The Chinese Communists were still uncertain of strong Soviet support. They wanted it and needed it, but at the same time, they were preparing the terrain for a future declaration of independence. That year the Chinese Communists praised Mao's interpretation of Marxism as best suited to Chinese conditions, a sign they were laying the groundwork for staking out a claim to ideological autonomy. When, a month later, Moscow signed a new treaty with the Nationalists, the Chinese Communists can hardly be blamed for wondering about the USSR's commitment to international Communist solidarity.

In this climate of uncertainty the Communists had tried to keep their options open by making overtures to the United States about a proposed alliance. But they insisted they would open relations only on the basis of equality and respect for China's territorial sovereignty. The Truman administration showed little interest. This left the Communists with little alternative but to hope for help from Moscow, even though Stalin, astonishingly, declined to repudiate the recently concluded treaty with the Nationalists until it became clear the Communists would win. The United States continued to pour money and military supplies into Guomindang coffers, as it had done since Pearl Harbor, despite growing signs that the Nationalists had lost popular support and with it the ability to prevail. As late as December 1948, by which time a Communist victory was beginning to look probable, American arms and ammunition were still arriving for the Nationalists.

American support for the Guomindang contributed to a rising tide of anti-American sentiment that spread far beyond Communist circles. The general view was that it was hypocritical of the Americans to purport to be mediating in order to help China achieve peace and reunification, while contributing so actively to the Guomindang war effort as in effect to make possible the continuation of the civil war. Many Chinese thus blamed the Americans for protracting the civil war. But they had other concerns. Individually and in the press growing numbers of Chinese expressed great anxiety that American support of the Guomindang government would drag China willy-nilly into the Cold War between the United States and the Soviet Union on America's side. Chinese wanted the opportunity to formulate an independent stance. In the eyes of many, Guomindang dependence on American support, with the implication that American policies were going to decide China's fate, risked opening a new chapter in foreign imperialism in China. Americans also did not endear themselves to patriotic Chinese by their often high-handed behavior in China, including the 1946 rape by two U.S. marines of a Beijing University student of prominent family that became a cause célèbre.

After 1945 reservations about America were also fueled by the U.S. policy of rebuilding Japan's economy after the war. Chinese across the spectrum feared a resurgence of militarism in Japan and thought that an American-Japanese alliance could bode only ill for China. They envisaged possible scenarios in which Japan, rearmed with American assistance, sent troops back to China either to combat communism or to fight in a war against the Soviet Union. After all that China had suffered, it was not a prospect the Chinese relished.

News of a growing American military presence on Taiwan, where by the late 1940s the Guomindang were preparing to reestablish the Nationalist government after their defeat in the civil war became inevitable, also began to cause great alarm among patriotic Chinese. Even independent newspapers not aligned with the Communist cause drew attention to America's interest in Taiwan and declared unacceptable the possibility that Taiwan, only recently restored to China after fifty years of Japanese occupation, might soon be detached by another foreign power. As America assumed the unwanted title of leading imperialist nation in China, the goodwill toward Americans that Chinese had once felt—because the Americans had cast off the yoke of British imperialism and because of their record of philanthropy in China—steadily dwindled away to nothing.

Bringing Foreign Domination to an End

In 1949 the Communists won the civil war. Proclaiming, "The Chinese people have stood up: China will never again be an insulted nation," Mao announced the establishment of the People's Republic of China.[8] The new government set about implementing some of its long-postponed goals. Bringing foreign privileges in China to an end had been an important goal of the May Fourth Movement. The continued presence of foreign industries, businesses, and missions remained as a visible reminder of the era of foreign domination. But in late 1949 Mao's new government not only had to remake China in a new image but also faced gargantuan tasks of postwar reconstruction. On the one hand, it was alert to the possibility that continued reliance on foreigners, many of whom continued to harbor a patronizing attitude toward China, risked subverting the momentum of the revolution. But it also recognized that it would be counterproductive to throw all the foreigners out posthaste. It thus made adroit use of foreigners to keep running essential services—such as electric power and telephones in Shanghai, both foreign-run—and as targets of hostility against whom it could unite groups of Chinese not yet convinced of the desirability of a Communist regime. As a short-term measure it took advantage of foreign-funded businesses to save itself money and keep Chinese employed. In determining their treatment of foreigners in China, therefore, the Communists weighed association with the imperialist past against present expediency and acted accordingly.

Among those whose loyalty the Communists identified as uncertain were Chinese living in the treaty ports, who had become habituated to the presence of foreigners in their midst. Much of the huge urban work force, vital to the success of the revolution, came into this category. To bring them under their control, the new Communist government encouraged those working for foreigners to bring grievances against their employers, and it rarely found against them in labor disputes. It also energetically publicized cases in which foreigners were alleged to have mistreated Chinese, to illustrate the imperialists' iniquitous attitudes of superiority.

Foreign missionaries' assumption of superiority had always been a particular source of contention with China. Now the day of reckoning had come. The new government allowed missionaries to stay for the time being only to the extent that they could provide needed education in foreign languages and technical subjects or that foreign funding for their colleges could save the Chinese state some money until the schools could be integrated into a national educational system. There were severe limitations to Chinese toleration. Catholics in particular encountered Communist opprobrium, mainly because the focus of their mission effort had been evangelical, whereas Protestants had moved steadily in the direction of educational and social welfare activities. Catholics were also especially suspect, as they had always been, because they were known to have strong links to outside authority. Moreover, they had become large landowners and hence helped prop up the very structure of land tenure that the new government intended to abolish. Finally, their insistence on priestly celibacy raised accusations that they wished to depopulate China, a claim that seems especially unfair given

Catholic views on contraception and in the light of China's subsequent policies of population limitation. Thus, as the Communist government moved to restrict foreign missionaries, Catholics were its first objects of censure.

In small but significant ways the Communists set about reclaiming the terrain of culture. They required all official communications thenceforth to be in the Chinese language, for as a July 1949 newspaper declared, the use of English—customary on, for example, electricity bills (bear in mind that the power company was foreign-run)—"betrays a strong sense of colonial influence," so that such measures were necessary "to uphold China's national prestige."[9] Foreigners now found that interviews with Chinese officials must be conducted through an interpreter, whether or not one was needed. Moreover, organizations staffed by foreigners who knew no Chinese, such as the Customs Service, immediately had to replace longtime foreign employees with Chinese, leaving the abruptly out-of-work foreigners with little option but to leave the country. Similarly, the new authorities moved to restrict foreign films, although this proved more unpopular. It took some time before attendance levels at the imports of Soviet cinema reached those once found at Hollywood movies.

Some diplomats formerly accredited to the Nationalists remained in China after the Communist takeover, but the Communists refused to recognize their diplomatic identities or special privileges. Britain, pressed by commercial interests still optimistic about the China market, was among the first to recognize the People's Republic. American trade concerns in China, on the other hand, were not influential enough to overcome rising anti-Communist sentiment in the United States. Now that the Communists had come to power, the Truman administration showed no inclination to change its mind about them. In early 1950 American ex-diplomats left China. Before long their countrymen would return to fight Chinese troops in Korea.

The self-assertion of the government of the People's Republic was the logical outcome of a process of evolving nationalism that had begun at least fifty years earlier. Around the turn of the century, learning from the West and adopting Western methods in one form or another had seemed to many to be China's best bet for survival. After 1919 Westernization as a technique of nationalism became considerably more ambiguous. After 1925 patriots no longer considered recourse to Westernization an acceptable option at all. By 1949 Chinese had achieved the revolutionary goal of ending the old-style foreign domination and set about creating a distinctively Chinese style for the new People's Republic.

CHAPTER SEVEN

Culture and Conflict, 1949–1997

The Chinese people have stood up.
China will never again be an insulted nation.[1]

—Mao Zedong, 1949

After the Communist victory in the war for control of the Chinese mainland, the stability and durability of the new regime remained uncertain. Domestically, even apart from the imperative of remolding the country along revolutionary lines, China was in urgent need of wholesale reconstruction after more than a decade of foreign and civil war. In order to rebuild the country, China needed to make use of members of the "bourgeois classes"—scientists, entrepreneurs, teachers, and technicians—but their overseas education raised the fear they were politically unsound and susceptible to imperialist subversion.

Internationally China's desire for autonomy now had to contend with the threat of active opposition, even a nuclear attack, by an increasingly anti-Communist United States. American technological supremacy had been well established since the dropping of the atomic bombs on Japan in 1945. Even after the Soviet Union's explosion of its own bomb in September 1949 had offered some hope for deterrence, it was impossible to feel any confidence that the United States would not deploy this new and deadly weapon against China. With reason, China felt extremely apprehensive about the world situation in general and American intentions in particular.

The Cold War polarization of the world into blocs dominated by two superpowers, the United States and the Soviet Union, suggested that China's most sensible strategy in the face of U.S. hostility was to tilt toward the Soviet Union. But Soviet behavior over three decades had furnished China with ample evidence of its dubious reliability as an ally. In the emerging climate of the Cold War, then, China found it necessary to align itself with one powerful but untrustworthy superpower, the Soviet Union, against the other, an extremely powerful and antagonistic United States. But the price Stalin exacted for Soviet support was the retention of strong Soviet influence in China's northeast (Manchuria) and in Xinjiang, a strategy he hoped would insulate the Soviet Union from encirclement by the United States. Among other things, this demand served to remind China that both political ideological bonds and China's territorial integrity ranked lower in the hierarchy of Soviet priorities than Soviet security.

Moreover, the enemy was near at hand. The world was still, psychologically and militarily, geared for war. The Chinese Nationalists (Guomindang), who had taken refuge on the island of Taiwan in 1945, were unambiguous about their firm intention of recapturing the mainland. American lamentations about the "loss" of China to communism made continued U.S. military support for the Guomindang a virtual certainty, while Stalin made clear he would not risk war with the United States over Taiwan. Not much farther away, American troops were still occupying defeated Japan, while Korea, newly released from Japanese colonial rule in 1945 into a joint American-Soviet trusteeship, was effectively divided into mutually antagonistic northern and southern zones by late 1946, occupied respectively by Soviet and U.S. forces.

This chapter explores two vital and interconnected aspects of the Chinese People's Republic that, taken together, epitomize China's recent interaction with the West and, to a lesser extent, the rest of the world. First, we examine the main thrust of China's formal foreign policy. Second, we explore China's relationship to Western culture in its broadest sense.

Here there is some considerable divergence between China's official stance and the approach adopted by ordinary Chinese people. At times the official demonization of "the West" has been an integral part of Chinese revolutionary strategy, designed to strengthen China through popular unity against a supposed common enemy. Animosity toward capitalist societies has at times extended to any kind of cultural association, broadly conceived, with outsiders, a policy that made any and all foreign links fraught with risk. One might be denounced, for instance, because of an overseas relative, a Western education, a Christian connection, a predilection for Beethoven, or even some more inadvertent and tenuous relationship, such as a conversation struck up on the street by an unwitting foreigner. Campaigns against such subversive foreign imports as free speech or the desire for greater political participation have partly been motivated by the inherited awareness that imported goods almost never come detached from their cultural context; Mao himself knew from his many years in the political wilderness that ultimately it is impossible to expunge unwanted ideas altogether. In short, the maintenance of cultural purity has been problematic.

Outside official circles, Chinese attitudes toward the West have confronted subtler issues. Some men and women, echoing the strategies of their late Qing and early republican predecessors, have sought to draw on the West as a source of alternative ideology whereby they can offer resistance to a repressive state. But decades of exposure to nationalistic propaganda produced by that very state (often for the very purposes of repression) have made Chinese intellectuals acutely self-conscious about cultural independence. They are thus caught in a bind. They can resist the state in the realm of culture by appeal to Western models, or they can resist Western culture in the name of nationalism, but in so doing, they risk willy-nilly lending their support to state policies.

Much of the history of the People's Republic concerns these issues of self-reliance and independence and related questions about what Chinese people mean by "the West" and how they have used it in different ways and for different purposes. The first test of new China's ability to address these conundrums was the Korean War of 1950–1953.

The Korean War

In 1950 sporadic armed conflict between northern and southern Korea in the years following World War Two escalated into full-scale civil war. In June of that year troops from the north, many of whom were veterans of the wars in China, invaded the south, quickly devastating South Korean troops and American occupation forces and capturing the capital city of Seoul. Three months later American soldiers landed at Inchon, near Seoul, which they recaptured. They then fought their way northward with some success, only to be driven back by the unexpected entry into the war in November of several hundred thousand "Chinese People's Volunteers," following an initial Chinese foray a month earlier. A savage war ensued, with great loss of life, punctuated by American threats to deploy nuclear weapons in Korea or China or both.

Many observers, on the assumption that North Korea was acting under orders from Moscow and with substantial Soviet aid, feared that the Korean War would soon develop into a third world war. In fact, the Soviet Union's role in the invasion and the extent of its subsequent military assistance remain somewhat nebulous. Certainly it wished to avoid provoking the United States into taking military action against itself and, as a corollary, to block any rapprochement between China and the United States. For these reasons the Soviet Union left all the actual fighting to Korean and Chinese forces and, at a critical early juncture in the war, failed to provide promised air support. This failure caused both North Koreans and Chinese to conclude that Moscow had in effect contributed to their high level of casualties. One result of this perception was that subsequently North Korea was much more favorably inclined toward China than to the Soviet Union, with which it dealt more out of necessity than choice. Another was, as we shall see, that China began more actively to come to terms with the perils of dependence on outsiders.

American assumptions that the Soviet Union was behind events in Korea aroused new fears about the spread of bolshevism that greatly affected U.S. conduct of the war. One early casualty was American judgment about China. U.S. policy makers failed to grasp the complexities of the three-way relationship among Mao, Stalin, and the North Korean leader Kim Il Sung, leading them to underplay the possibility that China might well come to North Korea's aid. Moreover, their habitual disparagement of Chinese military capabilities led to a near-fatal underestimation of the Chinese People's Volunteers' ability to fight. No less significant than these miscalculations, the United States deployed its naval forces in the strait between Taiwan and the Chinese mainland, in a clear demonstration that it would continue to stand by Chiang Kaishek against the Communists.

China's decision to enter the Korean War derived from the assessment that both its domestic and its international interests were crucially at stake. Even before the outbreak of war there had been considerable anxiety about possible attempts by the United States to collude with the Nationalists in sabotaging the revolution from within or to back a Nationalist invasion. With this went the Communists' ever-deepening doubts about the reliability of China's educated middle classes, which radical party leaders still suspected were insincere in their support.

On the home front in late 1950 Mao launched a nationwide campaign to "Resist America, Aid Korea." Intended both to reinforce external security and to bolster the strength of the party within the country, this campaign boosted morale through an all-out appeal to nationalism. Its success persuaded Mao of the efficacy of such tactics for political gain. The flood of anti-American sentiment it unleashed also placed in a perilous position those who had received their education in the United States, including not a few who had returned home from abroad specifically in order to contribute their foreign-learned skills to rebuilding new China after 1949.

Neither the North Korea–China side nor the South Korea–United States side really won the war, which lapsed into a protracted stalemate benefiting no one. After a truce in 1953—the Korean War has never been formally ended—the real losers were the Koreans. Their country was devastated, and the political divisions bequeathed by a half century of Japanese colonial occupation, a significant element of the original conflict, remained unresolved. Neither side drove out the other; any territorial gains were for the most part recovered, and the dividing line between north and south was not substantially changed.

New World Standing

For China the Korean War was profoundly important in a number of ways. First, it brought to the forefront of Chinese policy-makers' attention their already existing sense that in the long term, divergent interests would make a Sino-Soviet alliance unworkable. In this way the war both played a part in the Sino-Soviet split of the early 1960s and underscored China's need to acquire the capability to go it alone. Mao and other leaders began to focus on the principle of self-reliance that later they would be compelled to translate into reality. Second, the mass mobilization campaigns of the Korean War era were only the first of many in which Chinese were called to action by anti-imperialist, often specifically anti-American propaganda. The politics of mass mobilization and the years of antiforeign activism left a lingering influence on the mind-set of Chinese of all persuasions; making outsiders the scapegoat for problems of whatever origin became to some extent a habit of mind.

Third, the failure of the Chinese People's Volunteers to drive the Americans out of the Korean peninsula confirmed that notwithstanding the pervasive propaganda about "people's war," Mao's theory about the irresistible power of numerical advantage and presumed superior morale, the reality was that technological superiority still counted for more. Pragmatic recognition of this persuaded Mao that China must acquire whatever advanced military technology the superpowers had, including the atomic bomb. The knowledge that the United States possessed nuclear weapons lent a potentially terrible substance to its threats against China, while the uncertainty about Soviet willingness to back China in a crisis to the extent of deploying its own nuclear weapons further reinforced Chinese determination to ensure that "whatever they have, we must have," a decision arrived at in early 1955.

A fourth extremely significant consequence of the Korean War was that it greatly enhanced the international stature of the Chinese Communist Party (CCP). At the beginning of the war the CCP was seen by many as a possibly temporary regime dominated by Moscow and one whose continued political power was by no means certain. By the end of the war, three years later, the CCP and the People's Republic had proved a formidable force to be reckoned with. Although China had suffered immense numbers of casualties and been forced into retreat, it had stood up to the United States, the most powerful nation in the world and, to boot, the leading imperialist. It had compelled the United States to reach a compromise in Korea and to deal on equal terms at the negotiating table with the Chinese Communists, whom they so much detested. As General Peng Dehuai (1898–1974), then senior People's Liberation

Army commander in Korea, noted in a speech made in late 1953, "The time has gone forever when the Western powers are able to conquer a country in the East merely by mounting several cannons along the coast."[2] This situation strengthened China's confidence about pursuing a number of other goals in East Asia, among which the resumption of control over Tibet was a high priority.

China had effectively controlled the mountainous nation on its western frontier from the early eighteenth century, when the Qing had incorporated Tibet into their expanding empire. Tibet had, however, always retained a fair degree of autonomy, and since the early twentieth century it had been more or less independent. In the thirties and forties Chinese Communist leaders had consistently expressed their intention of reincorporating such areas as Tibet and Xinjiang into the Chinese polity as "autonomous regions," and in 1950 they took steps to bring this objective to fruition.

In 1950 and 1951, taking advantage of the fact that most of the world's attention was riveted on Korea, China had first invaded and then occupied Tibet relatively free from international protest. The Dalai Lama, spiritual and political leader of Tibet, remained in Tibet until 1959, when he fled into exile in India in murky circumstances. By then the foreign powers were ready to condemn Chinese actions in Tibet, including widespread killings and the suppression of Tibetan culture, moves that appeared to signal an intention to destroy Tibetan independence. But the powers' long inaction since the original Chinese invasion limited their credibility and made it possible for China to reject their criticisms as interference in its internal affairs. It was a claim that many foreigners, haunted by postimperial guilt and their own problems of postwar construction, were willing to accept. Tibetan independence fighters thus garnered little support internationally, although the United States' covert encouragement of resistance efforts for a while aroused their hopes.

By the early 1950s the People's Republic had become a significant player on the international stage, even though Taiwan still retained China's seat at the United Nations. It now had the international prestige—and the consummate diplomat, Zhou Enlai—to represent its interests at international conferences. Most notably, at Geneva in 1954 Zhou successfully forced the Vietminh leader Ho Chi Minh to compromise with France on postwar arrangements that primarily suited Chinese interests.

Zhou also played a leading role at Bandung in 1955, at the first international conference of newly independent Asian and African nations. Reiterating China's peaceful intentions, he endeavored to address the concerns of such nearby countries as Malaya and Indonesia that China was using those countries' large overseas Chinese populations to back the international spread of communism. On this issue Zhou had to tread very carefully, because remittances sent home by overseas Chinese were an important source of foreign exchange for China. That year China signed a dual nationality treaty allowing overseas Chinese to choose their citizenship, but allegations of Chinese support for Communist groups abroad continued, amid occasional outbreaks of violence against Chinese immigrants—some of long standing—whom local communities resented for their evident prosperity.

In the early decades of the People's Republic China actively sought to assume the leadership among the nations of the third world, to which they wished to spread the word about socialist revolution and successful resistance to imperialism, at the same time securing support in the international arena and denying it to the Soviet Union and Taiwan. In Southeast Asia, as we have just noted, this goal was viewed with considerable suspicion, both because of China's proximity and because of the presence of sizable overseas Chinese populations. But in at least some parts of Africa, China's message was much more welcome. To Tanzania, Angola, Mozambique, Ghana, and other African countries, China sent material aid and provided military training and supplied funding and manpower for economic development projects. It also hosted African students at schools within China, teaching both its ideology of revolution and its tried-and-true methods of guerrilla warfare. The point here, at its simplest, is that the oft-cited "fact" of China's international isolation at this time is misleading. More accurately, in the 1950s and 1960s China was isolated from the United States and to a lesser extent Europe, and later from the Soviet Union, but it was fully engaged with many other non-Western nations.

China and the Soviet Union

In the early 1950s the Soviet Union delivered extensive military, technical, and financial aid to China. It sent experts and advisers and generally served as a model for the People's Republic. Particularly after the Korean War, Chinese intellectuals, whose political attitude had always been suspect, began to find themselves increasingly passed over for employment in favor of Soviet experts. Those who went overseas to study now went to Moscow; no one went to the United States any more.

But the close relationship between the Soviet Union and China did not last. When Stalin died in 1953, Mao saw his chance to enhance his already considerable prestige by creating a distinctively Chinese revolution based on his own theories, known as Mao Zedong Thought. At the same time, he sought to seize the leadership of the worldwide Communist movement, causing resentment among Stalin's less prestigious successors and thwarting Soviet ambitions to extend its influence around the world. After the 1956 anti-Soviet, anti-Communist uprisings in Hungary and Poland the Soviet Union needed to shore up its support; partly for that reason, Soviet leader Nikita Khrushchev undertook that year to help China build its own atomic bomb. But as China saw it, the Soviet Union continued to act in a condescending way toward it, treating it as a junior member of the ideological league and a technological bumpkin.

The 1956 uprisings had other repercussions in China. Attributing them to repression against intellectuals and to the isolation of the Eastern European Communist parties, Mao issued a call to "Let a hundred flowers bloom, let a hundred schools of thought contend." His purpose in launching the Hundred Flowers Movement was to avoid the kinds of problems that had arisen in Eastern Europe; he hoped to revitalize intellectual life by allowing more freedom in academic debate and to use intellectuals' criticisms to improve political and bureaucratic efficiency.

The call for debate let loose a flood of criticisms that, from the party's point of view, exposed the alarming vitality of bourgeois, liberal ideas. The movement ended in June 1957, thirteen months after it had begun, when Mao implemented a policy of harsh repression that stemmed the flow and, besides, brought China into line with other Communist regimes across the world. This period of repression was known as the Anti-Rightist campaign. Debate was stifled, and intellectuals were subject to censure; some of those who fell from favor at this time were banished to remote parts of the country for ten or twenty years.

This repression partly related to Mao's assessment of the de-Stalinization campaign in the Soviet Union. The dismantling of the

Stalin personality cult, begun in 1956, had at first served as something of a curb on Mao's power. But this spurred Mao to condemn de-Stalinization as a sop to capitalist interests and to move to reinforce his own power by squelching his critics.

The Anti-Rightist campaign merged into what was to become one of the most utopian, most disastrous episodes in the history of the People's Republic, the Great Leap Forward of 1958–1961. Essentially this was an economic program intended to raise China to the industrial level of Britain and the United States within a short time, leapfrogging over the socialist stage of development envisaged in classic Marxist theory to arrive much more quickly at the goal of a communist society. The principal methods were the collectivization of agricultural production and living, the decentralization of industrial production, and self-reliance.

Overall the Great Leap Forward resulted in the death from starvation of tens of millions of Chinese, particularly during the Three Hard Years of 1960–1962. Moves toward collectivization and rapid industrialization were in every sense counterproductive. It took some little time before the exhilarating prospect of catapulting the nation into the revolutionary future gave way to a recognition of the harsh realities. The fate that had befallen so many of those who had spoken out in the Hundred Flowers Movement—disgrace and banishment—gave pause to many would-be critics within China. Even as ravenous people were scavenging for wild grasses to assuage their hunger, local officials vied with one another to report breathtaking successes, putting pressure on others to match or surpass their imaginary production figures. Growing political divisions among the leadership further contributed to the failure to halt in mid-Leap. Concealing the full magnitude of the disaster was possible in part for these reasons and in part because there were very few foreign observers in China who might have been able to contradict phony reports or to muster support from international relief organizations. For by the early 1960s China had fallen out not only with the United States, with which it had again come to the brink of war over Taiwan in 1958, but also with the Soviet Union.

During the Great Leap Forward, in a logical outcome of earlier campaigns to promote politics over everything else, it became markedly preferable to be "red" than "expert"—that is, it was better to be able to boast a "good" class background (to come from a worker or poor peasant family) and to be free from the contaminating effects of a foreign education (Western or Soviet) than to be technically skilled but ideologically tainted. The preference for political correctness over technical knowledge meant that Chinese men and women of good class backgrounds were promoted to positions requiring scientific and technical knowledge in areas such as physics or engineering, regardless of their training. This tactic deepened the revolution but, in the name of self-reliance, hindered industrial progress.

Moreover, despite the rhetoric, China's need for Soviet expertise had not diminished. At just the same time as Great Leap advocates were trumpeting the phenomenal potential of the revolutionary will of the masses, China's demands for Soviet military aid were greater than ever, particularly in light of China's plan to build its own nuclear weapons. What Mao appears to have meant by self-reliance was, then, not at all technological independence, but only a diminution in Soviet political influence, which in his view threatened to dilute the indigenous purity of the Chinese Revolution.

In the late 1950s Sino-Soviet relations became acutely strained. There were many points of difference. The fundamental distinction was that Mao's confidence in the redeeming power of politics led him to the view that it would be possible to survive a nuclear attack, whereas Khrushchev considered this unlikely. Thus Mao was ready to confront the possibility of nuclear war, whereas Khrushchev was increasingly inclined to seek ways to prevent it. Khrushchev's fear that Chinese combativeness would drag the Soviet Union into a nuclear war with the United States was a major factor in the final Soviet decision to withdraw from China.

Disagreement arose over mutual accusations that Soviet blueprints were less than state-of-the-art and that Chinese copies of an advanced American missile Moscow had somehow obtained and passed on were crucially incomplete. Further disputes arose over Soviet demands to install a long-distance radio transmitter in China with which to keep in contact with submarines in their Pacific fleet, which China rejected as an infringement of its sovereignty by means of infiltration of its intelligence and communications systems. Fortified by enhanced self-confidence and unnerved by the spirit of détente between the Soviet Union and the United States that temporarily followed Khrushchev's summit with U.S. President Dwight Eisenhower in 1959—China at last accused the Soviet Union itself—the great anti-imperialist—of imperialism.

Sino-Soviet cooperation on China's nuclear project came to an abrupt end in 1960, at the height of the Great Leap Forward. Although China had seen the split coming, an eventuality that the propaganda about self-reliance anticipated, it was taken aback by the speed of the Soviet withdrawal. In the space of a few months all Soviet technical experts had been withdrawn. Almost half the promised equipment and raw materials for the strategic weapons program never reached China. Soviet and Eastern European artistic, literary, and musical experts were also withdrawn from their assignments all over China, leaving a huge vacuum in the arts and education worlds. In time those who had struggled to learn the Russian language found that it was politically unacceptable, even dangerous to admit to such a connection to the treacherous former ally. In 1962, when the Soviet Union as well as the United States supported India in its border war against China, China's isolation from both superpowers emerged in stark relief.

Despite the setbacks of Soviet withdrawal, however, China exploded an atomic bomb in 1964. As a top priority national security project, the nuclear program received the active protection of the top leadership from the potentially damaging effects of continuing political campaigns against intellectuals, experts, and overseas education. The dire need for technical expertise outweighed the risks inherent in the supposed counterrevolutionary class affiliations of the best scientists and engineers. This need was made all the more pressing by the growing presence of U.S. forces in Indochina.

CHINA AND THE VIETNAM WAR

The Chinese Communists had long expressed solidarity with oppressed people and their revolutions around the world, although Vietnam and China were traditional enemies. It was the fear China would export its success, as the Soviet Union had to Eastern Europe, that underlay much postwar American foreign policy, especially toward China and Southeast Asia. By the late 1950s Mao had come to the opinion that the overextension of American power was in China's interests because eventually the United States would hang itself with its own overextended rope (the "noose" strategy). Hence, although China did not actively intervene in Vietnam, where revolutionaries had continued to make progress after the failure of the 1954 Geneva talks to bring an end to hostilities, it encouraged the Vietnamese Revolution in the hope that this would in the long term reduce America's ability to implement the threat of armed intervention, nuclear or otherwise, in the continuing impasse over Taiwan.

By the early 1960s disagreements within the Chinese Communist Party, especially the realization that the Great Leap Forward had been a devastating mistake, had produced rifts among party leaders and greatly undermined Mao's prestige within China. Out of a desire to recover both his own political power and the momentum of the revolution, Mao increasingly referred in his speeches to the immediate and grave threat posed to China by the forces of foreign imperialism. The United States' avowal in late 1963 that it intended to expand its involvement in Vietnam provided the perfect pretext for rallying the Chinese people to unite against foreign aggression.

But China had to act cautiously because it could not risk actually provoking the United States to attack it. It was to deter such an eventuality, after all, that China had devoted such intense attention to completing construction of its atomic bomb. China issued belligerent public pronouncements but at the same time secretly let the United States know that, although China intended to support the Vietnamese Revolution, it did not seek war with the United States. It would defend itself against U.S. invasion, but it would not initiate a conflict. For China, then, the Vietnam War was a highly delicate matter. On the one hand, it was critically important that war with the United States remain no more than a threat and not be allowed to become a reality. On the other hand, the possibility of war helped activate the extraordinary mobilization that became the Cultural Revolution.

The Cultural Revolution

The Cultural Revolution was a mass movement based on class struggle and had much to do with a sense of insecurity about foreign culture. It lasted officially for "ten bad years"—from 1966 to 1976. Mao launched it for several reasons. First, as we have seen, he wished to consolidate his own power and to dispose of his critics in the party leadership. Second, articulating a theory of "continuous revolution," he wished to give the generation come to maturity since 1949 a taste of revolution firsthand, in order to revitalize the nationalist-infused ideological élan that had brought the Chinese

Communists to power in the first place. Third, he wished to eliminate lingering bourgeois influence in China and the continued social and political predominance of those who labored with their minds over those who labored with their hands. In Mao's view, this situation impeded China's progress toward the genuinely egalitarian society originally envisaged by the revolution.

"Bourgeois influence" became a code phrase for any form of foreign connection. Everything foreign was publicly condemned as antirevolutionary and anti-China. During the most violent attacks on intellectuals, schools and universities closed down, and many intellectuals were dispatched to rural areas to live and work among the peasants in order that they might become closer to and learn from the most revolutionary social class. Many were subjected to horrifying physical and mental abuse and were publicly disgraced, leading to imprisonment and even death. Yet notwithstanding the suffering, many found the volatile conditions of the Cultural Revolution liberating after the stifling atmosphere of the early People's Republic and later recalled it with considerable nostalgia.

Possession of books, especially translations of foreign works, routinely led to confiscation and punishment during this period. But foreign culture did not absolutely disappear. It simply went underground. In the cities, particularly in Beijing, illicit copies of foreign novels—Balzac, Hemingway, and Lorca, for example—were clandestinely passed from hand to hand, to be avidly devoured and passed on in great secrecy. Music by the Beatles played in underground salons, whose members also shared their nonsocialist artworks among themselves. Even in the countryside intellectuals sent to work among the peasants sometimes managed to obtain or keep their books, including banned foreign translations. A scholar who read German literature in the malodorous privacy of a pigpen epitomized such efforts. In short, foreign culture in diverse forms found ways to survive in China despite official condemnation and despite aggressive neighborhood vigilance on the part of individuals seeking to prove their own revolutionary zeal.

The conflict between revolutionary purity and professional expertise came to a head during these years. But because national strength remained China's chief ambition at the highest levels, in special cases the crucial need for technical expertise was secretly allowed to prevail over political imperatives. National security was deemed a special case, as it had been in the case of the atomic bomb. For that purpose, also, the leadership created what became known as the Third Front, shifting major military-industrial installations deep into the interior of China, as a protection against possible superpower attack, much as the Nationalists had done during the wartime Japanese occupation. Military factories were built on a massive scale in remote and mountainous areas. The Third Front had mixed results, but like the self-strengthening projects of the late nineteenth century, it left an important legacy: it greatly facilitated the later development of Chinese industry, including military industry. Chinese leaders' desire to pursue that path eventually led to rapprochement with the United States.

In the 1960s and 1970s the Cultural Revolution focused international attention anew on the goals of the Chinese Revolution. Its reverberations spread all around the world. In the United States, for instance, many feminists and socialists looked to China as a model of greater equality to which they might aspire. In Europe, Chinese students' leading role in the Cultural Revolution influenced the widespread mass student demonstrations of 1968. In Southeast Asia the Khmer Rouge under Pol Pot derived inspiration from Maoist ideology, with unpredictable and often terrible results. Some two hundred thousand ethnic Chinese in Cambodia—about half the Chinese population—were killed, often for their urban as much as for their racial origins; many Cambodians who favored the Cultural Revolution also perished. In Latin America several pro-Chinese groups sprang up; one of them, the Peruvian organization known as Shining Path (Sendero Luminoso), became a powerful guerrilla movement that has endured as a political force until the present. Shining Path openly paid tribute to Maoism and demonstrated its ideological debt by, for example, its work among the common people and its commitment to violence. Notwithstanding the antiforeign propaganda pervasive in China at the time, it is not altogether clear that those then in power actually desired their country's complete separation from the rest of the world, but in any event these examples show that absolute isolation was impossible.

Normalization of Relations with the United States

The outwardly xenophobic strains of the Cultural Revolution and the related mistreatment of intellectuals were the particular accomplishment of the Gang of Four, the radical group associated with Mao's wife, Jiang Qing, and army leader Lin Biao. By the end of the decade of the 1960s Lin Biao's power was second only to that of Mao, who declared Lin his successor even as he began to express doubts about his ambitions. The power struggle that ensued had much to do with China's international position.

In early 1966 the Soviet Union signed a mutual defense pact with Mongolia and stationed troops in Mongolian territory within reach of Beijing. Within a few years the Soviet invasion of Czechoslovakia in 1968, the Brezhnev doctrine of limited sovereignty for socialist states, and Sino-Soviet border clashes in 1969 all greatly heightened China's apprehensions about imminent Soviet attack. In Chinese perceptions, the Soviet Union became a more immediate threat than the United States, which was deeply distracted by its engagement in Vietnam and had, besides, so far showed little sign of attacking China. Moreover, the deep divisions over the war within the United States suggested that the hard-line anticommunism of an earlier era was beginning to fade.

U.S. President Lyndon Johnson's decision not to run for re-election, in the wake of the 1968 Tet offensive in Vietnam, further persuaded Mao that America was on the defensive. Proceeding on this assumption, and out of a sense of acute vulnerability, China edged toward the normalization of relations with the United States, as a way both of moving on from the chaos of the early years of the Cultural Revolution and of obtaining advanced technology from abroad. Supporters of rapid economic progress backed this move, but others condemned any rapprochement as capitulation to the imperialist enemy.

Among those who opposed normalization was Lin Biao. He and the radicals saw this policy as part of a more general move to restore normal political structures. From their point of view, that was undesirable because it would strengthen their political opponents, notably Zhou Enlai. Lin's opposition to normalization thus formed an integral part of the struggle for power. At the same time, it was not implausible because continued U.S. involvement in Vietnam did pose at least a potential threat to China. From Lin's perspective, moreover, continuing skirmishes with the Soviet Union, which an alliance between China and the United States would presumably discourage, were a proven way for him to enhance his power because they enabled him, as army commander, to assume the mantle of a national savior.

Lin Biao died in 1971 in a plane crash, allegedly while fleeing to Moscow following an unsuccessful attempt to assassinate Mao. His death came shortly after a secret visit to China by U.S. National Security Adviser Henry Kissinger. Within a few months the People's Republic of China replaced Taiwan at the United Nations, and U.S. President Richard Nixon, once a ferocious opponent of communism, visited China, thus formally ending its isolation from the Western world.

On February 28, 1972, after intense negotiation, the joint U.S.-China Shanghai Communiqué set out the parameters of the new relationship. Two of the most important aspects concerned the withdrawal of American troops from Vietnam and a major shift in United States policy on Taiwan. According to this, the United States agreed to recognize Taiwan as part of a single China and set out its intention of gradual military disengagement from what could now be claimed as "China's internal affairs" on the island. From China's point of view, such a public statement was prerequisite to the normalization of relations, even though it fell short of a proposal for imminent reunification with Taiwan. For political reasons on both sides, it took seven years before the exchange of ambassadors marked the full normalization of relations. Nonetheless, the Shanghai Communiqué played a major role in reincorporating China into the global capitalist economic system.

Normalization also brought back into the foreground of Chinese concerns all the old questions about autonomy and dependence. No less in the late twentieth century than in the late nineteenth, it was well-nigh impossible to limit the terms of a relationship with outsiders to commercial exchange and technology transfer. Foreign ideas, beliefs, and values, from rock music to economic capitalism to political democracy, were simply impossible to keep completely under control.

Some of the consequences of this dilemma were a little incongruous. In the late twentieth century Western liberals, philosophically more kindly disposed than their conservative counterparts toward overall Chinese revolutionary goals, laid an emphasis on human rights and democracy that seemed to pose a more subtle threat to Communist authority than did mere capitalism. For that reason, Chinese authorities preferred dealing with conservative Western leaders, whose links to international business interests made them far less likely to criticize China for its authoritarian government and poor human rights record.

AFTER MAO

Mao's death in 1976 formed part of a series of momentous events that year. Zhou Enlai died in January, and in the spring nationwide demonstrations, purportedly in Zhou's honor, indicated the presence of simmering discontent; in Beijing, official attempts to crush the pro-Zhou demonstrations led to a violent incident centered on Tiananmen Square. In early July top military commander and strategist Zhu De died. Three weeks later a massive earthquake shook the industrial city of Tangshan, only a hundred miles from Beijing, with the loss of hundreds of thousands of lives. Traditionally Chinese believed that natural disasters portended disharmony in human society. Although such beliefs were anathema to the staunchly antisuperstitious Communists, many people privately regarded the earthquake as a sign that the extremism of the past few years must come to an end, as well as a possible indication of impending upheaval. When Mao died in September, then, the third major leader to die within a few months, many regarded the earthquake as cosmic confirmation of figuratively earth-shattering events.

After a period of intense political maneuvering, in which the fall of the Gang of Four shortly after Mao's death signaled a halt to radical politics, Chinese leaders began to focus attention on pulling the country back together again after the social and economic dislocations and the political mayhem of the past few years. In 1975 Zhou Enlai had reiterated an earlier call for sweeping reforms in four broad areas: agriculture, industry, defense, and science and technology. Known as the four modernizations, these goals now received high priority. They became the focus of a campaign to reunite the country after the deep divisions brought about by the Cultural Revolution. This project also included an important new departure: the gradual opening to trade with nonsocialist countries.

In late 1976 the United States elected a president (Jimmy Carter) whose commitment to freedom from oppression around the world prompted him to make human rights a factor in U.S. foreign policy, including its policy toward China. Although subsequent presidents often gave human rights relatively low priority as they formulated foreign policy, Western attention thereafter continued to focus on such issues. To many international observers, however, the United States' own social inequalities invalidated its credibility as a critic, while its singling out of China on human rights, as it apparently glossed over abuses elsewhere in the world, was tantamount to bad faith. It strongly suggested that after all, the United States had yet to overcome its Cold War–era demonization of China.

The chief contenders for leadership of the nation after Mao's death were Hua Guofeng, a hitherto relatively minor player who held the position of vice-premier, and Deng Xiaoping, a veteran revolutionary who had been the particular protégé of Premier Zhou Enlai's. An early member of the Chinese Communist Party, he had held a variety of government positions in the 1950s but fell from power early in the Cultural Revolution. Reinstated in 1973, he disappeared from view once more after Zhou's death in early 1976, as the Gang of Four sought to eliminate all potential opposition in anticipation of Mao's death. After that event and the fall of the Gang of Four, Deng reemerged as a contender for the leadership despite attempts by Hua Guofeng's supporters to block him.

The contest for the succession remained unresolved when, in early 1978, handwritten posters appeared on a wall near Xidan Street in central Beijing, objecting to the official verdict that the 1976 outpouring in honor of Zhou Enlai had been a counterrevolutionary plot. To many this bold demand seemed a natural outgrowth of the public criticisms of the Cultural Revolution era. In an unexpected outcome it achieved its desired result within six months.

Posters on what soon became known as Democracy Wall began to express a broad spectrum of dissatisfactions, ranging from criticism of residual radicalism and those who promoted it to complaints about individual injustices and calls for human rights and democratic reforms. Crowds gathered, relishing this new forum for debate, copying the posters by hand and circulating them among their friends. At the same time, several dozen underground periodical magazines containing polemical literary writing and other not-so-veiled political commentary started to appear. It was something unprecedented under the People's Republic, the kernel of an organized dissident movement.

But as the 1978 activists soon discovered, the relatively liberal climate did not last for long. The overturning of the negative verdict on the 1976 Tiananmen incident, and the toleration of the fledgling democracy movement itself, were beneficiaries of the ongoing power struggle rather than an indicator of an official embrace of Western political ideals. In other words, Deng Xiaoping, by now in the ascendant, wished to represent himself as a reformist alternative to Hua Guofeng.

In December 1978 a man from a high-ranking party family, Wei Jingsheng, put up a poster in which he called for a "fifth modernization," democracy. Wei's call brought together a number of like-minded people, some of whom began to criticize the political system itself even more openly. But this "Beijing Spring" was short-lived. In March 1979—very shortly after Deng Xiaoping's triumphant visit to Washington marked the normalization of relations with the United States and the final confirmation of his accession to power—signs of a crackdown began to appear. Official publications accused those who wrote in unofficial magazines and signed their names to wall posters of collusion with foreigners. Before long Wei, who had gone on to criticize Deng Xiaoping personally, was sentenced to fourteen years in prison.

Wei Jingsheng became a symbol of the new ambiguities. In some circles in China, and throughout the liberal West, his calls for democracy made him a hero, but in China the political times moved on, and other dissidents came to surpass Wei in the public mind. Some saw Western admiration for Wei, and his transformation into a symbol of the oppressiveness of new China, as a sign of the resurgence of the old attitude that outsiders knew what was best for China. Proponents of this view dismissed Wei's supporters within China as dupes of foreign imperialism but at the same time lay open to the accusation that they themselves were little more than mouthpieces of the official Chinese government viewpoint.

THE 1980s

By 1980 Deng Xiaoping had launched China on a series of economic reforms generally intended to give freer play to market forces in China. First he sought to modernize the agricultural sector by ending collectivization and permitting farming households to work on their own account and by a major shift toward commercialization. One major consequence of these changes was that the relative unprofitability of growing food crops led to a decline in food production by the mid-1980s. As a result, far fewer people could subsist on the land, so that millions of farm workers had to find other work.

These changes in the countryside were followed by wide-ranging urban economic reforms, among which the most important were a new sanctioning of the profit motive and the abolition of the "iron rice bowl" system, which guaranteed pay for workers in state enterprises irrespective of profitability; the removal of governmental controls on prices; and the creation of a free labor market (in which the newly redundant rural workers also offered themselves for hire). Among other things, private enterprise became far more competitive than it could be under a system dominated by state ownership.

Third, Deng adopted an open-door policy that allowed a rapid and massive increase in foreign investment in China, particularly by the nations of the capitalist West. The results were dramatic, with a fourfold increase in foreign investment in the ten years to 1988 and a further incremental rise over the course of the next decade. At the same time, however, China began to incur a growing foreign debt.

Deng's economic reforms led to startling results. Internationally, by the end of the 1980s China had become one of the world's leading economic powers. Domestically the pursuit of profit became, for the first time under the People's Republic, not just acceptable but an act of patriotism. At the same time, the standard of living increased enormously, particularly in the cities, where a vigorous consumer culture enjoyed official encouragement. But with these changes came a greater disparity between rich and poor and between urban and rural dwellers. A new migrant population, many of whom moved from the countryside to the cities in search of opportunity, became a fact of Chinese life. So did violent crime and corruption, the inevitable accompaniments to the changes in the economy.

A significant side effect of Deng's reforms was that Westerners became much more of a commonplace in China. International tourism surged as more and more parts of the country became accessible to foreigners. The foreign exchange this boom produced helped China pay some of the bills for the imported technology fueling the four modernizations. But not all foreign visitors complied with what the Chinese authorities apparently regarded as a tacit contract to spread the good word about socialism's achievements in return for access.

Accompanying the economic reforms and the new openness to the Western world was a relaxation of official control over cultural matters. During the late 1970s and early 1980s many victims of the Cultural Revolution were officially rehabilitated, some posthumously, and the opprobrium officially attached to intellectual status again dissipated. Moving beyond the athletic exchanges ("Ping-Pong diplomacy") that had marked the beginning of the process of normalization of relations with the United States, the government permitted an influx of Western culture, in the form of plays, movies, and other forms of artistic expression that had nothing to do with socialist construction.

At the same time, Chinese writers and artists began experimenting with new form and content, in a surge of intellectual excitement at the relaxation of the old constraints on their creativity. One striking new genre was scar literature, which described and criticized the wide-ranging mistreatment people had suffered during the Cultural Revolution, a rich fount of source material. But this direction alarmed hard-liners in the party and the army, whose political power was still considerable, since many of the poignant tales of suffering were in part addressed against their own earlier excesses. Deng himself, much touted in the West for his reforms, had already shown his ambivalence about cultural freedoms in the crackdown on Democracy Wall. Over the next several years a series of campaigns were mounted against malign influences from the West, characterized as "spiritual pollution," "bourgeois liberalization," and "peaceful evolution" to capitalism. These campaigns demonstrated that even though China now was a sovereign state increasingly powerful on the international scene, its authorities nonetheless felt tremendous ambivalence about the infiltration of cultural influences on the coattails of economic development.

Since the Cultural Revolution years, when the official line had been that everything foreign was bad almost by definition, Chinese men and women, and especially Chinese youth, had developed a keen interest in the outside world. But many had only incomplete knowledge of the West, which made them highly idealistic about, for example, the perfections of a society governed by the rule of law. Many fell prey to "study abroad fever." Young people studied English obsessively in order to pass the language tests necessary for admission to

American universities and devoted enormous energy to forging useful connections with visiting scholars and other foreigners.

China began to send students abroad as part of a general broadening of international exchanges. At first most who took part in such programs were senior scholars, but by the later 1980s there was a steady flow of younger Chinese students overseas. Chinese authorities struggled to exercise control over those who went abroad to study through a careful selection process, but this became more difficult as students found ways to fund their studies privately—for instance, with the help of a relative living abroad. A major issue was whether the students would return home or whether China would in effect suffer a brain drain of its best and brightest young men and women.

Students who did return experienced a number of difficulties. A foreign degree was helpful in obtaining employment, but others who had not had the chance to go overseas often felt resentful. In the course of time intellectual divisions appeared between those whose academic training in the West gave them often profound new theoretical insights and those still in China who based their scholarship on the observation of actual conditions. These differences sometimes became acrimonious. Those overseas claimed that their distance from China gave them the advantage of perspective, while those at home asserted that that perspective was so grounded in alien cultural values and in the assurance that speaking freely carried no personal danger as to have become intrinsically less worthy of respect in a properly Chinese context, if not altogether irrelevant. The same kinds of conflict brought hopeless divisions between dissidents at home and those in exile.

Christianity under the People's Republic

Another contentious source of foreign values was Christianity. In the early days of the People's Republic the new authorities generally denounced religion as feudal superstition that had no place in a modern socialist state. This condemnation applied alike to foreign religions, such as Christianity and Islam, and to more or less indigenous religions, such as Daoism and Buddhism, that recognized a power higher than the state. All religions came under suspicion because they offered Chinese believers an alternative source of authority; unquestioning acceptance of the state was a necessary part of the anticipated transformation to communism.

Christianity was something of a special case. Apart from the blanket disapproval of religion, it suffered both from the upsurge of antiforeign sentiment and from the perception that it was a thinly disguised instrument of imperialism. On all counts it was utterly unwelcome. By the mid-fifties all Christian missionaries had been expelled, and any hint of association with Christianity bore with it the virtually automatic assumption of political untrustworthiness. Believers were forced to practice their religion in secret. Bishops were imprisoned for decades at a time.

Catholics in particular were subject to persecution because of their ties to the Vatican. The People's Republic resorted to a tactic that the Kangxi Emperor would have appreciated: It sponsored the creation of a Catholic Patriotic Association, all of whose members had to abjure any connection to Rome. Those willing to join could win freedom from persecution, while continued acknowledgment of papal authority remained illegal. Chinese Catholics were forced underground in large numbers. Discovery carried considerable personal risk. In a single case toward the end of 1996, for instance, more than one hundred Catholics were reportedly arrested, beaten, and imprisoned.

The People's Republic was more tolerant of other branches of Christianity, both because it had little choice and because they seemed to pose less of a threat. Although there was little chance that China would become predominantly Christian, Christianity remained alive and well in China at the end of the twentieth century, but its future remained uncertain. In the late 1990s attention to religious freedom for Christians around the world was beginning to become an issue in American political circles, with unpredictable consequences for those in China. Finally, whereas in Hong Kong under British rule many churches had functioned as bases for mission work on the mainland, China's resumption of control over Hong Kong seemed likely to influence their future direction.

HONG KONG, TIBET, AND XINJIANG

In 1984 China and Britain negotiated the terms for the return to China of Hong Kong upon the expiration in 1997 of the ninety-nine-year lease on the New Territories, on the Chinese mainland opposite Hong Kong Island. Contrary to British expectations, China made it clear it would not renew the lease. Given Hong Kong's dependence on the mainland for such essential resources as oil and water, Britain had little choice but to agree to return Hong Kong Island itself. One of Britain's few remaining colonial possessions, Hong Kong had by this time become a thriving center of capitalist enterprise, with a British governor and an English-style legal system with final appeal to the Privy Council in London. As a financial center, it offered a huge potential asset to a modernizing China.

In the 1984 joint Sino-British declaration, China agreed to maintain "one country, two systems" in Hong Kong. For fifty years after 1997 Hong Kong would remain a center of capitalism with some degree of autonomy. The agreement promised that during the fifty-year period society and politics would remain unchanged. Among other things, it was a possible model for the eventual reincorporation of Taiwan.

During the next thirteen years both sides tried to institute changes. Although Britain had ruled Hong Kong with a firm hand and had been extremely reluctant to share significant power, it hastily introduced a democratic process in Hong Kong before the colony reverted to Chinese rule. Under these last-minute British reforms, a new legislature was democratically elected, but Beijing soon appointed a provisional legislature to replace it. Changes also took place at the individual level. Many Hong Kong residents began to make preparations for the handover, for example, taking care about the free expression of opinion, as they tried to anticipate Beijing's presumed wishes. Other wealthy Hong Kongers moved away, including some of the huge corporations whose original fortunes had been made in the old opium trade. The vacuum they left was quickly filled by entrepreneurs from the Chinese mainland.

The impending return to Chinese control of the Portuguese colony of Macao in 1999 attracted less attention and less emotion in China. Portugal had played a far less important role in China's nineteenth-century history than had Britain, and Macao had never been so significant an international center as Hong Kong. In any event, after riots in the 1960s that were related to the Cultural Revolution and Portugal's own revolution in the 1970s, Macao had effectively already reverted to Chinese control some years before.

Tibet was another matter. Since the Dalai Lama had fled in 1959, great numbers of Chinese had been moved to Tibet, an "autonomous region" of the People's Republic that considered itself an occupied nation. Repression of Tibetans was widespread, amid accusations of genocide and the destruction of Tibetan culture. In 1987 the Chinese government brutally suppressed a Tibetan uprising and imposed martial law. Conditions were stringent. The merest mention of Tibetan independence might provoke arrest. Foreign journalists were expelled, but periodic reports of grave abuses, including torture, eventually reached the West, where activists began to take up the cause of a "free Tibet."

To Chinese chagrin, the U.S. government bowed to the pressure of the "free Tibet" lobby and announced the appointment of an official with special responsibility for Tibetan affairs, implying that it did not regard Tibet as an integral part of China. Within China itself Tibetan independence was hardly even at issue. The general view was that Tibet was and had long been a part of China and that Western criticism of Chinese behavior in Tibet was nothing more than yet another attempt to infringe on China's sovereignty by interference in its internal affairs.

Another source of anxiety about religious minorities was the reverberation of Islamic revivalism across Xinjiang from Central Asian states newly independent after the fall of the Soviet Union. In the late 1990s a series of bus bombings and a riot by Uighur Muslims in the west Xinjiang city of Yining prompted new calls for secession. Secular issues, including resentment of Chinese nuclear testing in Xinjiang's vast wastes, were important in the strengthening drive for independence. But what most concerned Beijing was the influence of Islam, which showed no inclination to retreat from its claims on the hearts and minds of Chinese citizens resident not only in Xinjiang but throughout the nation.

ADJUSTING PERSPECTIVE

In the last decades of the twentieth century, memories of the imperialist era still lingered in Chinese minds. The emergence of Japan as China's leading trading partner caused anxiety to some who feared that Japan's wartime goal of creating a Greater East Asia Co-Prosperity Sphere might after all come to fruition through economic infiltration. Hostility toward Japan was widespread among urban intellectuals, indignant at Japanese government efforts to whitewash Japan's war record in school textbooks. In Nanjing a memorial to the 1937 massacre was erected, attracting considerable attention. In the countryside recollections of wartime suffering remained vivid. Before the arrival of the first Japanese tourists in the late 1970s local inhabitants received intensive "education" from officials panicked about possible violence. But in the case of Westerners, curiosity about representatives of the former imperialist countries overcame any lingering hostility. In the late 1970s and early 1980s visitors from all countries reported crowds of Chinese thronging to catch their first-ever glimpse of a Caucasian. This fascination soon dissipated as Europeans and Americans once again became a common sight throughout the land, but for some time they continued to receive special treatment in China, an incongruous echo of the bad old days.

By late 1985 the uncertainties bequeathed by the Cultural Revolution years, the swings in cultural policy, and the dislocations and contradictions inherent in rapid economic development had begun to take their toll. Economic progress and material improvement provided personal satisfaction and made Chinese feel less scorned by outsiders for their backwardness and poverty. But as noted above, violent crime and corruption increased noticeably. Many of those charged with curbing corruption turned out themselves to be prime offenders, effectively obstructing a return to integrity and prompting widespread resentment. Against such a background, calls for greater freedom and greater political participation began once more to return to the surface.

In 1986 the well-known astrophysicist Fang Lizhi, who, like many of his academic colleagues, had spent years in political disgrace, provided a focal point for the expression of some of these concerns, particularly among students. Fang inspired many by his commitment to greater political openness and participation and was a leading figure in student demonstrations staged to protest the party's manipulation of local elections at the end of that year. The size of the demonstrations was too unsettling to disregard. Fang was removed from his academic positions and deprived of membership in the Communist Party. Hu Yaobang, a senior party leader widely regarded as a likely successor to Deng Xiaoping, was dismissed for failing to keep a lid on simmering discontents. At the time the arrests and the condemnations of bourgeois liberal tendencies issued by party leaders appeared once more to have put an end to the revived movement for democracy and greater civil rights. But in fact 1986 was the beginning of a continuum that came to a head three years later.

CULTURE AND THE NATION

In 1988 the extraordinary success of a six-part television documentary signaled the continued ambivalence Chinese felt about the relative merits of Chinese and Western culture, broadly conceived. *He shang* ("River Elegy") presented such national symbols as the Yellow River and the Great Wall in a highly negative light, portraying them as the sources of poverty, backwardness, and isolation: "The stubborn diseases of the old society are like silt carried in the Yellow River—accumulating day after day, it slowly elevates the river channel in the lower reaches and eventually precipitates a crisis."[3]

He shang called on Chinese intellectuals to take the lead in bringing China back to health, thus reversing the revolutionary narrative that gave priority to workers and peasants in the proper development of the state. Turning upside down many generally accepted facts of Chinese history and rewriting parts of Western history to suit its own purposes, it contrasted China with a dynamic West, on whose advanced science, technology, and democracy it heaped lavish praise.

The documentary's extraordinarily favorable account of the West, taken together with attacks on a broad range of Chinese failings said to have resulted from what was described as China's unduly hermetic history, was, in the view of many analysts, intended less as a paean to Western culture as such than as the revamped use of a familiar weapon: deploying the West to transform China, while nonetheless staking a claim to great patriotism. In doing so, however, *He shang* appeared to adopt a patronizing outsider viewpoint that in a different time and place many of the same Chinese who now extravagantly admired it would have denounced as cultural imperialism. Many did indeed condemn *He shang* on just such grounds, calling it anti-Chinese; they claimed it "vilified the Chinese people" and compared it to "pus oozing from a sore."[4] But its immense popularity—it was rerun on official TV stations only a couple of months after its initial showing, the script was a best sell-er, it was featured in many leading newspapers, and it received thousands of fan letters—suggested that the most patriotic Chinese, however much they may have resented "the West," still saw some utility, if not inevitability, in invoking it as a valuable source of ammunition against the official line at home. But by the end of 1988 *He shang* had been banned, and a few months later its author was in political disgrace.

The kind of criticism leveled against *He shang* surfaced repeatedly. It arose, for instance, in analysis of several Chinese movies shown abroad to international acclaim. Some considered that the foreign success of such movies as Zhang Yimou's *Raise the Red Lantern* and Chen Kaige's *Farewell My Concubine*, among others, was due to a cultural sellout. They charged that by pandering to presumed foreign expectations about China, the filmmakers in fact betrayed national culture by portraying not "real" China but what they thought a Western audience thought was the "real" China. In this view, the filmmakers' international success in putting Chinese movies back on the map was hollow. It was not at all the triumph for China that some people claimed it to be. Such circularity was not unusual in the debates about national identity and foreign influence that permeated cultural circles in the last decades of the twentieth century. Discussion about postmodernism, for instance, disputed at length whether this was too rooted in Western culture to be desirable for China, and whether in any case it was possible to experience postmodernism without first passing through some form of modernism, and whether China could be said to have done so.

Tiananmen, 1989

The year 1989 marked the fortieth anniversary of the establishment of the People's Republic and the seventieth anniversary of the May Fourth Movement. Anniversaries had often provided the government with the opportunity for nationalistic display, but on this occasion they also provided a basis for dissident action. Early in the year several prominent intellectuals, including Fang Lizhi, made a number of bold proposals in a letter to the paramount leader Deng Xiaoping. They called for "socialist democracy," suggesting that democratic reforms need not necessarily subvert the cause of the revolution. They called for the release of political prisoners and for freedom of expression. They framed their call in terms of national need, asserting that the relaxation of restrictions was vital for practical and intellectual progress and to enable China to leave behind the reputation for repression that still prevented full resumption of its former prestige in the world.

The death of Hu Yaobang, the senior leader dismissed over the 1986 demonstrations, provided a pretext for supporting these proposals. Thousands of students demonstrated in Tiananmen Square in April 1989. In addition to expressing their grief at the death of a party leader who had seemed to back them, they called for a reversal of the verdict on the events of 1986, an end to corruption, improved economic conditions, and greater participation in the political process. The demonstrations expanded into an occupation of Tiananmen Square, hugely symbolic as the site of the 1976 demonstrations and of the mass rallies of the Cultural Revolution a decade earlier, as the place where Mao had declared the People's Republic in 1949, and as the locus of antiforeign demonstrations in 1919.

The occupation of Tiananmen Square and the several thousand students on hunger strike created an extraordinary spectacle that completely overshadowed the visit of Soviet President Mikhail Gorbachev to Beijing in mid-May. This was to have been a momentous occasion, the first such visit since the Sino-Soviet split almost three decades before. Journalists from all over the world who had traveled to Beijing to cover the meeting reported instead on the student demonstration. Astonished overseas audiences became incorporated in the drama as Chinese students began to concentrate their demands on their calls for political participation, often in ways that they hoped would gain them international support. For example, the students erected a replica of the Statue of Liberty, which they called the Goddess of Democracy, in front of Mao's portrait in Tiananmen Square as a highly effective way to appeal to the sensibilities of American television audiences.

These were incomparably euphoric times for Chinese men and women accustomed to a restraint born of repression. Apart from students in Beijing and around the country, newly formed autonomous (nongovernmental) groups of workers began to join in the demonstrations. Citizens turned out to express their support. Journalists working for official newspapers and television channels, unprecedentedly, occasionally expressed views at variance with the party line. Senior scholars returned home from abroad. More than once the numbers of demonstrators in Beijing surpassed one million. An electric sense of excitement spread throughout the cities. As one middle-aged party member put it, for the first time in his entire life he was free from fear. In the largest upsurge of support for a political movement within China mounted by Chinese overseas since the time of Sun Yatsen and Kang Youwei, perhaps one million Hong Kong residents took to the streets to demonstrate their backing for the students and sent them quantities of money and supplies. Taiwan and Macao followed suit. But many of those watching the unfolding events felt a deep sense of foreboding.

By late May the moderate faction in the deeply divided government was losing ground to those who wished to suppress the demonstrations at whatever cost. The imposition of martial law should perhaps have sounded a clear warning bell, given earlier events in Tibet, but the momentum of the protests was almost irresistible. Demonstrators armed with the invincibility of youth persuaded the first approaching troops to turn back. But on the night of June 3 and into the next day, the army forced its way across the city, through barricades of vehicles and humans, to the center of the city, where they cleared the square by force. Hundreds, if not thousands—the numbers remain in dispute—died.

Chinese government attempts to restrict reporting of the Beijing massacre and the violence in many other cities were foiled by overseas Chinese and others who faxed in foreign news reports, prompting official accusations about the cultural imperialism of the West. The government denounced the students' nonviolent demonstrations as a counterrevolutionary rebellion caused by what Deng Xiaoping later characterized as "an international and domestic climate" in an attempt to "overthrow the Communist Party and socialist system" and to "establish a bourgeois republic entirely dependent on the West."[5]

Here Deng fell back on the saw that claimed in effect that those who opposed the government lacked patriotism, a quality only the government could properly define. This view underpinned many of the bitterest conflicts of the People's Republic era, but it was one with which, increasingly, Chinese men and women came to find issue as the twentieth century wound down.

Beyond the killings carried out by the People's Liberation Army, a number of workers were executed. Many of the student leaders and intellectuals accused of inciting them escaped abroad, where they became temporary celebrities. Others were arrested and served lengthy periods of imprisonment, enhancing their political credibility in a way that those who left the country would never be able to do. Fang Lizhi and his wife took refuge in the U.S. Embassy in Beijing. They remained there for many months before a graceful formula was found to allow them to leave the country. By this act Fang too lost much of his stature as a dissident leader because his action appeared to lend credence to charges that the movement was part of an international plot to subvert the Chinese government.

The association of democracy and human rights with the liberal West provided potent ammunition to the Chinese authorities and other conservative opponents. Appealing to an ill-defined Chinese nationalism, such people decried the 1948 Universal Declaration of Human Rights, to which war-torn China had not been a party, as cultural imperialism. These "cultural relativists" claimed that human rights were specific to the West and at odds with Asian and Chinese values. Pursuing this theme, they likened the attempts of Westerners to impose their views about human rights to the attempts of nineteenth-century missionaries to force Christianity down China's collective throat. Criticism by foreigners of China's continued oppression of dissidents was assailed as an unwarranted interference in China's internal affairs, a mantra that, as we have seen, was invoked frequently. Chinese antiliberals did not hesitate to draw attention to the shortcomings of the Western record on human rights, such as the British record in Northern Ireland and racial inequalities in the United States. Despite these arguments, however, and despite continuing arrests, a number of influential intellectuals within China continued, at some personal risk, to press for political reform and for the release of political prisoners.

CHINA AFTER TIANANMEN

Tiananmen and its repressive aftermath undermined the dwindling legitimacy of the CCP. Before long the collapse of the Soviet Union and the general discrediting of communism around the world further weakened the CCP's position. As the democratizing new governments in the former Communist countries ran into trouble, however, Chinese ambivalence toward what a Western model might be able to offer China began to deepen. The allure of order, even the oppressive order provided by the Communist government, remained strong. Better the Chinese devil they knew, perhaps, than the devil of foreign origin that they did not.

Chinese men and women, moreover, grasped all this, for however much the Chinese government might have desired to block out news of the rest of the world, this was no longer possible. In the 1990s the advent of the Internet made the flow of information even easier, although rules requiring registration of access to the electronic media were quickly introduced. It remained unclear whether and to what extent it would be possible effectively to enforce them. The numbers of Chinese men and women known to have Internet access remained a relatively small percentage of a population of one and a quarter billion.

Popular culture toward the end of the century showed a distinctly nationalist strain. Among the best-selling works published in the middle and late 1990s were *The China That Can Say No*, a low-brow and immensely popular diatribe against foreigners, broadly conceived. "Saying no" to almost everything became, for a while, all the rage. More specific was an attack on the media in the United States, *Behind the Demonization of China*, which built a case many found highly convincing by reference in particular to articles published since 1989 in the *New York Times* and the *Washington Post*. The authors found these articles to be almost uniformly negative and altogether lacking in the kind of objectivity those newspapers brought to their reporting of domestic issues. They concluded that the negative attitude represented the perspective of the U.S. government.

Many leading members of the government in the 1990s both lacked the prestige of a Mao Zedong or a Deng Xiaoping and were directly associated in the public mind with the Tiananmen massacre. To continue to govern with any authority at all they faced a choice: reversion to the politics of fear or allowing the economy so to expand that people's material lives improved significantly enough that they would forget their political grievances. The latter path seemed their best bet. If such economic expansion were skillfully managed, moreover, China's position in a world in which even the economic superpowers were showing signs of fragility would be enhanced.

Chinese economic growth in the 1990s was breathtaking, giving it immense political standing internationally. A tacit agreement between rulers and ruled allowed economic prosperity in return for not openly questioning the rulers' legitimacy. Foreign countries soon overcame their distaste for Chinese policies in their desire to tap the China market; occasional attempts to influence China's human rights policies or its actions in Tibet by threatening commercial sanctions were largely ineffective. Many Chinese believed that their political freedoms were steadily expanding, although they were still a long way off the standards found in Europe or the United States.

That ultimate Western threat to the Chinese status quo—democracy—refused to disappear. The argument that Chinese people were inherently unsuited to a democratic political system was definitively disproved by general elections held in 1996 in Taiwan. By this time Taiwan had become economically powerful despite CCP efforts to isolate it internationally. Although it was no longer dominated by the aging politicians who had accompanied Chiang Kaishek in the flight from the mainland half a century before, its political dispute with the mainland remained unresolved. Moreover, by this time calls for Taiwan independence had further complicated the issue.

To the government in Beijing, Taiwan's shift toward democracy seemed to confirm the unwelcome view that political liberalization was the inevitable consequence of economic liberalization. Events on the mainland and on the island of Taiwan had a distressing tendency to influence one another, as in the case of demonstrations for democracy that each experienced in 1986. At the time of the 1996 elections in Taiwan, Beijing conducted military exercises in the Taiwan Strait with a view to discouraging any move toward independence, but this only enlarged the vote for Prime Minister Li Denghui, a Guomindang member and native-born Taiwanese.

The Taiwan issue remained for China the single most important issue left over from the bad old days, but most people around the world expected it to be resolved peacefully, a view reinforced by occasional visits by mainland leaders to Taiwan and vice versa, as well as by Taiwan's heavy economic investment in the People's Republic. Yet in 1996, when the United States issued Li Denghui a visa for a private visit to a college reunion at Cornell University, Beijing protested vociferously ("interference in our internal affairs").

Nationalist sentiment began to cause the Beijing government a range of problems in "Greater China," as Hong Kong and Taiwan came to be called. Toward the end of 1996 Japanese claims to a set of islands they called the Senkaku and Chinese called the Diaoyu prompted vigorous protests from Taiwan and Hong Kong. Students and others on the mainland, spreading the word partly by the Internet, began to join in. Beijing, powerless to control Chinese from beyond the mainland, strongly discouraged these energetic demonstrations of nationalism. It did so for three reasons. First, it had no wish to compromise relations with Japan, since it valued Japanese power to make economic investments that would speed Chinese industrialization. Second, it wished to minimize the risk that any kind of political organization, even in a "good" cause, could turn sourly against their own authority. The impending return of Hong Kong to Beijing's control made this concern especially compelling. Finally, it hoped to preempt anyone else from seizing the nationalist initiative, wishing to retain that prerogative for itself as a much-needed source of legitimacy.

In early 1997 Deng Xiaoping finally died. The transfer of power to a new generation, headed by Deng's appointee, Jiang Zemin, took place without conspicuous upheaval, but Deng's passing had some fairly immediate results. It appeared to enhance the prospect of eventual reconciliation between Beijing and the Dalai Lama, already the subject of secret dialogues, because Deng had long been associated with China's Tibet policy. Dissident Wei Jingsheng, whom Deng reportedly regarded as a personal enemy, was released a few months after Deng's death, three years into a second long prison sentence imposed in 1995 after a brief period of liberty. The timing of his release, which came only a few weeks after President Jiang Zemin's state visit to the United States, led Americans and other Western observers to claim credit, but Chinese commentators, both official and unofficial, denied any connection between the two events. Joining the ranks of dissidents in exile, Wei moved to New York City. His release was followed by that of other political prisoners who were sent into exile abroad.

In late-twentieth-century China, two things stood out. One was the pursuit of material wealth. The other was a fervent nationalism evidenced, for example, in widespread excitement at Hong Kong's return to Chinese sovereignty. The depth and patent sincerity of the Chinese people's collective sense of national dignity and pride, inflated by a powerful sense of past wrongs, were immense, even though official support for such sentiments laid open the way to charges of manipulation. This kind of nationalism offered the government a further measure of legitimacy and helped it tap the enormous wealth of the overseas Chinese community, as the Qing had once done. It also made the condemnation of dissidence as unpatriotic rather more persuasive.

China's new economic power helped Chinese men and women around the world to hold up their heads in patriotic pride, even though economic instability elsewhere in East and Southeast Asia aroused considerable antagonism toward ethnically Chinese members of local communities. Nevertheless the ambivalence many still felt about national culture, and its relationship to the West and to foreign culture, remained unresolved, a sting in the tail of history.

Conclusion

In our contemporary world the notion of global interconnectedness has become commonplace, to a large extent because of the possibility of very rapid international travel and, in particular, because of the development of communications systems that make it possible to conduct transactions almost simultaneously around the world. But global connections are nothing new, even though the times and our conceptions of time have changed.

The evidence of history simply negates the long-standing myth, propagated since the eighteenth century primarily by Westerners frustrated by their inability to impose their will on China, of Chinese isolation and isolationism. Well before the advent of Europeans to East Asia, China was integrated into a wide-ranging network of commercial, intellectual, religious, and cultural contacts that linked it with the whole of Asia, the eastern Mediterranean, at least the northern part of Africa, and periodically even lands farther afield. From earliest times China sought out and took in a vast range of foreign imports, in the form of both material goods and new knowledge, and spread abroad its own material and spiritual civilization, most notably textiles, ceramics, and Confucian ideas of government, social organization, and human behavior. With those exports went many other traits of the cultural heritage, including Buddhism, transformed by its Chinese sojourn from its original Indian condition.

This age-old experience of international exchange brought China to a keen awareness of the perils of unrestrained interaction with others who might not share its values and traditions. In that view, when such encounters took the form of trade, they risked increasing commercial greed and exacerbating social inequalities. When they involved religion, they risked wooing Chinese converts away from strict allegiance to China and its political leadership. When they involved culture, more broadly conceived, there was no limit to what might be at stake. Recognizing that both foreign trade and foreign religions came unavoidably bundled with foreign cultures, many Chinese tended to the view that the potential consequences of allowing free circulation of any part of the bundle posed a potential threat to their political autonomy and distinctive cultural identity. In consequence they were, collectively, extremely cautious. To outsiders, that caution may have appeared more like exclusivism, but the record demonstrates that it in no way implied an inherent hostility to foreigners as such or to their material, intellectual, or spiritual civilizations.

The extraordinarily tenacious notion, that traditional China was almost hopelessly attached to its traditions, makes it particularly important in China's case to bear in mind the shared burden of responsibility for history. A careful examination of the facts suggests that time after time instances in which China did prove resistant to new ideas, new knowledge, and new ways of doing things cannot be wholly explained as the simple consequence of an ingrained hostility to innovation. Seventeenth- and eighteenth-century Chinese mathematicians and astronomers, for example, were skeptical about what Jesuit missionaries revealed to them concerning the latest discoveries in Europe not because of a reluctance to accept new ideas but because ecclesiastical restrictions on the missionaries had led them into such inconsistencies that it was plain to Chinese evaluating the new information that it was riddled with errors or at least contradiction. Chinese scholars were not scientific reactionaries, but they could hardly help concluding that the Jesuits were best not relied on. In the imperialist nineteenth century, Chinese resistance to Western demands for "free trade" led many Westerners to characterize China as profoundly conservative, but it would be more accurate to speak of China's insistence on independence in the face of Western aggression; what the West called free did not seem so to China. Much more recently Westerners who blame Chinese rhetoric about the evils of American imperialism for the lion's share of the mutual hostility between the People's Republic and the United States during the Cold War era fail to acknowledge the role of the American anti-Communist movement, which for years led the United States to treat the People's Republic as a virtual pariah.

The preceding chapters have, in addition, presented many illustrations of Chinese open-mindedness and its cousin, a pragmatic adaptability and willingness to experiment. More often than not China managed to reap advantage from new situations and new possibilities. One example emerged out of the gulf between propaganda and reality in foreign relations. In the ideal Chinese worldview, others acknowledged China's superiority and revolved in its orbit, but in the real world China recognized that this was not what happened. In practice China often had to acknowledge that at best it was no more than equal to other states and that at worst its weakness made it impossible to insist on equality, let alone superiority. In another example, dating from the late eighteenth century, the Qing emperor claimed in public China's complete indifference to foreign goods and manufactures but almost simultaneously sought to acquire European-style artillery, thus belying Western claims of Chinese indifference to technological innovation. An illustration of China's pragmatic ability to make the best of a bad situation was its adroit use of the nineteenth-century treaty system as both a shield and a sword. Compelled by the early "unequal treaties" to permit foreign residence in specified treaty ports, China vigorously resisted the establishment of additional foreign settlements beyond the designated areas. It also adopted the system of international treaties as a means of establishing Chinese diplomatic representation overseas. Finally, the degree to which Chinese intellectuals were willing to experiment with different political forms, all imported, during the late nineteenth and early twentieth centuries suggests an unusual degree of open-mindedness. The consistent purpose was salvation of the nation; in pursuit of that goal, Chinese proved ready to try whatever might be necessary, however new and however foreign its origin.

The configurations of global power have undergone countless shifts over the past few centuries. What has not changed much has been the way in which events in China have influenced and been influenced by those taking place elsewhere in the world; restraint and reserve are not the same as isolation. The global currents that have whirled and eddied throughout Chinese history flow on toward the next millennium.

Permissions

The author gratefully acknowledges the following for their generous permission to reprint copyright materials: Alfred A. Knopf and Jonathan Cape, Ltd., for material from Jonathan D. Spence, *Emperor of China: Self-Portrait of K'ang-hsi*, © 1974; Stanford University Press, for material from Frank Dikotter, *The Discourse of Race in Modern China*, © 1992, from Linda Cooke Johnson, *Shanghai: From Market Town to Treaty Port, 1074–1858*, © 1995, and from Elizabeth Perry, *Shanghai on Strike: The Politics of Chinese Labor*, © 1993; University of California Press, for material from Edward Schafer, *The Golden Peaches of Samarkand*,© 1963, and from Arnold Rowbotham, *Missionary and Mandarin: The Jesuits at the Court of Peking*, © 1942; Columbia University Press, for material from *Sources of Chinese Tradition*, ed. Wm. Theodore de Bary, © 1960; Editions Economica, for material from Jacques Dars, *La Marine chinoise du Xe au XIVe Siecle*, © 1992; University of Hawaii Press, for material from David E. Mungello, *Leibniz and Confucianism: The Search for Accord*, © 1977, and from David E. Mungello, *The Forgotten Christians of Hangzhou*, © 1994; Yale University Press, for material from Lynn Struve, *Voices from the Ming-Qing Cataclysm: China in Tiger's Jaws*, © 1993, from Jane Hunter, *The Gospel of Gentility: American Women Missionaries in Turn-of-the-Century China*, © 1984, and from *One Day in China: May 21st, 1936,* translated, edited, and with an introduction by Sherman Cochran and Andrew C. K. Hsieh with Janis Cochran, © 1983; Cambridge University Press, for material from Jacques Gernet, *China and the Christian Impact*, © 1982, and from Joseph Needham, *Science and Civilization in China*, volume 3, © 1959; Loyola University Press, for material from *East Meets West: The Jesuits in China, 1582–1773*, ed. Charles E. Ronan, S.J. and Bonnie B. C. Oh, © 1988; E. J. Brill, for material from H.T. Zurndorfer and L. Blusse, eds., *Conflict and Accommodation in Early Modern East Asia*, © 1993; Königshausen and Neumann, for material from *Religion und Philosophie in Ostasien: Festschrift for Hans Steininger am 65. Geburtstag*, ed. G. Naundorf, K-H. Pohl, and H-H. Schmidt, © 1985; Benjamin Elman, for material from *From Philosophy to Philology: Intellectual and Social Aspects of Change in Late Imperial China* (Cambridge: Harvard University Press, 1984); Harvard University Press, for material from Chow Tse-tsung, *The May Fourth Movement*, © 1960; Harvard University Council on East Asia Studies, for material from Lloyd L. Eastman, *The Abortive Revolution: China Under Nationalist Rule, 1927–1937*, © 1974, from James W. Polachek, *The Inner Opium War*, © 1992, and from Yeh Wen-hsin, *The Alienated Academy: Culture and Politics in Republican China, 1919–1937*, © 1990; Mouton de Gruyter, for material from Tsou Rong, *The Revolutionary Army: A Chinese Nationalist Tract of 1903*, © 1968; Princeton University Press, for material from William Stueck, *The Korean War: An International History*, © 1995; David Higham Associates, for material from Ma Huan, *Ying-yai Sheng-Lan* (The Overall Survey of the Ocean's Shores), translated from the Chinese text edited by Feng Ch'eng-Chün with introduction, notes, and appendices by J. V. G. Mills, © Hakluyt Society, 1970; Oxford University Press, for material from *The First Chinese Embassy to the West: The Journals of Kuo Sung-t'ao, Liu Hsi-hung and Chang Te-yi*, tr. J. D. Frodsham, © 1974; University of Washington Press, for material from Marilyn A. Levine, *The Found Generation: Chinese Communists in Europe during the Twenties*, © 1993, and from Tsi-an Hsia, *Gate of Darkness: Studies on the Leftist Literary Movement in China*, © 1968; *Bulletin of Concerned Asian Scholars,* for material from Stephen Field, "*He shang* and the Plateau of Ultrastability," © 1991; Arizona State University, for material from *Phoebus*, no. 6.1, © 1988; Penguin Books, Ltd, for material from *The Analects*, by Confucius, tr. D. C. Lau (Penguin Classics, 1979), © D. C. Lau, 1979.

Notes

CHAPTER ONE

1. Confucius, *Analects*, XI, 12, translated by D. C. Lau (London: Penguin, 1979).
2. See Wilma Fairbank, *Liang and Lin: Partners in Exploring China's Architectural Past* (Philadelphia: University of Pennsylvania Press, 1995), 69, for an account of the different types of pagoda and their relation to Indian stupas.
3. Duan Chengshi, *Yuyang Zazu*, c. 850, cited by Frank Dikötter, *The Discourse of Race in Modern China* (Stanford: Stanford University Press, 1992), 15. For other Chinese characterizations of foreigners, see Edward Schafer, *The Golden Peaches of Samarkand: A Study of Tang Exotica* (Berkeley and Los Angeles: University of California Press, 1963), 22. This section on the Tang is much indebted to Schafer's work.
4. Schafer, *Golden Peaches*, 28, citing a part of Yuan Zhen, "Faqu." Translation slightly altered.
5. Ibid., 54, citing Li Ho, "Long Ye Yin."
6. Han Yu's memorial cited in William Theodore de Bary, ed., *Sources of Chinese Tradition* (New York: Columbia University Press, 1960). Translation slightly altered.
7. *Chau Ju-kua: His Work on the Chinese and Arab Trade in the Twelfth and Thirteenth Centuries, Entitled Chu-fan-chï*, translated from the Chinese and annotated by Friedrich Hirth and W. W. Rockhill (St. Petersburg: Imperial Academy of Sciences, 1911; reprint, New York: Paragon, 1966), 144.
8. L. Hambis, *Marco Polo, la Description du monde* (Paris: Klincksieck, 1955); cited by Jacques Dars, *La Marine chinoise du Xe au XIVe siècle* (Paris: Commission française d'histoire maritime/Economica, 1992), 139.
9. Ma Huan, *Ying-yai Sheng-Lan* ("The Overall Survey of the Ocean's Shores"), 1433, translated from the Chinese text, edited by Feng Ch'eng-Chün with introduction, notes, and appendices by J. V. G. Mills (Cambridge, U.K.: Hakluyt Society, 1970), 173–74.

CHAPTER TWO

1. Cited by Rogers, "For Love of God: Castiglione at the Imperial Court," in *Phoebus* 6, referring to Arnold Rowbotham, *Missionary and Mandarin: The Jesuits at the Court of Peking* (Berkeley, University of California Press, 1942), 178.
2. David E. Mungello, *Leibniz and Confucianism: The Search for Accord* (Honolulu: University of Hawaii Press, 1977), 9.
3. Translated by Lynn Struve, *Voices from the Ming-Qing Cataclysm: China in Tiger's Jaws* (New Haven: Yale University Press, 1993), 237. The original letter is in the Vatican archives.
4. Jonathan D. Spence, *Emperor of China: Self-Portrait of K'ang-hsi* (London: Jonathan Cape, 1974), 72–73.
5. Jacques Gernet, *China and the Christian Impact*, originally published in French as *Chine et christianisme*, 1982; English translation (Cambridge, U.K.: Cam-

bridge University Press, 1985), 59, translating *Siku Quanshu Zongmu Tiyao*, chapter 34, note on Li Zhizao, ed., *Tianxue Chuhan*.

6. Cited by Gernet, *China and the Christian Impact*, 186. The papal bull in question was *Ex Illa Die*; it was followed in 1742 by another, *Ex Quo Singulari*.
7. Li Zhizao, note on Ricci's 1602 map, cited by Willard J. Peterson, "Why Did They Become Christians? Yang T'ing-yün, Li Chih-tsao, and Hsü Kuang-ch'i," in Charles E. Ronan, S.J., and Bonnie B. C. Oh, eds., *East Meets West: The Jesuits in China, 1582–1773* (Chicago: Loyola University Press, 1988), 142.
8. Albert Chan, S.J., "Late Ming Society and the Jesuit Missionaries," in Ronan and Oh, *East Meets West*, 171–72, citing Wang Zheng, *Chong-yi-tang Xu Bi* ("Miscellaneous writings of Wang Zheng").
9. Xu Dashou, cited in Gernet, *China and the Christian Impact*, 190.
10. Ibid., 191.
11. Nicolas Standaert, "Chinese Christian Visits to the Underworld" in H. T. Zurndorfer and L. Blussé, eds., *Conflict and Accommodation in Early Modern East Asia: Essays in Honour of Erik Zürcher* (Leiden: E. J. Brill, 1993), 58, translating Xiong Shiqi, *Zhang Mi-ke-er Yi Ji* ("Memoirs of Michael Zhang"), 8a–8b. The date of this work is unknown, but Yang Tingyun, who died in 1627, wrote a preface, so the memoir must have been written prior to that date.
12. E. Zürcher, "The Lord of Heaven and the Demons—Strange Stories from a Late Ming Christian Manuscript," in G. Naundorf, K-H. Pohl, and H-H. Schmidt, eds., *Religion und Philosophie in Ostasien: Festschrift für Hans Steininger am 65. Geburtstag*, (Königshausen & Neumann, 1985), 368–69, translating Li Jiugong, *Li Xiu Yi Jian* 2, 9b–10b.
13. David E. Mungello, *The Forgotten Christians of Hangzhou* (Honolulu: University of Hawaii Press, 1994), 56–57, citing the Jesuit annual letter of 1678–1679, now held in the Jesuit archives in Rome. This description of the impact of Martini's body is largely taken from Professor Mungello's account.
14. Ma Shilin, comp., *Cheng'an Suo Jian Ji* ("Collection of Leading Cases [I Have] Seen"), edition of 1805, edited by Xie Kui, 16, 3b.

CHAPTER THREE

1. "Yingshi Maga'erni Laipin An" ("The Case of the English Macartney Embassy and Their Gifts"), *Chang Gu Cong Bian* (Collected Historical Records) (Beiping, 1930–1943), 3, 16–24, at 19b.
2. A tael was worth about one-third of an English pound at this time. A high-ranking official might earn about twelve thousand taels annually; most ordinary commoners would be unlikely to see as much as one thousand taels in their entire lifetimes.
3. Sir George Staunton, *An Authentic Account of an Embassy from the King of Great Britain to the Emperor of China*, 3 vols. (London: G. Nicol, 1797), 1, 49.
4. Cited by Joseph Needham, *Science and Civilization in China*, vol. 3: "Mathematics and the Sciences of the Heavens and the Earth" (Cambridge, U.K.: Cambridge University Press, 1959), 456.
5. Nathan Sivin, "Wang Hsi-shan," *Dictionary of Scientific Biography*, XIV (New York, 1970–1978), 160.
6. Qian Daxin, *Qian Yan Tang Wen Ji*, cited by Benjamin Elman, *From Philosophy to Philology: Intellectual and Social Aspects of Change in Late Imperial China* (Cambridge: Harvard University Press, 1984), 83.
7. *Lettres édifiantes et curieuses écrites des missions étrangères*, 14 vols. (Lyons, 1819;

originally published in Paris, 1702–1776, and subsequently rearranged), 3, 427.

8. Arnold Rowbotham, *Missionary and Mandarin: The Jesuits at the Court of China* (Berkeley: University of California Press, 1942), 98, 247.
9. *Archivum Romanum Societatis Jesu*, Jap.Sin., 184, 261–62; letter of Jean-Mathieu de Ventavon, S.J., to Father Imbert, S.J., November 4, 1772.
10. Unpublished letter of Father Bourgeois dated October 30, 1769, possibly in the Xujiahui library, Shanghai, cited by Louis Pfister, *Notices biographiques et bibliographiques sur les Jésuites de l'ancienne mission de Chine, 1552–1773* (Shanghai: Imprimerie de la Mission Catholique, 1932), 914.
11. Cited by Fu Lo-shu, *A Documentary Chronicle of Sino-Western Relations* (Tucson: University of Arizona Press, 1964), 273–74. Translation slightly altered.
12. Jean-Joseph Marie Amiot (1718–1793), letter written from Beijing to Henri Bertin in France, July 1, 1788, located in the Bibliothèque de l'Institut de France, 1517, 52.

Chapter Four

1. This quote represents a composite of different remarks on the subject made by Qing authorities. For the originals, see *Qing Jiaqing Chao Waijiao Shiliao* ("Materials on the Foreign Relations of the Jiaqing Reign of the Qing Dynasty"), 4, 21b–23b, cited by Fu Lo-shu, *A Documentary Chronicle of Sino-Western Relations*, 394, and *Yuehaiguan Zhi* 29, 9–15, also cited by Fu, 612. I have slightly modified Fu's translation.
2. Dispatches from U.S. Consuls in Canton, 1790–1906, File Microcopies of the U.S. National Archives (Washington, 1947) 101, vol. 1, February 21, 1790, to April 20, 1834. The petition is dated February 10, 1814. The archives contain the Chinese original, an English approximation (reproduced here), and a Spanish/Portuguese version. Partial English translations may be found in Fu Lo-shu, *Documentary Chronicle*, 391–92, and Frederic D. Grant, "The Failure of Li-ch'uan Hong: Litigation as a Hazard of Nineteenth-Century Foreign Trade," *American Neptune*, vol. XLVIII, no. 4 (Fall 1988), 243–60.
3. James W. Polachek, *The Inner Opium War* (Cambridge: Harvard University Press, 1992), 165, citing *Yapian Zhanzheng* ("The Opium War"), 6 vols. (Shanghai: Shenzhou Guoguang She, 1954), 4, 22.
4. Linda Cooke Johnson, *Shanghai: From Market Town to Treaty Port, 1074–1858* (Stanford: Stanford University Press, 1995), 181, citing Cao Shang, "Yihuan, beichang ji," 8b–9a.
5. See Gerald Graham, *The China Station: War and Diplomacy, 1830–1860* (New York: Oxford University Press, 1978), 117–18, 183, 215–18, cited by Jonathan Spence, *The Search for Modern China* (New York: Norton, 1990), 158.
6. See J. Y. Wong, *Anglo-Chinese Relations 1839–1860: A Calendar of Chinese Documents in the British Foreign Office Records* (New York: Oxford University Press/The British Academy, 1983), entries for 1844 and 1849 passim.
7. Documents on Chen's case are in the Public Record Office, London. For a summary, see Wong, *Anglo-Chinese Relations, 1839–1860*, 212–15.
8. Cited by Johnson, *Shanghai*, 186.
9. *Chinese Emigration: Report of the Commission Sent by China to Ascertain the Condition of Chinese Coolies in Cuba* (Shanghai: Imperial Maritime Customs Press, 1876; reprint, Taipei/Chengwen, 1970), 7, cited by Lynn Pan, *Sons of the Yellow Emperor: The Story of the Overseas Chinese* (London: Secker & Warburg, 1990), 47 (figures on Cuba); 48 (quotation).

10. Jonathan D. Spence, *God's Chinese Son* (New York: Norton, 1995), 241, citing P. Clarke and J. S. Gregory, *Western Reports on the Taiping: A Selection of Documents* (Canberra: Australian University Press 1982), 189.

CHAPTER FIVE

1. *Shanghai Beike Ziliao Xuanji*, 321–12, cited by Elizabeth Perry, *Shanghai on Strike: The Politics of Chinese Labor* (Stanford: Stanford University Press, 1993), 40.
2. See Albert Feuerwerker, "The Foreign Presence in China," in John K. Fairbank, ed., *The Cambridge History of China*, vol. 12, *Republican China 1912–1948*, part I (Cambridge, U.K.: Cambridge University Press, 1983), 129–31.
3. Kang Youwei, "Shang Qingdi Di'er Shu" ("Second Letter to the Emperor"), in Jian Bozan, ed., *Wuxu Bianfa* ("The Reform Movement of 1898"), 4 vols., (Shanghai, 1953), vol. 2, 145; cited by Jonathan D. Spence, *Gate of Heavenly Peace: The Chinese and Their Revolution, 1895–1980* (New York: Viking, 1981), 11.
4. *The European Diary of Hsieh Fucheng, Envoy Extraordinary of Imperial China*, translated by Helen Hsieh Chien (New York: St. Martins, 1993), 65.
5. See Thomas L. Kennedy, "China's 19th-Century Military Reforms: A Reassessment Based on Some Recent Writings." Unpublished paper, 1994, 46.
6. Munitions production figures for the Jiangnan Arsenal are taken from Thomas L. Kennedy, *The Arms of Kiangnan: Modernization in the Chinese Ordnance Industry, 1860–1895* (Boulder, Colo.: Westview, 1978), 164, citing Wei Yungong, *Jiangnan Zhizao Juji* ("Record of the Jiangnan Arsenal") (Taibei: Wenhai, n.d.), 3, 2–38. Shipbuilding figures are taken from Kennedy, ibid., 161–62, citing Wei and other Chinese records.
7. *Li Wenzheng Gong Zougao* ("Memorials of Master Li Wenzheng [Li Hongzhang]") 9, 31–35, cited by Kennedy, *Arms of Kiangnan*, 47–48.
8. Guo Songtao, in J. D. Frodsham, translator and annotator, *The First Chinese Embassy to the West: The Journals of Kuo Sung-t'ao, Liu Hsi-hung and Chang Te-yi* (Oxford: Clarendon Press, 1974), 98.
9. Captain Paul Schlieper, *Meine Kriegs-Erlebnisse in China, Die Expedition Seymour* (Minder-in-Westfalen: William Köhler, 1902), 12–14, cited by Jane Elliott, "China Described by Her Enemies: The Writings of Western Soldiers Who Fought in the China Campaign in 1900." Unpublished manuscript, 1997, 248, note 234.
10. Shanghai Mercury, *Shanghai by Night and Day* (Shanghai, 1902), cited by Yeh Wen-hsin, *The Alienated Academy: Culture and Politics in Republican China, 1919–1937* (Cambridge: Harvard University Press, 1990), 58.
11. Soumay Tcheng, *A Girl from China*, as told to Bessie Van Vorst (New York: Fred A. Stokes, 1926), 77–79, quoted in Jane Hunter, *The Gospel of Gentility: American Women Missionaries in Turn-of-the-Century China* (New Haven: Yale University Press, 1984), 233.
12. Anna Hartwell, cited by Hunter, *Gospel of Gentility*, 230.
13. Marilyn A. Levine, *The Found Generation: Chinese Communists in Europe during the Twenties* (Seattle: University of Washington Press, 1993), 19, citing Wang Yunwu, "Cai Jiemin xiansheng de gongxian" ("The Contributions of Mr. Cai Yuanpei"), *Dongfang zazhi*, vol. 37 (April 1940), 4.
14. Kang Youwei, cited in Charlotte L. Beahan, "The Women's Movement and Nationalism in Late Ch'ing China." Unpublished Ph.D. dissertation, Columbia University, 1976, 142, citing Howard S. Levy, *Chinese Footbinding: The History*

of a Curious Erotic Custom (New York: Walton Rawls, 1966), 72.

15. *Dong Fang Za Zhi* (1904), 5, 6, and 7, cited by Chia-lin Pao Tao, "The Anti-footbinding Movement in Late Ch'ing China: Indigenous Development or Western Influence?" Unpublished paper presented to the Association for Asian Studies, Washington, D.C., April 1993.

CHAPTER SIX

1. Shanghai Students' Union, The *Students' Strike: An Explanation*, a leaflet published in English in 1919 and cited by Chow Tse-tsung, *The May Fourth Movement* (Cambridge: Harvard University Press, 1960), 93.
2. *Daqing Lichao Shilu*, Guangxu, 371, 7a, cited by Jonathan D. Spence, *Gate of Heavenly Peace: The Chinese and their Revolution, 1895–1980* (New York: Viking, 1981), 14.
3. Translated by C. T. Hsia in "Yen Fu and Liang Ch'i-ch'ao as Advocates of New Fiction," in Adele A. Rickett, ed., *Chinese Approaches to literature from Confucius to Liang Ch'i-ch'ao* (Princeton: Princeton University Press, 1978), 230–32, cited by Leo Lee, "Literary Trends I: The Quest for Modernity, 1895–1927," in *The Cambridge History of China*, vol. 12, part 1 (Cambridge, U.K.: Cambridge University Press, 1983), 455.
4. Zou Rong, *The Revolutionary Army*, 24, translated by John Lust (The Hague and Paris: Mouton & Co, 1968), 81.
5. Qu Qiubai, *Wenji* ("Collected Literary Works"), 4 vols. (Beijing: 1954), 1, 23, translated by Tsi-an Hsia, *Gate of Darkness: Studies on the Leftist Literary Movement in China* (Seattle: University of Washington Press, 1968); cited in modified form by Spence, *Gate of Heavenly Peace*, 135.
6. This quotation is a composite of two cited by Lloyd L. Eastman, *The Abortive Revolution: China under Nationalist Rule, 1927-1937* (Cambridge: Harvard University Press, 1974), 68. The citations are taken from "Xin Shenghuo Yundong zhi yaoyi" ("Essential Information about the New Life Movement"), compiled by Xin Shenghuo Congshu she (Society for Collectanea on the New Life [Movement]), (Nanjing: 1935), 111; and Iwai Eiichi, *Ranisha ni kansuru choosa* ("An Investigation of the Blue Shirts"), issued by the Research Department of the Foreign Ministry, marked "secret" (1937), 37–38.
7. "A Letter from the Northeast" in *One Day in China: May 21st, 1936*, translated, edited, and with an introduction by Sherman Cochran and Andrew C. K. Hsieh with Janis Cochran (New Haven: Yale University Press, 1983), 207–8.
8. Mao Zedong, "The Chinese People Have Stood Up," in *Selected Works of Mao Tsetung* (Beijing: Foreign Languages Press, 1977), vol. 5, 15–18.
9. *Dagongbao*, July 24, 1949, translated in *China Press Review*, vol. 939 (July 28, 1949), cited by Beverley Hooper, *China Stands Up: Ending the Western Presence, 1948–1950* (Sydney and London: Allen and Unwin, 1986), 74.

CHAPTER SEVEN

1. Mao Zedong, "The Chinese People Have Stood Up," in *Selected Works of Mao Tsetung* (Beijing: Foreign Languages Press, 1977), vol. 5, 15–18.
2. Quoted by William Stueck, *The Korean War: An International History* (Princeton: Princeton University Press, 1995), 362, citing Zhang Shuguang, "Military Romanticism: China and the Korean War, 1950–1953." Draft manuscript, March 1992.
3. *He shang* ("River Elegy"), "Sorrows," translated by Stephen Field, "*He shang*

and the Plateau of Ultrastability," *Bulletin of Concerned Asian Scholars* (June 1991), 12–13.

4. Quotations (from a high-ranking Beijing official and the dean of National Taiwan University, respectively) are from Frederic Wakeman's review of *River Elegy* in *New York Review of Books* (March 2, 1989), 19.
5. Deng Xiaoping, "Zai Jiejian Shoudu Jieyan Budui Jun Yishang Ganbu Shi De Jianghua" ("Speech upon Receiving Army Commanders of Beijing Troops Carrying Out Martial Law), *Renmin Ribao* ("People's Daily"), July 28, 1989, 1.

Further Readings

In general, those seeking further information should refer to the many volumes of the *Cambridge History of China* and to specialist journals, where much of the latest research is appearing. Among the many excellent publications in the latter category, probably the most useful in this context are *Asia Major*, *Australian Journal of Chinese Affairs* (now *China Journal*), *China Quarterly*, *Journal of Asian Studies*, *Journal of World History*, *Late Imperial China*, *Modern Asian Studies*, *Modern China*, and *T'oung Pao*. Collections of articles on particular topics from these and other journals and edited volumes have been reprinted, see under Russell-Wood, below. Where specific articles are referred to in the text, they are included in the list below, which is highly selective and is intended only as a starting point. Items cited in full in the notes are not included in the bibliography

Adas, Michael. *Machines as the Measure of Men: Science, Technology, and Ideologies of Western Dominance.* Ithaca and London: Cornell University Press, 1989.

———, ed. *Technology and European Overseas Enterprise: Diffusion, Adaptation, and Adoption.* Aldershot, U.K., and Brookfield, Vt.: Variorum, 1996.

Bergère, Marie-Claire. *The Golden Age of the Chinese Bourgeoisie.* Cambridge, U.K.: Cambridge University Press, 1989.

Blussé, Leonard. *Strange Company: Chinese Settlers, Mestizo Women, and the Dutch in VOC Batavia.* Dordrecht, Holland, and Riverton, N.J., Foris Publications, 1986.

Boxer, C. R. *Fidalgos in the Far East, 1550–1777.* The Hague: M. Nijhoff, 1948.

———. *South China in the Sixteenth Century: Being the Narratives of Galeota Pereira, Fr. Gaspar da Cruz O.P., and Fr. Martin de Rada, O.E.S.A. 1550–1575.* London: Hakluyt Society, Second Series, vol. CVI (1953).

Brook, Timothy. *The Confusions of Pleasure: Commerce and Culture in Ming China.* Berkeley and London: University of California Press, 1998.

Chen Jian. *China's Road to the Korean War: The Making of the Sino-American Confrontation.* New York: Columbia University Press, 1994.

Chen Xiaomei. *Occidentalism: A Theory of Counter-Discourse in Post-Mao China.* New York and Oxford: Oxford University Press, 1995.

Coble, Parks M., Jr. *Facing Japan: Chinese Politics and Japanese Imperialism, 1931–1937.* Cambridge: Harvard Council on East Asian Studies, 1991.

———. *The Shanghai Capitalists and the Nationalist Government, 1927–1937.* Cambridge: Harvard Council on East Asian Studies, 1986.

Cochran, Sherman. *Big Business in China: Sino-Foreign Rivalry in the Cigarette Industry, 1890–1930.* Cambridge: Harvard University Press, 1980.

———, ed. *Inventing Nanjing Road.* Forthcoming.

Cohen, Paul A. *China and Christianity: The Missionary Movement and the Growth of Chinese Antiforeignism, 1839–1939.* Cambridge: Harvard University Press, 1963.

———. *History in Three Keys: The Boxers in History and Myth.* New York: Columbia University Press, 1997.

Cranmer-Byng, J. L. *An Embassy to China: Lord Macartney's Journal, 1793–1794.* London: Longman, 1962.

Cumings, Bruce, *The Origins of the Korean War.* 2 vols. Princeton: Princeton University Press, 1981, 1990.

Cushman, Jennifer. *Fields from the Sea: Chinese Junk Trade with Siam during the Late Eighteenth-Century and Early Nineteenth Centuries.* Ithaca: Cornell University Southeast Asia Program, 1993.

Dirlik, Arif. *Anarchism and the Chinese Revolution.* Berkeley and London: University of California Press, 1991.

Duara, Prasenjit. *Rescuing History from the Nation: Questioning Narratives of Modern China.* Chicago and London: Chicago University Press, 1995.

Esherick, Joseph W. *The Origins of the Boxer Uprising.* Berkeley, Los Angeles, and London: University of California Press, 1987.

Fairbank, J. K., ed. *The Chinese World Order: Traditional China's Foreign Relations.* Cambridge: Harvard University Press, 1968.

———. *Trade and Diplomacy on the China Coast: The Opening of the Treaty Ports, 1842–1854.* Cambridge: Harvard University Press, 1953.

Flynn, Dennis O., and Arturo Giraldez, eds. *Metals and Monies in an Emerging Global Economy.* Brookfield, Vt.: Variorum, 1997.

Franck, Irene M., and David M. Brownstone. *The Silk Road: A History.* New York and Oxford: Facts on File Publications, 1986.

Gardella, Robert. *Harvesting Mountains: Fujian and the China Tea Trade, 1757–1937.* Berkeley: University of California Press, 1994.

Garver, John W. *Chinese-Soviet Relations, 1937–1945: The Diplomacy of Chinese Nationalism.* New York: Oxford University Press, 1988.

Goncharov, Sergei N., John W. Lewis, and Xue Litai. *Uncertain Partners: Stalin, Mao and the Korean War.* Stanford: Stanford University Press, 1993.

Greenberg, Michael. *British Trade and the Opening of China, 1800–1842.* Cambridge, U.K.: Cambridge University Press, 1951.

Grunfeld, A. Tom. *The Making of Modern Tibet*, 2d ed. Armonk, N.Y.: M. E. Sharpe, 1996.

Hao Yen-p'ing. *The Comprador in 19th Century China: Bridge between East and West.* Cambridge: Harvard University Press, 1970.

Harley, J. B., and David Woodward, eds. *The History of Cartography*, vol. 2, book 2, *Cartography in the Traditional East and Southeast Asian Societies.* Chicago: University of Chicago Press, 1994.

Harrell, Paula. *Sowing the Seeds of Change: Chinese Students, Japanese Teachers, 1895–1905.* Stanford: Stanford University Press, 1992.

Hay, Stephen N. *Asian Ideas of East and West: Tagore and His Critics in Japan, China and India.* Cambridge: Harvard University Press, 1970.

Hershatter, Gail. *Dangerous Pleasures: Prostitution and Modernity in Twentieth-Century Shanghai.* Berkeley, Los Angeles, London: University of California Press, 1997.

Hevia, James L. *Cherishing Men from Afar: Qing Guest Ritual and the Macartney Embassy.* Durham and London: Duke University Press, 1995.

Honig, Emily. *Sisters and Strangers: Women in the Shanghai Cotton Mills, 1919–1939.* Stanford: Stanford University Press, 1986.

Howland, Douglas. *Borders of Chinese Civilization: Geography and History at Empire's End.* Durham and London: Duke University Press, 1996.

Hu deHart, Evelyn. "Latin America in Asia-Pacific Perspective." In Arif Dirlik, ed. *What's in a Rim.* Boulder, Colo.: Westview, 1993.

Hung, Chang-tai. *War and Popular Culture: Resistance in Modern China, 1937–1945.* Berkeley, Los Angeles, London: University of California Press, 1994.

Hunt, Michael H. *The Genesis of Chinese Communist Foreign Policy.* New York: Columbia University Press, 1996.

———. *The Making of a Special Relationship: The United States and China to 1914.* New York: Columbia University Press, 1983.

Jansen, Marius. *China in the Tokugawa World.* Cambridge: Harvard University Press, 1992.

Karl, Rebecca. *Secret Sharers: Chinese Nationalism and the Non-Western World at the Turn of the Twentieth Century.* Durham and London: Duke University Press, forthcoming.

Kim, Samuel S., ed. *China and the World: Chinese Foreign Relations in the Post-Cold War Era.* Boulder, Colo.: Westview, 1994.

Kraus, Richard Curt. *Pianos and Politics in China: Middle-Class Ambitions and the Struggle over Western Music.* New York: Oxford University Press, 1989.

Lach, Donald F., and Edwin J. van Kley. *Asia in the Making of Europe*, vol. 3, *A Century of Advance*, book four: "East Asia." Chicago and London: Chicago University Press, 1993.

Leonard, Jane Kate. *Wei Yuan and China's Rediscovery of the Maritime World.* Cambridge: Harvard University Press, 1984.

Levathes, Louise. *When China Ruled the Seas: The Treasure Fleet of the Dragon Throne, 1405–1433.* New York: Simon and Schuster: 1994.

Lewis, John W., and Xue Litai. *China Builds the Bomb.* Stanford: Stanford University Press, 1988.

———. *China's Strategic Seapower: The Politics of Force Modernization in the Nuclear Age.* Stanford: Stanford University Press, 1994.

Li, Lillian. *China's Silk Trade: Traditional Industry in the Modern World, 1842–1937.* Cambridge: Harvard University Press, 1981.

Lin Man-houng. "Currency and Society: The Monetary Crisis and Political-Economic Ideology of Early Nineteenth-Century China." Unpublished Ph.D. dissertation, Harvard University, 1989.

Liu, Lydia. *Translingual Practice: Literature, National Culture, and Translated Modernity.* Stanford: Stanford University Press, 1995.

Liu Xinru. *Ancient India and Ancient China: Trade and Religious Exchanges, A.D. 1–600.* Delhi: Oxford University Press, 1988.

Meisner, Maurice. *Li Ta-chao and the Origins of Chinese Marxism.* Cambridge: Harvard University Press, 1967.

———. *The Deng Xiaoping Era: An Inquiry into the Fate of Chinese Socialism, 1978–1994.* New York: Hill and Wang, 1996.

Morse, Hosea Ballou. *The Chronicles of the East India Company Trading to China, 1635–1834.* 5 vols. Oxford: Clarendon Press, 1926.

———. *The International Relations of the Chinese Empire.* 3 vols. London, Longmans, Green, 1910–1918.

Mungello, David. *Curious Land: Jesuit Missionaries and the Origins of Sinology.* Honolulu: University of Hawaii Press, 1985.

Murray, Dian. *Pirates of the South China Coast, 1790–1810.* Stanford: Stanford University Press, 1987.

Ng, Chin-keong. *Trade and Society: The Amoy Network on the China Coast, 1683–1735.* Singapore: Singapore University Press, 1983.

Pritchard, Earl H. *The Crucial Years of Early Anglo-Chinese Relations, 1750–1800.* New York: Octagon Books, 1970.

Reardon-Anderson, James. *The Study of Change: Chemistry in China, 1842–1949.* Cambridge, U.K.: Cambridge University Press, 1991.

Rigby, Richard W. *The May Thirtieth Movement: Events and Themes.* Canberra: Australian National University Press, 1990.

Rossabi, Morris, ed. *China among Equals: The Middle Kingdom and Its Neighbors, 10th–14th Centuries*. Berkeley and London: University of California Press, 1983.

———. *Voyager from Xanadu: Rabban Sauma and the First Journey from China to the West*. Tokyo, New York, and London: Kodansha, 1992.

Rowe, William T. *Hankow: Commerce and Society in a Chinese City, 1796–1889*. Stanford: Stanford University Press, 1984.

———. *Hankow: Conflict and Community in a Chinese City, 1796–1895*. Stanford: Stanford University Press, 1989.

Russell-Wood, A. J. R., ed. *An Expanding World: The European Impact on World History, 1450–1800*. Birmingham, U.K.: Ashgate, 1997.

Schwarcz, Vera. *The Chinese Enlightenment: Intellectuals and the Legacy of the May Fourth Movement of 1919*. Berkeley: University of California Press, 1986.

Schwartz, Benjamin I. *In Search of Wealth and Power: Yen Fu and the West*. Cambridge: Belknap Press of Harvard University Press, 1964.

Shambaugh, David. *Beautiful Imperialist: China Perceives America, 1972–1990*. Princeton: Princeton University Press, 1991.

Shiba Yoshinobu. *Commerce and Society in Sung China*, translated by Mark Elvin. Ann Arbor: Michigan Center for Chinese Studies, 1970.

Smith, Richard J. *Mercenaries and Mandarins: The Ever-Victorious Army in Nineteenth-Century China*. Millwood, N.Y.: KTO, 1978.

Snow, Philip. *The Star Raft: China's Encounter with Africa*. New York: Weidenfeld and Nicolson, 1988.

Spence, Jonathan D., *The Memory Palace of Matteo Ricci*. New York: Viking, 1984.

Spence, Jonathan D., and John E. Wills, Jr. *From Ming to Ch'ing*. New Haven: Yale University Press, 1979.

Steensgaard, Niels. *The Asian Trade Revolution of the Seventeenth Century: The East India Companies and the Decline of the Caravan Trade*. Chicago and London: University of Chicago Press, 1973.

Subrahmanyam, Sanjay. *The Portuguese Empire in Asia, 1500–1700: A Political and Economic History*. London and New York: Longman, 1993.

Tsai Jung-fang. *Hong Kong in Chinese History: Community and Social Unrest in the British Colony, 1842–1913*. New York: Columbia University Press, 1993.

Viraphol, Sarasin. *Tribute and Profit: Sino-Siamese Trade, 1652–1853*. Cambridge: Harvard University Press, 1977.

von Glahn, Richard. *Fountain of Fortune: Money and Monetary Policy in China, 1000–1700*. Berkeley and London: University of California Press, 1996.

Wakeman, Frederic, Jr. *The Great Enterprise: The Manchu Reconstruction of Imperial Order in Seventeenth-Century China*. Berkeley and London: University of California Press, 1985.

———. *Policing Shanghai*. Berkeley, Los Angeles, London: University of California Press, 1995.

———. *The Shanghai Badlands: Wartime Terrorism and Urban Crime 1937–1941*. Cambridge, U.K.: Cambridge University Press, 1996.

Waldron, Arthur. *From War to Nationalism: China's Turning Point, 1924–1925*. Cambridge, U.K.: Cambridge University Press, 1995.

———. *The Great Wall of China: From History to Myth*. Cambridge, U.K.: Cambridge University Press, 1990.

Waley-Cohen, Joanna. "China and Western Technology in the Late Eighteenth Century." *American Historical Review*, vol. 98, no. 5 (December 1993), 1525–44.

Wang Gungwu. *The Nanhai Trade: The Early History of Chinese Trade in the South China Sea*, 2d ed. Singapore: Times Academic Press, 1998.

Wills, John E., Jr. *Embassies and Illusions: Dutch and Portuguese Envoys to K'ang-hsi, 1666–1687.* Cambridge: Harvard University Press, 1984.

———. *Pepper, Guns and Parleys: The Dutch East India Company and China, 1662–1681.* Cambridge: Harvard University Press, 1974.

Wong, R. Bin. *China Transformed: Historical Change and the Limits of European Experience.* Ithaca, N.Y., and London: Cornell University Press, 1997.

Yahuda, Michael. *Towards the End of Isolationism: China's Foreign Policy after Mao.* London: Macmillan, 1983.

Yen Ching-Hwang. *Coolies and Mandarins: China's Protection of Overseas Chinese during the Late Ch'ing Period (1851–1911).* Singapore: Singapore University Press, 1985.

Yu Ying-shih. *Trade and Expansion in Han China; A Study in the Structure of Sino-Barbarian Economic Relations.* Berkeley: University of California Press, 1967.

Zhuang Guotu. *Tea Silver, Opium and War: The International Tea Trade and Western Commercial Expansion into China in 1740–1840.* Xiamen: Xiamen University Press, 1993.

Index